Between North and South

Women's Diaries and Letters of the South
Carol Bleser, Series Editor

Between North and South

The Letters of Emily Wharton Sinkler 1842–1865

Edited by

Anne Sinkler Whaley LeClercq

University of South Carolina Press

UNIVERSITY OF SOUTH CAROLINA *BICENTENNIAL*

© 2001 University of South Carolina

Published in Columbia, South Carolina, by the
University of South Carolina Press

Manufactured in the United States of America

05 04 03 02 01   5 4 3 2 1

Library of Congress Cataloging-in-Publication Data

Sinkler, Emily Wharton, 1823-1875.
    Between North and South : the letters of Emily Wharton Sinkler, 1842-1865 /
edited by Anne Sinkler Whaley LeClercq.
    . p. cm. — (Women's diaries and letters of the South)
    ISBN 1-57003-412-5 (alk. paper)
    1. Sinkler, Emily Wharton, 1823-1875—Correspondence. 2. Plantation life—
South Carolina—Santee River Region—History—19th century. 3. Plantation
owners' spouses—South Carolina—Santee River Region—Correspondence.
4. Women—South Carolina—Santee River Region—Correspondence. 5.Women—
South Carolina—Santee River Region—Social life and customs—19th century.
6. Santee River Region (S.C.)—Biography. 7. Charleston Region (S.C.)—
Biography. 8. Philadelphia (Pa.)—Biography. I. LeClercq, Anne Sinkler Whaley,
1942- II. Title. III. Series.
F277.S28 S57 2001
975.7'78—dc21   2001004913

To my mother, Emily Whaley
and my grandmother, Anne Sinkler Fishburne

Contents

Illustrations

Series Editor's Preface

Between North and South: The Letters of Emily Wharton Sinkler, 1842–1865, edited by Ann Sinkler Whaley LeClercq, is the fourteenth volume in what had been the Women's Diaries and Letters of the Nineteenth-Century South Series. This series has been redefined and is now titled Women's Diaries and Letters of the South, enabling us to include some remarkably fine works from the twentieth century. Published by the University of South Carolina Press, this series includes a number of never-before-published diaries, some collections of unpublished correspondence, and a few reprints of published diaries—a potpourri of nineteenth-century and, now, twentieth-century southern women's writings.

The series enables women to speak for themselves, providing readers with a rarely opened window into southern society before, during, and after the American Civil War and on into the twentieth century. The significance of these letters and journals lies not only in the personal revelations and the writing talent of these women authors but also in the range and versatility of the documents' contents. Taken together these publications will tell us much about the heyday and the fall of the Cotton Kingdom, the mature years of the "peculiar institution," the war years, the adjustment of the South to a new social order following the defeat of the Confederacy, and the post–1900 "New South." Through these writings, the reader will also be presented with firsthand accounts of everyday life and social events, courtships and marriages, family life and travels, religion and education, and the life-and-death matters that made up the ordinary and extraordinary world of the American South.

Between North and South begins in 1842 with the marriage of Emily Wharton, a daughter of a distinguished Philadelphia family. Emily, at the age of nineteen, became the bride of Charles Sinkler, a midshipman in the United States Navy who was stationed in Philadelphia. The groom, the son of a very wealthy cotton planter in upper St. John's Parish, sixty miles from Charleston, South Carolina, brought Emily to South Carolina to live among his family. LeClercq, the great-great-grand-daughter of Emily, writes in *Between North and South* that she retrieved Emily's letters from the attics of relatives in both Philadelphia and in the South, to piece together the fully textured life of this appealing nineteenth-century woman. Emily, though reared and educated in a cultured and lively Philadelphia family, fell deeply in love with a southerner and moved south. For the remainder of Emily's life she traveled between Charleston and Philadelphia, spending the winter months on the Sinkler plantations and the spring and much of the summer among her relatives in Philadelphia. Emily's beautifully expressive letters reveal that she endeared herself to all who knew her both in the cosmopolitan north as well as in the agrarian ante-bellum south. Her correspondence also shows Emily, who grew up in a developing industrial metropolis, to be an intelligent observer of a strikingly different culture—that of the isolated, lonely, and quiet life of a cotton plantation in the South Carolina lowcountry, surrounded by African American slaves and a white French Huguenot community.

With the coming of the Civil War, Emily and Charles stayed on their plantation and their eldest son, Wharton, enlisted in the Confederacy. *Between North and South* is an absorbing story of a northern daughter reared in one world, who embraced another culture so fully that she became a southern "Sinkler woman" *par excellence.*

Between North and South is almost a mirror image of another volume in our series, *Best Companions,* edited by Eliza Cope Harrison. The latter book contains the correspondence of Eliza Middleton Fisher of the illustrious Charleston, South Carolina, family, and her mother, Mary Hering Middleton, following Eliza's marriage into a prominent Philadelphia family and her move there in 1839. Emily Sinkler was a northerner who moved south, and Eliza Fisher was a southerner who moved north. They were contemporaries and part of a close-knit antebellum elite class. They even traveled regularly by steamship between Philadelphia and Charleston at the same time of year, frequently at the height of the hurricane season; both women describe their stormy close calls in correspondence home. Their stories beautifully complement each other.

CAROL BLESER

Preface

ONE SNOWY DAY IN 1991 I found a warm nook in my attic in Knoxville, Tennessee, and began poring through old family papers and relics. My librarian preservation instincts were piqued by a wonderful family receipt book filled with everything from how to cure hiccups, to certain remedies for mosquito bites and bed bugs, to three ways to prevent drunkenness, all intermingled with delicious directions for French rice pudding, corn pone, rice blancmange, trifle, charlotte russe, and much more. So began the journey into my family's ancestral past and, in particular, into the life and longings of my great-great-grandmother, Emily Wharton Sinkler. When my prying fingers loosened a paste-in on the frontispiece, there, written below in lovely script, were the words "Emily Wharton Sinkler, Charleston, 1855."

With three months of research leave from my position as head of the Undergraduate Library at the University of Tennessee, I began the laborious task of creating a culinary history. There were many delightful discoveries about food practices and culinary traditions in the antebellum South Carolina lowcountry. I shuddered at the thought of the poor drunken husband who was dosed on ipecacuanha, a harsh cathartic causing vomiting. I wondered at the use of a hair wash that called for cantharides, a beetle used in native cultures as an aphrodisiac. It was intriguing to note that diarrhea might be cured with a concoction of fennel seed combined with soot from a wood fire, plus rhubarb.

I began the delightful and challenging task of cooking from scratch. I learned to make delicious rice puddings. I experimented with chocolate custards, omelet soufflés, plum puddings, buttermilk bread, Sally Lunn, cornbreads, and much more. My kitchen became a science laboratory where I whipped up and served anything that could be concocted with basic nineteenth-century plantation ingredients. The receipts of Emily Wharton Sinkler showed the remarkable way that plantation women used the commodities at hand—eggs, cream, milk, rice, corn, wheat, and potatoes—and combined these simple but elegant ingredients with different spices and in different combinations to make puddings, blancmange, omelet, meringue, pone, cake, bread, pie, custard, and more.

My mother, Emily Whaley, aided me in this enterprise. We often cooked as a team in her wonderful kitchen at 58 Church Street in Charleston. She had a sure method for translating gills, teacups, and pinches of this and that into accurate measurements. During these cooking classes we talked about family traditions, and I learned the stories of great-great-grandmother Emily. Soon I discovered that the family had preserved fifty-five of her letters. What began as a culinary effort became a biographical one, ending with over ninety-six of her letters.

As I pored through Emily's poignant, humorous letters home to her family in Philadelphia, I began to wonder and dream about her real life. I learned what it was like to have whooping cough and to travel by sea in a sailing ship between Philadelphia and Charleston when hurricanes were unpredictably present. Emily's story created a powerful impression in terms of the actual day-to-day life of women in the antebellum South.

Emily Wharton had been reared and educated in the cultivated family of Thomas Isaac Wharton at 150 Walnut Street in Philadelphia. In the 1840s Charleston and Philadelphia were intimately connected by the fact that each was a U.S. naval port and also by the intricacies of cotton culture. Charleston provided the raw materials for the burgeoning piecework looms and mills of early industrial Philadelphia. Southern families sent their daughters and sons to boarding schools in Philadelphia. Philadelphia businessmen were frequent boarders at the Charleston Hotel and the Mills House. It was through this interconnection that Emily Wharton met Charles Sinkler, a lieutenant in the U.S. Navy. Emily married Charles Sinkler in 1842 at the age of nineteen and moved to Eutaw Plantation on the Santee River, sixty miles from Charleston. There she faced a difficult adjustment to life in a French Huguenot, slave-based, cotton-culture family and community.

Emily's story was told, in part, in *An Antebellum Plantation Household: Including the South Carolina Low Country Receipts and Remedies of Emily Wharton Sinkler,* published by the University of South Carolina Press in 1996. There I used brief excerpts from Emily's letters to highlight her life in the South Carolina lowcountry. The principal emphasis of the book was the preservation and explication of Emily's receipt and remedy book. After I had completed the book, I discovered forty additional letters by searching the attics of South Carolina and Philadelphia relatives. Suddenly, I had a very definitive account of Emily's life from her arrival in Charleston in 1842 through the Civil War. I realized that Emily's own voice told a more powerful tale than my words and excerpts.

Emily had become a very real, vibrant person. I felt that her extraordinary vitality had a message that would appeal to any individual living today. I wanted to save her past as an inspiration for contemporary life. Much as we travel to foreign countries for the feeling of adventure found in exposure to another culture, so going back in time to the antebellum South and to plantation life at Eutaw and Belvidere might provide a window of opportunity for exploring how we live today.

There are many qualities evident in Emily's letters and life that are still relevant today. She had an eagerness to try the new and to be contemporary. For example, Emily and her sister-in-law Anna Linton Sinkler sang the songs of Jenny Lind, who was touring the United States in 1850. They also sang the operas of Donizetti, Bellini, and Rossini at the time they were being written and first produced. At Belvidere and Eutaw Plantations, evening musicals were not a special event but the essential entertainment of the nighttime house. Emily was immersed in the best writing of her time: the works of Charles Dickens, Washington Irving, and Charlotte Brontë were read aloud for daily entertainment in the Sinkler parlor.

Another quality evident in Emily's life and those of her friends was her deep spirituality. In Emily's day, an individual's oath and word were sacred, based on a deep commitment and belief in the power of God. The Episcopal church was an integral part of Emily's everyday life. She was the leader of the ladies' guild, and Charles was a vestryman in three different churches. When Emily discovered that the laws of South Carolina forbade schooling for African Americans, she established a church where she taught young and old how to read through songs and the prayer book.

Emily and Charles lived an agrarian life. Through their farming and gardening they were in touch with the earth and the cycle of the seasons. Flower gardening, vegetable planting, and cotton culture were all an essential part of the Sinkers' way of life. Their oneness with the land is a quality that reverberates with meaning today as we attempt to save the South from strip malls and over-development. It is far simpler today to buy our vinegar, wine, and jams from the local supermarket than to be out in the hedgerows picking blackberries in summer to make our own vinegar, wine, and jams. But the delight in creating her own concoctions was crucial to Emily's and her family's livelihood at Belvidere and Eutaw.

Emily immersed herself in the African American culture that surrounded her. African American culture was an integral part of plantation life. Emily learned how to cook from her kitchen help, how to use ashes to leaven bread, how to season soups with potherbs, how to combine rice and cornmeal into delicious cakes. Many of her remedies, such as inhaling the smoke of the jimsonweed for asthma, were absorbed from African American culture. She loved the chants, spirituals, and music which surrounded her and which became a part of Sinkler family festivities, such as plantation Christmas celebrations.

As with any good documentary work, I have utilized the primary sources of the time—newspapers, wills, censuses, maps—to give a more complete understanding of Emily's words and letters. Endnotes are there to amplify and to lead the reader to other sources. Through the textual bridges, I hoped to create the ambience and patina of Emily's daily life so that the reader would become absorbed in her adventures and experience her life firsthand. For ease of reading by current-day readers, some features of the holographic text have been standardized to current usage. Books and journal titles, for instance, and the names of ships have been italicized for easy identification; handwritten dashes have been edited to a standard length; and capitalization has generally been edited to conform to twenty-first century practice.

Emily was a pioneer in the old-fashioned sense of the word. She learned how to make do in a rural, isolated environment. She invented alternatives for everyday necessities. She managed and husbanded the resources of the plantation. Her letters show the significance of the role of the caretaker, generally a woman, to the economy, health, and hygiene of the antebellum South. Emily lived her life successfully in two very different worlds: Philadelphia, with its cosmopolitan air; and Charleston and rural South Carolina, where slave culture was an essential part of life. Emily was a remarkable person in that she lived between these two worlds and managed to endear herself to those whose lives she touched in both.

Upper St. John's Parish was a small microcosm of the rural, antebellum South. The French Huguenot community of Eutawville that included the Sinklers' two plantations, Eutaw and Belvidere, was a distinct sociological and cultural entity. Yet in many ways, Emily and her friends lived lives not all that different from other women at this time in the South. They lived in a patriarchal, paternalistic society where the opportunities for women were circumscribed. They had fewer opportunities than men to fulfill roles outside of the domestic/religious sphere.

This book is dedicated to the many Sinkler women who have gone before me. Their courage, determination, and love of life gave rise to the epigram "those Sinkler women." More particularly, it is dedicated to my grandmother, Anne Wickham Sinkler Fishburne, whose work *Belvidere*[1] inspired this book. Her voluminous research and copious files of letters and notes have been of invaluable help. This work is also dedicated to my mother, Emily Wharton Fishburne Whaley, whose books *Mrs. Whaley and Her Charleston Garden*[2] and *Mrs. Whaley Entertains: Advice, Opinions, and 100 Recipes from a Charleston Kitchen*[3] provided me inspiration to undertake this work.

Between North and South has found a comfortable home with congenial companions in USC Press's Women's Diaries and Letters of the South publication series. Documentary editor and history professor emerita Carol Blesser, Ph.D., is general editor of the series. She selected this book for inclusion and contributed a helpful preface. Finally, I want to thank my colleagues Susan Frohnsdorff, whose careful editing has greatly improved the accuracy of this work, and Dr. David Heisser of The Citadel's library faculty, whose superb scholarly scrutiny has been very helpful in the editorial process; and Dr. Alexander Moore, whose unfailing support and insights have been deeply appreciated.

ANNE SINKLER WHALEY LECLERCQ

Notes

1. Anne Sinkler Fishburne, *Belvidere: A Plantation Memory* (Columbia: University of South Carolina Press, 1949).

2. Emily Fishburne Whaley, *Mrs. Whaley and Her Charleston Garden* (Chapel Hill, N.C.: Algonquin, 1997).

3. Emily Fishburne Whaley, *Mrs. Whaley Entertains: Advice, Opinions, and 100 Recipes from a Charleston Kitchen* (Chapel Hill, N.C.: Algonquin, 1998).

Wharton Family of Philadelphia

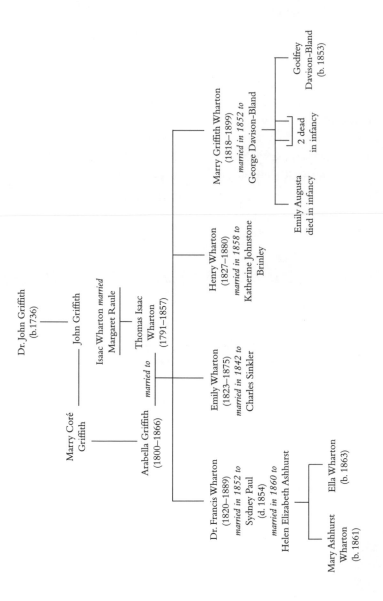

Sinkler Family of South Carolina and Philadelphia

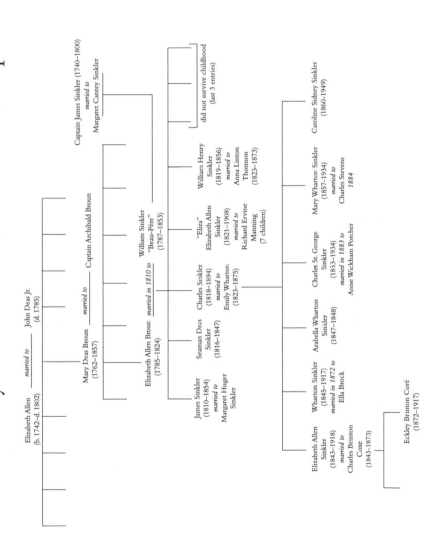

*Between
North and
South*

I

From Whence She Came—
Family and Philadelphia,
1823–1842

THE WORLD OF CHARLESTON seemed fresh and strange to Emily Wharton Sinkler when she arrived in 1842. She was the nineteen-year-old bride of Charles Sinkler. Charles lived at Eutaw Plantation in Upper St. John's Parish in lowcountry South Carolina.

Upper St. John's Parish was bordered by the Santee River and Swamp. In this remote, isolated area, Emily found new friends, different customs, and a landscape and culture that were the antipodes of her native Philadelphia. Yet, Emily was alive and welcoming to this strange environment that was so different from her beloved native Philadelphia. She immediately set about sharing the novelty and excitement of daily life with her Philadelphia family through weekly letters to each member.

Emily was born into a cultured, prominent Philadelphia family on October 12, 1823. The Thomas Isaac Whartons lived at 150 Walnut Street in the heart of old Philadelphia. They were Episcopalians and worshiped at St. Stephen's Church located at 19 South Tenth Street. Thomas Isaac Wharton was a lawyer with an office in his home, as was the custom then.

Philadelphia in the antebellum years was a cultural center where art, theater, music, and publishing thrived. It was a commercial port of significance, with imports of porcelain, silks, velvets, and other fine products from France, Italy, and Britain. It was a craft center without peer, where silversmiths and furniture makers flourished. Carriage shops created all kinds of horse-drawn vehicles, from plain wagons to fancy barouches. It was a center for dry goods stores, where bolts of cloth crammed the shelves. It was the nation's first industrial city. Its coal-driven steam power plants were to make possible mass production of textiles, locomotives, and household machines, such as the Franklin stove.

Immigrants from Ireland, along with escaped slaves and freed African Americans, transformed the city of brotherly love established by the Quakers. The highly ethnic, white, and Protestant city was plagued by riots among members of the Native American party, Irish Catholics, and freed African Americans.

Emily missed her family and poured out her frustration, loneliness, and acute observations to them in letters that she numbered by individual recipient so that she would have a means for tracing every letter. She had personal writing days for each family member. The mail went daily from Vances Ferry on the banks of the Santee River, down the Santee Canal, to the Cooper River, and so into Charleston. There it was placed on coastwise steamboats and delivered to Wilmington, Delaware, and from there to Philadelphia. Mail service took approximately four days. The Sinklers also used a "factor," an individual hired especially for the purpose of expediting receipt and delivery of mail and packages. He also made all their arrangements for travel. The Sinkler family's factor was first Mr. J. Chapman Huger, whose business was on the Commercial Wharf. Later their agent was Mr. Harris Simons, whose place of business was on Adger's Wharf.[1]

Emily's extended family included her grandmother, her father, her mother, and three siblings. Grandmother Mary Coré Griffith, or "Grand Marty," was married to John Griffith, a merchant of Philadelphia, but had been early left a widow. Mary Coré lived at Charlie's Hope on the Delaware River and was something of a spendthrift, splurging all her money on acres of roses grown in rows like corn for her bees. It is said that she spent twenty-five thousand dollars on her apiary alone. She was eccentric and extravagant. She also wrote novels and stories. She was mentioned by Sir Walter Scott in the preface to *The Heart of Midlothian* and by Maria Edgeworth in her famous *Letters*. For Emily she was an adored grandmother with whom she spent wonderful summer vacations away from the yellow fever and cholera epidemics of Philadelphia. It was from Grand Marty that Emily learned her love of gardening. Mary Coré Griffith had created a garden that was pungent with the sweet aroma and perfume of hundreds of old-fashioned roses. On a warm spring day the glorious, huge, fruit-like blooms fashioned a rainbow of pinks, mauves, crimsons, blood reds, and velvety roses. Mary Coré's garden was the summer playground of her granddaughter. In this idyllic landscape, free from the city cares of Philadelphia of the 1830s, Emily learned to love gardening.

"Papa," called "Wharton" by his colleagues, was the distinguished jurist Thomas Isaac Wharton. He had graduated from the University of Pennsylvania in 1807 and studied law in the office of his uncle, William Rawle, a leader of the Philadelphia bar. In 1830 he was elected a member of the American Philosophical

Society. He was active in the Library and Athenaeum Companies. The Historical Society of Pennsylvania was started in Wharton's home at 130 South Sixth Street. "Papa" was Emily's intellectual mentor, sending her copies of such periodicals as *Godey's Lady's Book, Graham's Magazine, Household Words, Neal's Saturday Gazette,* and the *Illustrated London News,* as well as daily newspapers, especially the *Ledger* and the *Philadelphia Evening Bulletin.* He provided her a monthly allowance and was her lifeline to Philadelphia shopping and merchandise, sending her everything from breakfast herring to new ploughs from the store Ogles and Watsons. He was also a beloved Santa Claus, showering her with fabric for stylish new outfits, boxloads of bonbons, and music.[2]

"Mamma," Arabella Griffith Wharton, was of a sweet and loving disposition but afflicted with poor health and eye problems that prevented her from writing her darling Emily with any frequency.

Emily's three siblings, Frank, Mary, and Henry, were her faithful correspondents and yearly visitors. Frank, the eldest, practiced law with his father and went on to become a professor of theology at Cambridge, England. Mary was Emily's confidant, pen pal, and coach in terms of style, fashion, and housekeeping. Mary sent Emily receipts for ginger cookies and chocolate cake from the *Germantown (Pa.) Telegraph.* Henry, Emily's beloved younger brother, was a rascal and an imp, full of charm, wit, and good times. He practiced law with his father and became a noted Philadelphia prosecutor and member of the Philadelphia bar. The three northern siblings visited Emily at Eutaw and Belvidere on a regular basis.

The Philadelphia of Emily's girlhood was a thriving metropolis and Delaware River port. Located between the Schuylkill and Delaware Rivers, the city was laid out in a rectangular grid whose east-west streets (Walnut, Chestnut, Locust, Pine, etc.) were named after trees and whose north-south streets were numbered from the wharf-lined Delaware River back to Twenty-first in the area of Fairmont Park. The red brick houses were uniformly three or four stories and were side by side with their neighbors. Shiny, white marble stoops and doors with silver knockers carried one up to the ground floor, frequently an office. Emily's house at 150 Walnut Street fit this pattern of comfortable row houses. It was the location of her father's law office as well as the family town house.

Church for Emily and the Wharton family was St. Stephen's Church at 19 South Tenth Street, which had been constructed in 1823. The Gothic stone structure had two matching stone towers, like battlements on either side of a broad, terraced entrance. The dark structure had been designed by William Strickland and was later decorated by Frank Furness and Louis Comfort Tiffany. Inside, eight arches framing lavender, pink, and green stained glass windows dominated the small, intimate church. Emily referred to the interior as being "Geshick rose." Cylindrical chandeliers provided a soft, green-toned light. Emily was christened here in 1823.

Summertime for Philadelphians was spent in country houses in suburbs such as Germantown or Chestnut Hill. Thick forests of old oaks stood out dark against the rolling red hills with their fields and farms, providing a country-like setting. Philadelphians also voyaged to Cape May on the tip of New Jersey. A daily steamer, the *Ohio,* left the wharf on the Delaware River, often with as many as 250 on board for the several-hour trip to Cape May. Cape May's guesthouses were large, gingerbread-type frame structures with broad verandas looking out to the Atlantic Ocean. Lovely beds of hollyhocks and roses framed the Victorian-style houses. Advertisements in the daily newspaper touted the efficiency and comfort of the ride: "The Steamboat Ohio will leave Dock Street wharf on Wednesday morning at 8 a.m. for The Cape and return the following day. Fare, $1., including meals and carriage for hire to the Island. Ticket for the season, $12 . . . A new wharf at the Cape for easy landing of passengers."[3]

It was important to be out of Philadelphia during the summer because of disease. There were epidemic outbreaks of malarial fevers, Asiatic cholera (1832 and 1849), smallpox (1852), yellow fever (1853), dysentery, scarlet fever, and tuberculosis. Malaria and tuberculosis were relatively slow killers, whereas cholera killed with terrifying speed and ugliness.[4] There were 2,314 cases of cholera in 1832, resulting in 985 deaths, and the 1849 epidemic resulted in 1,012 deaths.[5]

While summers were spent away from the epidemics and heat of Philadelphia, winters for the young Wharton children were spent in schooling. Emily spoke Italian, German, and French and was well versed in English literature. She learned at school how to read aloud and project her voice. She also played the piano, the melodeon, and the guitar. She sang and played the piano as part of the family's evening entertainment. She acquired these skills at one of the female institutes or seminaries that provided education for young women in Philadelphia. An advertisement in the *Germantown (Pa.) Telegraph* for the Rydal Mount Female Institute gives a glimpse into the educational expectations for young women: "The classics and modern languages, music, drawing, and other popular accomplishments, [are taught, while] propriety and elegance of manners, and conversation receive proportionate attention. $25 [required] for a 5–month session. Mrs. Fales is the headmistress . . . Located in salubrious Germantown, her course of instruction and system of order and discipline are well calculated to afford young ladies every facility for formation of good habits and the attainment of a solid and useful education."[6]

While Emily and her sister, Mary, were educated in Philadelphia, her brother Frank attended a boarding school in Burlington. His course of instruction was undoubtedly quite different from that which Emily and Mary received. For example, an advertisement for A. Bolmar's Institute for Boys in West Chester, which was only a four-hour ride from Philadelphia, noted the following: "The

most particular attention is paid to the morals, health, manners and personal neatness of the pupils . . . The course of instruction: orthography, reading, writing,
arithmetic, geography, the use of Globes, English grammar, composition, history,
book-keeping, algebra, geometry, mensuration, surveying, Latin, Greek, French,
Spanish, and German languages. Lectures in Chemistry and Astronomy. $250 per
annum."[7]

Philadelphia in the 1830s and '40s was becoming a transportation hub. In
1842 the Reading Railroad initiated service from Philadelphia to Pottsville, and
by 1847 it was considered the greatest freight road in the United States, carrying
passengers, coal, and other heavy freight.[8] Horse-drawn omnibuses provided
transportation within the city. There were regular routes for main streets, and
daily service was provided to Germantown and the other suburbs.[9]

Emily traveled between Philadelphia and Charleston on the coastwise sailing schooners that were replaced by steamships in the early 1840s. Her favorite
schooners were the *Emma* and the *Southerner,* but she was later to travel on the
Columbus and the *Osprey.* These sail steamboats made regular trips between
Philadelphia and Charleston and Savannah that typically took only four days.[10]
However, Emily and Charles were frequently traveling in August and September
at the height of the hurricane season, and so it is not surprising that she experienced the howling winds, thirty-foot waves, and driving rain of terrifying storms.

Emily's life followed a typical pattern. Fall and winter months, including
October, November, December, January, February, and March, were spent at
Eutaw and Belvidere Plantations. Spring and summer months—April, May, June,
and July—were spent with the Whartons in Philadelphia. The early fall months
of August and September, when it was still hot in the South, were spent in various locations such as Virginia, Sullivan's Island in South Carolina, or Flat Rock in
North Carolina. When fall weather permitted, Emily, Charles, and the children
returned to Eutaw and Belvidere, enjoying the excitement of planning for
Thanksgiving and then Christmas.

Emily's very first letter home (from a total of ninety-six letters which sur-
vive) tells of her narrow escape from a hurricane. It also reveals her surprise at
seeing African American slaves in church. In Charleston it was the custom for
slaves to attend church along with their owners. Philadelphia of 1840 had very
few slaves and 19,833 freed African Americans out of a total city population of
93,665.[11] However, because of racial segregation in housing, African Americans
were isolated from whites in Philadelphia, and thus Emily was not accustomed to
seeing African Americans *en masse.*

On arrival in Charleston, Emily and Charles stayed at Stewarts, a small
Charleston inn, on Chalmers Street. Emily loved Charleston from the first moment
she put her foot on the steps of Stewarts, with its broad piazzas, private rooms,

each with its own fireplace, and an adjoining garden redolent with the perfume of the tea olive. Emily's new circle of friends included Lizzie Middleton, Harriet Huger, and Harriet Ravenel. They shopped on King Street at Mme. Payot's and bought pretty flowers and lace to make caps and mantuas. They drove out Broad Street for a view of the spectacular crimson and violet fall sunsets over the marshes of the Ashley River.

ૐ ૐ ૐ

Charleston, Monday Morning, [November] 1842

My Dear Mamma,

I cannot resist the temptation of writing again to day although I am afraid if I write every day it will be rather a tax as to postage. I told Mary in a letter I wrote on Saturday that we should leave to-day but we have altered our route and do not go until to-morrow and then go through in a day instead of stopping a night on the way. We leave here in the cars at 8 in the morning and go 25 miles in them and then meet the carriage which will carry us home by 1/2 past 2.

Yesterday we went to church morning and afternoon to St. Philip's of which Mr. Campbell is assistant rector. He was out of town so we did not hear him preach. St.Philip's is the handsomest church I was ever in. It has entirely a different look from the Philadelphia churches and is the very antipodes of its namesake. All the pews, altar and pulpit in short everything which is generally white with us is walnut there and the church is filled with splendidly carved pillars, very elaborately done. The ceiling is also beautiful. They have two things different from us. They have a clerk who repeats all the responses and gives out the Psalm and Hymn in the most stentorian voice. They also sit down while singing. There is a most perfect monument in the church I ever saw. It is the last work of Chantry. It is erected to the son of Bishop [Robert] Smith and the figure alone cost three thousand dollars.[12] Chantry was very unwilling to do it and died very soon after.

My good behavior was very much tried in church and I am sure you will pity me when you know the cause. There are seats against the wall arranged for the black people. When I came into church they had not yet come but on looking round once it was almost too much for me. They were all very old people on our side—such dressing. There was one old man in particular who seemed near 100. He was dressed in woolen pantaloons of a very grotesque cut with a flying Josey over it, a long scarf round his neck and on his head an immense white turban. All the women dressed with bonnets pitched exactly in the oddest way. They had prayer books and repeated the responses and sung, all rocking themselves to and fro. You can imagine what a sight it was for me to see 20 of them.

There is a perfect little boy about 8 who waits or rather assists at table here and whose mouth is distended with grins at the attention I pay him. I asked him yesterday at dinner if he had been to church. He said, no he didn't love to go. I gave him a little advice on the subject and yesterday afternoon when I came back from church as I came along the piazza, I saw him capering along making all sorts of grimaces. Been to church Missy—been to church and been a very good boy there. In the evening we heard him talking on the stairs to a little girl about the sermon. His great delight is to go with bare feet but as soon as he sees me coming he slips on his boots.

On Saturday we returned some visits and I went to King Street and bought some very pretty flowers and some lace to make a cap. Mme. Payot has a shop here at which I got them. We took a very pleasant drive. Every body here owns a carriage and very fine horses. I know my way perfectly about. After church Lizzie Middleton and I walked out Broad Street and as she was in a hurry to get back to prayer at Mrs. Heywards before tea I walked back with her, then went home alone without the slightest trouble. The streets are not all straight and there is not one house in Charleston like any I have ever seen in Philadelphia. They are all with a great air of age and respectability. I have not seen one new house. A great many are built with brick and the others dark stone. They have generally very high steps and almost all Piazzas and gardens in front, which look now very green owing to the wild orange and evergreen trees.

We paid a strange visit on Saturday to Mrs. Alfred Huger the wife of the gentleman who wrote to me.[13] She is not at all young and the day was very cold being ice in the Street. Conceive of her then coming into the room dressed entirely in white cambric with a light Tartan Cap on her head. I was taken aback much more so when she rushed up to me, put her arms around my neck and kissed me several times calling me Cousin Emily. She was a Miss Rutledge and a great belle but is now at least 88. Her manners are generally very cold and they said she paid me a great compliment. In the evening her husband came to see us. He looks much like Mr. Wilcocks, [and] entered the room deliberately, marched up to me, took my hand and kissed it with great impressment. He quite embarrassed me with compliments. He is very amusing, has a great deal of dry humor. He talked for a long while about my not answering his letters and insisted on my calling him Cousin Alfred. We are to dine with him to-day and will have an amusing time. Lizzie Middleton has been very kind. She staid here on purpose to see me and has been every day. She went round and told her friends to come and see me so there has been a succession of Hugers and Loundes here. I have seen very few as I have been out a great deal. I have seen the Campbells frequently. They have given us the most pressing invitation to come and stay with them at Beaufort as long as we like. Indeed every one here is as kind as possible. Every day a message is sent offering us the carriage for all day. I am going to-day to leave cards and shall take Susan Campbell to drive and to make a few little purchases.

It is very cheerful here, at dark always a good many gentlemen come in to see us and they bring round some coffee and a waiter full of enchanting little cakes made by the old black women. The bed-room looks so nice too when I go up there, the wood-fire is just lighted, the curtains of the bed drawn.

You would like Seaman Sinkler very much. I am quite delighted with him. He is so very attentive and kind. He has just been here to say that he has packed up a whole collection of books and sent them for me to the country. He has picked up a great many in Paris as he has lived there 3 years. He has sent on to the Eutaw among other books a perfect treasure. It is a receipt book of French receipts that he got in Paris teaching how to make all sorts of things. We were talking last night about French bonbons and this book is full of receipts how to make them. He knows how to do them himself and is now having made for me some pate de Guimauve and Sirop de Guimauve which he is going to send to me with a root of Guimauve so as I can make it myself. If I can get any opportunity I will send some on to you.

Give my best love to all my friends and say I will write as soon as we are settled. Do give my love to Helen Cox if you see her. I should like very much if Robert has time if he could take this letter to her to read and any other you think she would like. My best love to all. Mr. Sinkler sends his best love. To Frank I will write next. Tell Henry the letter after that is to him but he must let others read it and not keep it the way he does D. Ingrahams' letter. Every one congratulates us on the escape we had in the Wilmington boat. All who expected us were very much alarmed and thought the boat would never reach Charleston. It certainly did blow terribly. Ever affectionately yours, Emily

II

New Family, New Places—
Charleston and Eutaw
Plantation, 1842

EMILY WAS TO SPEND MANY happy days visiting in Charleston. However, Charleston was most frequently a stopping place where she embarked for her yearly summer trips to Philadelphia. Emily's destination was Eutaw Plantation on the banks of the Santee River. The swampy, low-lying region on the Santee River in Upper St. John's Parish was an isolated area of cotton plantations. There were twenty-two plantations located in the alluvial land along the Santee River. The Santee Canal and the Cooper River connected the plantations to Charleston. The Sinkler clan into which Emily married was of Scotch descent. The brothers James and Peter came to Upper St. John's Parish in 1785, when Captain James Sinkler of Revolutionary War fame was given a land grant to Belvidere Plantation.

When Emily arrived in Upper St. John's Parish, her father-in-law, William Sinkler, owned four cotton plantations: Eutaw, Belvidere, Wampee, and Apsley. The pineland town of Eutawville provided a summer retreat from malaria for the plantation owners. The Rocks was the parish church. While the Sinklers were of Scotch ancestry, the other families—Porchers, Gaillards, Mazycks, Palmers, Ravenels, Cordes, Marions, Dwights, and Gourdins—were French Huguenot. The area was isolated, accessible to Charleston by barge on the Santee River and Santee Canal and, after 1833, by "the cars," or railroad, from a station at Branchville, some twenty miles from Eutaw and Belvidere Plantations.

The French Huguenots had come to Upper St. John's after the revocation of the Edict of Nantes in 1685. They found in the somber beauty of the Santee Swamp, with its forest walls of oak and cypress, an area inhabited only by wild animals and widely separated villages of Santee Indians. A map of Upper St. John's Parish from 1865 stated, "Here dwelt a people in peace and contentment, whose ancestors had fled from tyranny in other lands. They tilled the ground and roamed the forests and at last, all was well with their world."[14]

Emily's new Sinkler in-laws were avid hunters, expert farmers, and passionate horse racers. William Sinkler, her father-in-law, farmed Eutaw Plantation with the assistance of 103 slaves. His racetrack was known throughout South Carolina for its private races, and the African American trainer Hercules was considered the best in the region. William Sinkler had built Eutaw Plantation in 1808, marrying the beautiful Elizabeth Allen Broun in 1810. He was left a widower with five young children—James, Seaman Deas, Charles, Elizabeth, and William Henry—by Elizabeth's untimely death in 1824.

Emily's husband, Charles, born July 8, 1818, was a member of the United States Navy from 1836 to 1847. He was stationed in the Gulf of Mexico on the U.S. brig *Perry* during the Mexican War and was wrecked on the Florida Keys in the hurricane of October 11, 1847. While Charles was off in the Navy, Emily lived with her in-laws at Eutaw Plantation. Charles had an adventuresome spirit and had sailed around the world twice on the *U.S.S. Columbia*. Charles was a serious, somewhat stern man whose devotion to work and the Lord were equal. He was to become a warden of the Episcopal church at both the Rocks and St. Philip's. He had been educated at the College of Charleston, delivering an address entitled "On Eloquence" upon his graduation April 4, 1834. Emily always addressed her husband as Mr. Sinkler.

Charles had three brothers, James, Seaman Deas, and William Henry. Seaman Deas Sinkler lived in Charleston, where he was a respected doctor. He had received his medical training in Paris. He was to become Emily's closest confidant, as they shared a mutual love of books, literature, and music, especially opera. James Sinkler married Margaret Huger of Charleston and lived with his family at a neighboring plantation called Wampee. William Henry Sinkler, the youngest of Charles's brothers, farmed Eutaw Plantation with his father. William Henry was married to his first cousin, Anna Linton Thomson, who was to become Emily's best friend and confidant. The two shared a love of music and gave many evening concerts for family and friends. Anna was known for her magnificent contralto voice, while Emily had a beautiful soprano voice. Elizabeth Allen Sinkler, called Eliza, Charles's only sister, married Col. Richard Irvine Manning II in 1845. She was the housekeeper, or lady in charge, at Eutaw Plantation, and Emily quickly learned the manners and mores of Southern women from Eliza. When Eliza married in 1845 and moved to Homesley Plantation thirty miles away in the Santee sand hills, Emily's close circle of friends was greatly diminished.

Upon arrival at Eutaw Plantation in the crisp fall of 1842, Emily found herself immediately thrown into preparations for a Sinkler family Christmas celebration. She discovered that the warm fall days were full of country activity, from walking and riding to evenings full of music and reading aloud. Emily settled happily into life on the banks of the Santee Swamp at Eutaw Springs. The walls of dark cypress trees and the deep black water of the springs were all strange to Emily. The hoot of the night owl, the cry of the blue heron, the scream of a Carolina panther, or the cry of the tame Eutaw peacocks were all foreign sounds to her city-trained ears.

Emily's days were timed to the rising sun, to the full red moon of October, to long, sunny autumn afternoons when she would walk out the sandy white Eutaw avenue beneath the gray-green, mossy, live oak trees. She loved the company of Eliza Sinkler, and the two were accompanied by barking terriers and swift greyhounds.

Eutaw was a large frame house with big central rooms, a front hall, two side extensions, large piazzas, and big double chimneys. It had been built in 1808 by Emily's father-in-law, William Sinkler, whom Emily affectionately called the *beau-père*. A contract, or "indenture," was made on March 28, 1808, between William Sinkler and Benjamin King, the builder, for a lordly sum of $450 to build a house "forty feet in length, and thirty nine feet in breadth, one and a half story high, the first story to be twelve feet in the clear ... The two front rooms are to be finished with flat paneling chairboard high, beaded within, with capping & molding above, and wash boards below, with double architraves to the doors and windows, and a chimney piece and breast work suitable thereto ... The Piazza to be the length of the house and ten feet wide in the clear, to have a neat floor tongued and grooved, five columns and two half columns against the house ... and to have a flight of steps at each and descending to the grounds with newels, rails, ballisters."[15] The resulting house was an elegant, lowcountry farmhouse that was to become a Sinkler gathering place for a century and a half.

As reflected in Emily's next letter, the house brimmed with the energy of an ongoing party. The "they" referred to as "dancing on the Piazza for three days" were the slaves—an unusual and revealing Sinkler Christmas custom. Emily also speaks of "marking" linen so as to prepare it for embroidery. Ladies spent much time sewing and embroidering.

Eutaw
November 22, 1842

My dear Frank,

Your part of a letter was gratefully received and although a longer letter would have been more satisfactory yet I felt as if I had no right to complain although I am sure my letters are long enough to give me a right to expect something in return. However I am in hopes of getting this evening a very copious one from some member. Yesterday was Sunday and I thought of you all going off to church and Sunday school—Geshick rose painted before me in very vivid colors. Mr. Dehon [Rev. William Dehon] has not yet come and Mr. Sinkler went off at ½ past 10 to the Pineland where he made a very good beginning with six boys. Eliza and I read the service and one of Melville's sermons in Anna's room as she is quite sick. We had quite a good imitation of Sunday papers, 2 *Banners,* 1 *Recorder* and several *Gospel Messengers.*

I wish you could have seen me in the afternoon. I went on the back steps as usual to feed the poultry about 200 in number. They have got very free with me and a rooster yesterday stood on my foot to eat the grains of corn off it. You would have laughed to see me going down to the creek followed by a black boy with a basket of corn and a whole set of waddling ducks who were straining every nerve to keep up with me. Being Sunday there were a large crowd of Negroes on the bridge to see me feed the ducks in the creek. The ducks dive in the most amusing way quite to the bottom after corn. As soon as I am seen every black child exclaims at the top of its squeaking voice, Huddy missus, howdy missus! They are exceedingly affectionate, indeed rather too much so.

I do hope you will be here for Christmas. They dance then on the front piazza for three days. They are all very anxious here for you to come. I rather think you will back out of getting up at four o'clock as Mr. Sinkler has done this morning to go hunt deer and a wild cat. The weather was lovely yesterday. Eliza and I took a long walk in the morning. It was so warm that we only wore our sunbonnets and no shawls. We were accompanied by two most interesting terriers and two grey hounds.

Mr. Sinkler Sr. returns from town tomorrow. He took two letters with him for Philadelphia which I hope you have received before this. It is quite an event in the country for anyone to go to town and numerous are his commissions. He is going to bring up a guitar for Anna and myself. Brother Seaman, Mr. Stephens and Mr. Jones of the Navy are going to come up from Charleston. I am sorry for Eliza as I cannot answer for gay young midshipmen. When you come will you please ask Papa to buy me such a toothbrush as he got me in the summer and send it by you. You must also go to my friends and get letters for me. Insist on having letters even if they have written the day before. Of course every member of the family must write including Baker. Give my love to her and Mrs. Hope and tell Baker everything has carried beautifully.[16] The boxes of the Schooner Emma have not come yet but I expect them this week. I wish you would bring me some pretty and easy new duet. Something very simple for Anna and myself to sing. I have marked a great many things and have succeeded very well. I am quite industrious and have almost finished a beautiful black silk apron which I wish Mama could see as it is quite a model of neatness and ingenuity. This will have to be a shorter letter than usual as the boy goes soon to the Post Office. By Thursday's mail I will write a long letter to Papa and one to Aunt Hannah. With best love to you all, I am your affectionate sister, Emily.

Eutaw Nov. 25th 1842

My dear Henry,

I suppose you would like to hear an account of our journey from Charleston here. We left there on Tuesday morning at 8 o'clock in the cars in which we journeyed for 2 hours where we stopped at a place called Inabinetts. Now don't fancy as I did a flourishing little town. Inabinetts is nothing but a deserted log house with neither windows nor doors. There we met horses from the Eutaw and I think you would all have been very much amused could you have seen our cavalcade. First came Sampson, a black boy about 18 mounted on a white mule with a dirt drab coloured overcoat just fastened by a button around his neck and flying to the four winds, an old jockey hat on his head and an umbrella in his hand. He went first to show us the way. Next we came in our little carriage with the top down and the apron up and closing the procession came the baggage in a very singular looking affair. We did not reach the Eutaw until 4 o'clock. The road was very bad. Half the way through thick pine forests which seemed of interminable length and so thick the road so narrow and winding that you could literally see nothing but pines. We went through a great many swamps. In so many places there was no name for them. We were half the time in water and once or twice in little creeks in which the water came quite up to the hub of the wheels and the horses would stop to drink. I never felt so cold hardly in all my life and was very tired when we reached the Eutaw. There was a most hearty welcome. We found Eliza and her father, William and his wife, their Aunt Mary and little Anna Sinkler Mr. James Sinkler's daughter.

You cannot think how nice every thing is here. The house is very pretty outside. Down stairs is the dining room and drawing room. On the left wing is my room and Mr. Sinkler's dressing room, and on the right wing is Eliza's room and her father's. I am sitting now in the drawing room with a little table drawn before a large oak fire with 2 tall spermaceti candles writing on a perfect sandal wood desk which came out in the Columbia from Charleston.

Mr. Sinkler and William went out on a foxhunt yesterday morning early. Indeed he and his brothers are constantly on horseback.

Yesterday Eliza and I went to walk accompanied by little Anna. We went to Belvidere a decayed plantation. Eliza warned me beforehand of an old black woman who was very queer who lived there, but said she hoped we would not see her. Unfortunately we encountered her at the gate and although I am accustomed to extreme affection on the part of the African Race, she quite exceeded anything I have ever seen before. On being told who I was she was at first perfectly dumbstruck. She could only say Mas Charles lady three or four times and then she caught hold of me and almost squeezed me to death, embraced me in the most extraordinary way. I could not get away from her and she kept chattering all the while but as her teeth are all gone and it is hard enough anyway to understand the plantation negroes I could not make out anything she said. Eliza said she was apostrophizing Mas Charles who used to kill her such good squirrels. As soon as I could get away from her she commenced her wants to Eliza and they were exorbitant enough. These I could understand very well. Oh Missy do send old Missy some fine Castile soap and please Missy some new frock and plenty "bacey." We got away from her and went into the house hoping she would have gone, but no she was waiting for us at the gate with the greatest alacrity. You would have laughed could you have seen how Eliza and I rushed past her but she caught hold of little Anna and commenced her wants. . . .

Anna has just come in the room. She wishes to be remembered to you and says she remembers you perfectly at the Yellow Springs. Eliza sends her love to you. So you see you are highly regarded. We breakfast here at ½ past 8, dine near 4 and have supper at 8. You would like the different sorts of hot cakes they have. They make nice bread which is very nice toasted. Eliza made some very nice ice cream or frozen custard which you would have liked.

You have no idea what a quantity of birds there are about. The weather has been delightfully mild out of doors and the songs of these birds fill the air. I have seen several mocking birds and there are plenty of partridges. Today after diner we went out to feed the poultry. Sampson got a basket of corn and you never saw such a sight of waddling ducks, gay roosters, swelling turkeys, and strutting bantams, and weak eyed geese and small necked guinea fowls about 100 in all. After that I have been making taffy at the fire in an outer room surrounded by an admiring group of young boys. It was pronounced excellent by all hands and Mr. Sinkler, Sr. says he will never buy candy again. I do hope everyone intends writing as long letters as I write. I shall always write by both mails but you must all remember the mails are very irregular. My very best love to all. Ever affectionately, E.S.

Only a month later Emily was beginning to feel comfortable with her new family's customs. She was also learning the ways and habits of the African American slaves, which were so different from the freed African American servants she had known in the Wharton household in Philadelphia. But most of all, as we see in these next letters, Emily was homesick, missing her brothers, sister, and friends.

Eutaw, December 1ˢᵗ, 1842

My Dear Mamma,

The boy is going to the Post Office today and I do hope I will get letters. Do you know that this is my fifteenth letter and I have only received one in reply. I hope however that I am to be rewarded soon. You would laugh to see the mail-bag. On Mondays Mr. Gaillard a neighbour sends, on Thursdays we send. Each bag is large enough to contain all the correspondence of South Carolina but it never has more than a half dozen letters at the utmost. Eliza is an inveterate correspondent. She has eight intimate friends who are written to constantly. Anna never writes. Do you think Frank will come? I hope he will. I am sure he will be delighted with every thing but would advise him not to go on too high a key at first as to horses. He will soon get tired out. I would like him very much to bring me something when he comes. I will say it now for fear I forget it. I want him to bring me a wax doll for Huger Sinkler. If Mary will buy it I will be much obliged. I want a very simple small undressed one. Huger is a perfect creature of 3 years old. The first day she saw me somebody asked her before me if she did not love her Aunt Emily. She persisted for a long time in saying no and would give no reason why. She would not tell me or her Aunt Eliza but at last said she would tell one of her sisters. After a great deal of whispering it came out that, "me don't love Sonnys' daw Mudder as she no bring me a wax baby." It seems that this is her acme and she thought I certainly would have brought her one.

Everything has gone on as usual. My *beau-père* returned from town day before yesterday and among other things brought a very handsome guitar for Anna and myself. I am going to try to teach her a little but I doubt my abilities very much as you know I am not very great at that sort of thing. The Schooner Emma has arrived and my boxes will be here tomorrow probably and Anna and I intend practicing duets very diligently when she recovers. I think my voice has improved very much since I have been here. In looking over a Charleston paper on Monday evening I observed the list of passengers in the Wilmington boat and the names at the head of the list were Miss Drayton and Miss Wharton. Poor Mary what a fall she had. I was very much startled when I read the letter you said Sunday might have recorded a most tragic event but I thought it was Sunday night and then went on and was not relieved until I read she was not hurt. Was it cold in Philadelphia? For the last two days here it has been quite cold but today it is lovely. I am going soon to take a drive. We took a lovely one yesterday afternoon. I suppose Grandmama is with you now. Do give her my love. I am continually reminded of her by Aunt Mary here.[17] She is younger than Grandma by 12 years but she has her ways very much. We have a very anxious time lately with poor Anna. She was taken very sick on Saturday but she would not have the Doctors until Monday when she was so ill we had to send for him twice once in the evening. She is recovering now but she has suffered a great deal. I don't know what we would have done without Aunt Mary, for of course Eliza and I had not an idea what to do and I would not have spoken to the Doctor without almost dying. She looks wretchedly and Aunt Mary thinks her constitution entirely ruined. And all owing to her ridiculous repeated imprudence. Mr. Sinkler sends his love and says he wants to write to you but I insisted on writing. Ever affectionately, Emily Sinkler

Eutaw, December 1st, 1842

My dear Papa,

I have not a very long time to write in but as I hope you think a short letter is better than none at all I have begun this one. What do you think your friend Mr. Peter has been doing lately—Writing the most ridiculous verses to Mrs. King in the *Lady's Book!*

That he should have chosen such a very trashy periodical. . . . Eliza takes it and I happened to open it and the first thing was a piece of poetry by the translator of Mary Stuart and William Tell . . . The Star of the West. Etc. In almost every *Lady's Book* there is a piece of verse in the same style.[18]

I think you would enjoy life here very much and the change would be very good for you. The Negroes would amuse you too much. The waiters are very much like Morris in some respects and talk very much in his style but the field servants are almost unintelligible. They are already making preparations for the three days dance at Christmas and are begging old clothes to make a figure in. They are allowed the use of the Piazza for three days. We wished for you at dinner yesterday very much. There was a pair of wild ducks on table, which were pronounced capital. Mr. Sinkler tells me to say they are infinitely superior to Canvass backs and red necks. They are duck and mallard I was told to say. There is an abundance of Partridges here. The yard is full of them but they are not allowed to be shot there. Snipe also abound. There are some very fine horses here although I believe you are not much of an equestrian according to Mamma.

I know you would like very much some of the old fashioned customs they have. Large oak fires in every room. After dinner and supper when the cloth is removed they place in the middle of the table an old fashioned carved silver stand holding four bottles of cordial and place two decanters on each side and some glasses. No one has touched it lately for Mr. Sinkler is afraid of his back and William has been away for the last three or four days. Tomorrow he and Brother Seaman make their appearance. Mr. Alfred Huger in Charleston talked a good deal of Mr. Rawle and Mr. Scott said he was in the same class in college with Mr. Rawle.[19] I hope he has not been getting in any scrapes lately. Do dear Papa write very soon and make the others write. This is the 16th letter home, 12th to the family and I have only had one letter. Franks I don't count much. I begin to feel a little discouraged. Send an immense package of letters by Frank. I wish now and then you would send a newspaper—some Saturday paper I would like as they generally have a great deal of news in them. I have not seen a Philadelphia paper since I left. My next letter shall be much better. I must stop now. Ever affectionately your daughter, Emily

Only a few days later, Emily was again writing her "Papa," filling him in on how she spent her days. Religion was an important and central part of the Sinkler family routine. Each day began with morning prayers where selections would be read from the Bible and from the Psalms. All would kneel for prayers. Sunday was a day entirely devoted to prayer and church. Only religious tracts or newspapers were read on Sunday. Emily was used to the strict observance of Sunday, for in Philadelphia any street with a church, and almost all had churches, was roped off during Sunday service. This habit brought all traffic in Philadelphia to a halt on Sundays.

Emily refers in this letter to her father's dislike of "crossed" letters. Because paper was costly it was the custom to turn the last sheet sideways and write vertically between the horizontal lines. It is no wonder that Mr. Wharton found this custom irritating, as the resulting confusion made reading difficult. Emily also refers to "Grand Mama," who was Mary Coré Griffith and was a writer of some note.

ə ə ə

Vances Ferry, So Ca
Dec 6, 1842 Recd. 14th
T. I. Wharton, Esq.
150 Walnut Street
Philadelphia, Penn
Eutaw, December 5th, 1842

My dear Papa,

I was very glad to receive your letter. I was on the lookout for some time and at last at 6 o'clock in the evening I saw the boy come galloping up the avenue with the bag on his shoulder. It was brought to me and I was delighted to find one in your handwriting, as I expected a treat. You can judge of the extent of the correspondence of Mr. Gaillard's family and ours when that was the only letter in the bag and the little Banner and 2 Charleston Papers, the only newspapers. I was very much amused with the account of the new Prayers, Henry, etc. Your messages were all faithfully delivered. Mr. Sinkler Sr. said a great many complimentary things. Eliza desired me to say that her appetite has greatly increased. My sense of truth does not permit me to second her assertion. I hope you will write me very often just such letters. Tell Mary that I expect answers to both my letters before I write again to her. Has she seen any Metcalves lately?[20]

Perhaps you would like to know how we spend our days, thinking as we are in the country that interesting dialogue, "I see no toys and shops, etc. How do you pass your time!!" Breakfast is from half-past 8 to quarter of 9. I get up after 7. Mr. Sinkler five mornings out of seven gets up at four or five and mounts a horse and goes off to shoot wild ducks or deer or foxes. All the family assembles at 9:30 for family prayers. There is a great variety of hot cakes, waffles, biscuits. I don't take to all these varieties however and always eat toast for breakfast and supper. They make excellent wheat bread and toast it very nicely by the coals. Hominy is a most favorite dish. They eat it at all three meals. It is what is called grits in Philadelphia. We take breakfast in the hall and sit there all the morning.

Soon after breakfast our little carriage comes to the door and we set off to take a drive. The whole equipage is quite *comme il faut*. The carriage is perfectly plain just holding two persons. The horses are very dark brown with plain black harness. When we set out the dogs come running up so we have a cortege of two greyhounds and two terriers generally, one a perfect creature looking like a little horse; not much esteemed by the family. I have named him Spry. We are always preceded by Sampson on horseback to open gates. We are home at 12 or 1 and I then read and sew etc. until dinner time.

Mr. Sinkler goes off with his brothers to hunt and shoot partridges until dinner. They are always as you see on horseback. But you would be surprised to see how different Mr. Sinkler looks. He has grown fat already and has an excellent color.

We dine between half-past 3 and 4. Eliza is an excellent house-keeper. The ice cream here is really the best I ever tasted. After dinner I go out and feed the poultry which are now very well acquainted with me and are exceedingly obstreperous if I am late, standing at the foot of the steps and calling vociferously. I have a great favorite among them, the frizzly fowl. Its feathers are all put on the wrong way, which gives it the most ridiculous look. We have supper at 8 or half-past which is very much like breakfast except we have cold meat and after the cloth is removed wine and cordials. In the evening we have music, both piano and guitar.

The weather is exactly like Spring here and I suppose it is not very cold in Philadelphia. Yesterday was Sunday and as we had no church Eliza read the service and I read a sermon while Anna performed the part of Congregation. Next Sunday we hope to have church at the Parish church. Mr. Dehon, son of Bishop Dehon, is the rector.[21] After our service Eliza and I took a walk up the avenue which is nearly a mile long and the sun felt like midsummer. It was cold enough for ice on Thursday. The thermometer in the piazza after sundown was 64.

On our return Eliza and I found on the steps a young black woman whom after the accustomed salutation said she had brought a present. She had brought an apron full of eggs and wanted a calico dress in return to dance in at Christmas. She lives at one of Mr. Sinkler's plan-tations a few miles off and was a picture of affected modesty, keeping one hand before her face all the while and curtseying at every word. A boy of 16 came in the afternoon for a cast off frock coat to dance in. He said that William must give him one for Duck Peter had got a jacket given him and that he was ashamed to show his face. William gave him a frock coat and I wish you could have seen him going up the avenue grinning at every step and turning around to look if any one was looking at him. They are making great preparations for their dance though several are opposed to it on religious principles. They all call me Miss Emily but in speaking to me they say Missus.

I will stop now as I know gentlemen do not like crossed letters. In my next letter I will give you an account of the way the Negroes are arrayed. My Mr. Sinkler sends his most affectionate regards to you and Eliza desires her respects. Tell grand mama I wish she would write to tell me what work she is doing. Love to all. Your affectionate daughter, Emily

With warm weather continuing into December, Emily enjoyed visits from her neighbors, the Keating Simonses of Chickasaw Plantation. She had also spent the night with James and Margaret Sinkler at their plantation, Wampee, and enjoyed their children, Allen and Huger. As was the custom during duck hunting season, the Simonses brought the house a fine brace of wild ducks as a present. Emily, who loved music, was delighted to find that the African American slaves played the fiddle and that her young nieces and nephews enjoyed patting their feet to a good tune. One somber note was Emily's discovery that South Carolina laws prevented slaves from being educated. Emily fashioned a way around this law by instructing her servants using a religious pretext. And Charles, likewise, had a regular Sunday class with "the boys." Emily adored Charles's older brother Seaman Deas Sinkler, and, as seen in this next letter, she began to practice the music of Gaetano Donizetti, singing arias from *Anna Bolena, Puritani,* and *Lucia di Lammermoor,* especially for him.

Eutaw, December 10th, 1842

My dear Mary,

Brother Seaman returns to town on Monday morning early and I therefore intend writing by him instead of Vances Ferry P. O. which two last letters every one omits writing on the direction. Your letter was thankfully received along with Frank's and Helen Coxs'—what a poor shabby fellow Frank is! He is really too bad—never writes to me and gives Mr. Sinkler all the credit of writing while I am never noticed. I was very much surprised to find by your letter that you have had cold weather in Philadelphia. We have actually been suffering with warm weather. Imagine a Philadelphia May with sunshine. No fire, all the doors and windows open. To my great satisfaction it is cooler today as we have had rain. Every thing goes on very much the same here since I wrote last Monday. On Tuesday we dined at Wampee and on Wednesday had a bridal visit from Mr. and Mrs. Keating Simons who stopped on their way to Chickasaw, his place where we intend dining next week. We have had several visitors last week which is an event in the country, when we are sitting in the hall to hear it exclaimed there is a carriage coming up the avenue and the conjectures, etc.

I got into quite a scrape the other day—it is quite the custom to send presents of game, etc. and by way of a joke I told one of the servants always to bring me whatever came. We were sitting in the parlour with Mrs. Simons when Henry came in and gave a note to Eliza and told me there was a fine pair of wild ducks come. I immediately told Eliza they had been sent to me, and who had sent them. To my horror she replied Mrs. Simons. Of course they were not meant for me. I don't think it was noticed. We spent a night last week with Brother James and had a very pleasant time. He has very nice children. In the evening how you would all have laughed to have seen Allen and Huger dancing to the violin played by Orlando a blackey self taught—the door open and black heads of all sizes grinning in. We are all delighted to have Brother Seaman with us—he will certainly be back by Christmas again. Anna and I are practicing diligently *Norma* duets for him. My voice has improved very much since I have been here.

In looking over a Charleston paper yesterday I observed this under the head of news from Texas though I suppose you have long since heard it: "Mr. Napoleon B. Garnier was killed a fortnight ago in San Augustine by Gen. J. Pinckney Henderson. Garnier was a noted desperado and had threatened to shoot Gen. Henderson and was about to carry his menace into effect when the latter anticipated his enemy by stepping into a house where he obtained a gun and killed his enemy on the spot!" It is shocking. I should think that in this country he would be tried for manslaughter as it could not be entirely called self-defense as he went into a house to get a gun with the intention of killing. Do tell Frank he must go call on Miss Huger at Lizzie Middletons. They say she is exceedingly pretty and about 17, or 18. Lizzie has written me since I have been here and I wish Frank would go.

My boxes have come safely. Tell Mary Baker my box arrived perfectly dry but the book box got water in it and wet some of the books. They are now dried however. Mamma's picture has been shown and

Mr. Sinkler Senior and Eliza think it a capital likeness and Anna remembered her perfectly by it. I am quite ashamed of this letter. Little Anna has been standing by me all the while talking. She says do Aunt Emily say Huddy to your brother Henry for me. The baby calls me Anemone and Huger An' Emidy.

I wish I could do what Frank says with regard to the black children or frogs as he calls them but it is impossible. It is entirely forbidden by the laws of South Carolina and it would be very wrong for me to attempt to instruct them especially as Mr. Sinkler entirely disapproves of it. They are some of them very religious and have their own preachers. You will be glad to hear Mr. Sinkler meets with not the slightest opposition from any of the family and goes on Sunday to teach the boys. I would like to go and so would Eliza but it is 12 miles ride on a bad road on horseback so we don't think of it. There were no boys there last Sunday. I must stop now abruptly and will write better next time. Do all write soon. Your affectionate sister, Emily

P.S. Do don't let any one send me any sugar plums, I am disgusted with them. But if there is ever an opportunity and if you feel an inclination do send me a few honey figs like we used to have last winter and a little piece of sweet potato. Cool I am to think any one thinks to send me anything. Love to GranMarty be sure.

Emily's first Christmas at Eutaw was alive with festivity and the heady experience of being the center of attention as Charles's new wife. The entire Sinkler family assembled at Eutaw Plantation, and with only four bedrooms, it must have been something of a tight fit.

The first of many present boxes arrived from the Whartons. The inclusion of the *Illustrated London News* and periodicals such as the *Ladies Register,* the latter of which included current poetry, music, receipts, and fashions, was much appreciated at a time when the printed medium was the only method of keeping in touch. The reference to "the Wistar party cards" is to the gatherings held in Dr. Caspar Wistar's house in Philadelphia. Dr. Wistar was a noted Philadelphia doctor who held once-a-week soirees for Philadelphia's learned elite at which riddles and conundrums were posed and answered. At Wistar's death, Mr. Wharton continued to hold "Wistar Parties" in his house, where genteel company were invited.[22] Emily notes that Eliza had not changed her desultory eating habits despite receiving a delicious cake. Eliza, as the lady in charge of housekeeping, was extremely hard-working and slept and ate very little. Emily felt that she was working herself to an early grave.

Emily's first Christmas at Eutaw was a glorious occasion where black as well as white celebrated with dancing and fireworks for a full five days. The Sinklers turned the front piazza over to the African American community for three evenings of dancing, with music provided by African American slave fiddlers. As Emily notes, William Sinkler was "Maussa" to his slaves.

December 24, 1842

Dear Papa,

I have delayed writing until this Post as I wished to announce the safe arrival of the box. It has come safely and I cannot say how much I am delighted with everything in it. Mr. Sinkler Sr. is gratified and pleased with your remembrance of him in shape of the bottle and also the Wistar party cards. Eliza sends her respects to you and says that is the most acceptable cake you could possibly send to her. She was very much touched by the attention although I am sorry to say her habits are no better. The soap has been universally admired, it is indeed beautiful. The prayer book is the handsomest I ever saw and it is the very thing Mr. Sinkler wanted. He sends thanks to you and Mamma very much for them. He has gone with Seaman to shoot ducks or else would say more. Who thought of sending me the *Ladies Register*? It is the very thing I wanted. Do you know it contained the most charming receipts which Eliza and I are going to try. Last evening you would have been amused with the scene in the hall. Every member of the family, 10 in number was seated round the table each with one of the London Newspapers in his or her hand. Everyone is delighted with them. The sugar plums are delightful. I have not yet brought out that very cunning box of paté, but the others were placed on the table to be brought out every day after dinner. Every one of the name of Sinkler in this county pronounced them excellent. Brother Seaman who professes to be a judge of everything Parisian says they are bona fide.

Have you had a Merry Christmas in Philadelphia? I hope I will have a long account written to me of the proceedings. How much amused you would have been at every thing here. Early on Christmas morning before break of day the Negroes began to arrive from the different plantations of Mr. Sinkler and I was soon awakened by loud knocking on my door and then "Merry Christmas Masse Charles, may you have many many years. Merry Christmas Miss Emily, long life and prosperity to you." They went to every door in the house and made some such speech. One went to Brother James and said "Merry Christmas Massa, may you have tousand years and have me to drive you horse all de time." As soon as I came out of my room I was surrounded by all the House Servants eager to catch me. That is to say Merry Christmas, etc. first. Such laughing and screaming you never heard. Before breakfast everyone takes a glass of egg-nog, and a slice of cake. It is the universal custom and was not on this occasion omitted by anybody. As Christmas was kept five days egg-nog was regularly drank every morning. After breakfast a most amusing event took place. Every four or five minutes companies of women arrived to give their presents and wish Merry Christmas. They bring us presents each about half a dozen eggs and although they were all intended for their Missy (Eliza) I insisted upon having some, always to their great delight. I managed to collect about 100 eggs which of course the next day I gave to Eliza for her domestic purposes. All of the Negroes had their presents made them of new clothes and it was a perfect Babel what with their thanks and their excessive rapacity for more although each had a full share. Their maussa stood out on the Piazza helping them and of course a great deal of attention was paid to me as being Massa Charles new lady. Both he and I were very much congratulated all Christmas morning.

As I know you do not like crossed letters I will continue my account of the Negro festivities in a letter I am going to write to Mary. The whole family are assembled here keeping Christmas. Seaman has come from town. Brother James and his wife and five children are staying here and after dinner everyone of the name is collected round the table which can be said of very few families. Little Anna Sinkler came just now to ask if I was writing to you and say Huddy to you for her. She talks a great deal about Henry and feels the deepest interest in him. Give my best love to Mamma and tell her I will write to her next mail day. Goodbye dear Papa, Your affectionate daughter, Emily

III

Dealing with Pneumonia and Whooping Cough, Winter 1843

THE WINTER OF 1843 WAS to be a severe one for the Sinkler family. With the onset of cold weather, pneumonia and whooping cough spread throughout the plantations. Emily herself had a severe case of whooping cough, an infectious disease involving catarrh of the respiratory passages and characterized by spasms of coughing interspersed with deep, noisy inhalation. Emily's nephew caught pneumonia and died of it.

The Sinklers' burial ground was at St. Stephen's Episcopal Church in St. Stephen, South Carolina, which would have been at least a thirty-mile trek over bad roads from Eutaw. With death in the family, all the ladies went into mourning, wearing black. Emily's spirits were subdued by the death of James and Margaret Sinkler's third son, John Sinkler (1841–43).

Eutaw, January 18th 1843

My dear Mamma,

I can only write a very short letter to day, as dear little Johnny died last evening at 8 o'clock. I was over at Wampee in the morning and thought he was looking better than I had seen him for a day or two but he grew gradually worse after that. His grandfather went over as usual from the Eutaw at sundown and Anna and I expected him back at 7 or 8 o'clock but he did not return until nearly 11. You can have no idea how distressed the whole family is. All his uncles and Eliza have staid over at Wampee since he was first taken. This morning early Mr. Dehon was sent for and Anna and I carried the children over as the funeral service was to be read in the house and the body then carried to St. Stephen's Parish where is the family burying ground. It was the saddest scene I ever witnessed. Never did I see such agony as his father suffered. He took each one of his children into the little body. None of them of course can understand it except William the eldest and he is heart broken, his little summer duck he calls him. Everyone went in to see him but I could not go. I could not bear to see the little fellow laid out and even in the room when his little coffin was brought in and laid on a table in the middle of the room I did not look round once. I suffered enough without adding to it gloomy death feelings. You don't think it was wrong do you?

Immediately after the funeral service he was put in a carriage and his Uncle William and Uncle Charles have gone down to St. Stephen's with him and he will be buried to night and they will come back some time tomorrow, I hope, for they have not slept here (or any where much) for a week. Brother James is just setting off about now and will be there in time to see his little son put in the grave. This child was his darling and his pride. Although Seaman had prepared him for the child's death yet he had hoped to the very last. His poor mother though, for a week he has never been out of her arms once, and when they told her he was dead and took him from her arms she did not say a word or shed a tear. The only time she has shown any life was this morning. She said she must see him but the moment she did she fainted dead away and has been lying perfectly calm ever since. Eliza will I expect have a fit of sickness. Before the child was taken ill she looked wretchedly thin owning to her habits of eating nothing and sleeping only three or four hours at night but for a week she has literally taken nothing and sat up with him every night, not having taken off her dress once and now she is a perfect wreck.

Both she and Anna are going in mourning and I shall of course have to send to town by Seaman for a black silk dress and black ribbon for my bonnet and the dress can be very well made here, as there is an excellent mantua maker here. I never saw such an intelligent child. To the very last he was conscious and knew every one. He made signs for water when he wanted it and just before he died squeezed his grandfather's hand. His constitution was remarkably strong and both doctors say he stood what no other child could. On the plantation adjoining his fathers died only a few days ago old Mr. Gaillard from just the same disease, pneumonia. I have written dear Mamma but a dull letter but you will excuse it I know. I can think of nothing else now. I was disappointed in not hearing from any of you by the last mail. I have not heard now for three weeks nearly not since the 30th of December. Ellen McIlvaine and Susan Campbell wrote to me by the last mail. Love to all, I will write better next time. Ever your affectionate daughter, Emily

Emily herself did not escape disease and was sick with whooping cough for over two months. She describes the remedies available at the time for whooping cough. She also talks about the upcoming race events at Pineville, a town about twenty miles from Eutaw. There was a private racetrack at Eutaw, and Hercules, the African American trainer, was known statewide for his skill in training thoroughbred racehorses. Emily was bemused by the attention lavished on horseflesh by her Sinkler in-laws.

February was Race Week in Charleston, with four days of racing at the Washington Race Course (site of the present-day Hampton Park) put on by the South Carolina Jockey Club. The Jockey Club Ball was held during the week, as well as the Saint Cecilia Society Ball and the Military Ball of the Washington Light Infantry. There was a pavilion for the ladies at the track. Emily loved the bustle, excitement, and thunder of horses' hooves. The ladies had special seating in the grandstand. The price of admission was $1.50 for an omnibus and ten cents for each passenger, while a buggy and a pair cost seventy-five cents.[23]

Emily's father in law, William Sinkler, had three horses entered in the 1843 Race Week—Hero, Santa Ana, and Jeanette Berkley. He had just won the silver cup at the Pineville Races with Hero, his three-year-old. The Sinklers' racing silk color was red. The *Charleston Courier* described the events of each day's race in a daily column, "Race Week." "Every necessary arrangement has been made to preserve order and regularity for a gala week of pleasure and enjoyment . . . a period during which the courtesies and civilities of life are interchanged with our country friends. . ." On February 22, with a purse of $1,000, William Sinkler's Santa Ana came in second on the first race; on February 23, with a purse of $750, Mr. Sinkler's Jeanette Berkley came in second; on the third day of the race, with a $500 purse, Mr. Sinkler's Hero was the favorite and was also the winner. On the final day, for the three-mile heats, Mr. Sinkler's Hero was again the winner. "Thus ended a week of high enjoyment and pleasure and thus may it always be during the week that annually brings together the best blood and chivalry of Carolina and the bright and smiling faces and fair forms of Carolinas lovely daughters."[24]

In this next letter Emily begins to number each letter to each family member, so that she could find out whether her letters were reaching their destination.

❧ ❧ ❧

22d. I shall mark my letters after this
Eutaw February 6th, 1843

My dear Papa,

What can have become of Taylor? He has not been heard of in Charleston and I really cannot imagine where he has secreted himself. Brother Seaman came up from town yesterday and I fully expected he would bring the package but he had heard nothing of it and his name has not been seen in any of the lists of arrivals. I cannot think what is the reason you do not receive my letters regularly. Frank says in his last letter that mine come very irregularly. Now all you write never fail to make their journey in either four or five days after their post mark.

I have something to tell you which I think will surprise you. What do you think of my having the regular whooping cough? I did not intend to have said anything about it until it was all over but it is so much better now and I am afraid you might hear an exaggerated account of it that I thought it best to tell you myself. One of the servants had been up the country this fall where the whooping cough was raging and returned about two weeks after I got here. He had a cough but insisted upon it that he had never whooped. I shook hands with him and he was constantly about and the next thing was his brothers all got it and then it spread all over the Plantation. As soon as they had any suspicion they kept them all away from the house and I was not in the least afraid of catching it. Before Christmas I got a little cough and cold which I thought nothing of until four weeks ago when I began to whoop.

It is now just four weeks since I first began and the worst is now decidedly over. I am delighted I have had it for it has not been violent though I never had an idea what a distressing thing it was. Brother Seaman was up here about two weeks ago when it had nearly reached the height and said there was nothing to be done for it but time. He says now that it is on the decline and will not last many weeks longer. He gave me a little bottle of paregoric, squills, nitre etc. which I took one night but I did not sleep any the better for it so I left it off. About a week ago he sent me from town another bottle a mixture of ether, belladonna and opium, a most horrid tasting thing but it did not do me any good. I really have suffered a great deal. For ten days I was not able to leave my room and now I cannot taste or smell anything. I am just beginning to sleep at night but I used to have at least twelve fits in the night and every time I coughed be obliged to stand up in bed to get my breath. To show you how much better I am I only had three fits last night and three before breakfast. I have not been able to eat anything but liquids ever since I began and indeed I don't see much use in taking anything for the first fit I have after eating anything I cough every thing up without the slightest hesitation. That has been a symptom with all the Negroes on the Plantation. I am afraid I have been rather tediously minute but I thought Mamma would like to hear. I think it is a great blessing I have had it now for I have certainly had it lightly and Seaman says I have it very favourably. Of course it made me very weak when it was at the worse but I go out to ride every fine day and they all say I never looked better since I came here.

How Henry would enjoy being here now. The races are just beginning in a country town about 20 miles from here and the gentlemen are all full of it.[25] The races begin tomorrow and last for three days. The Charleston races begin next week. They have sent five horses from the stables here. Jeanette Berkley is the name of the horse. She is going to run both here and in Charleston and they think she has a good chance.

It is ridiculous the care they take of them, each horse has two boys to take care of him and a groom to take care of all of them. The horses eat the most dainty food and have to be rubbed with whiskey and actually drink it too. Every day before they take exercise they eat twenty eggs. Tell Henry I wish he could have seen Mr. Singleton's horses. They spent a night here on their way down. One named Kate Converse used to belong to William and he sold it to Mr. Singleton for 3,000 dollars after she had made 500 dollars in a race. I have just had an invitation to the Jockey Club Ball to which I shall not go. I hope I shall get a letter from home tonight by the mail. Give my best love to all. I shall write soon again. Ever dear Papa your affectionate daughter, Emily

Mr. Sinkler sends his love.

IV

Questions of Slavery and the Temperance Movement, Winter 1843

EMILY'S NEXT LETTER SHOWS some of her feelings about the slave-based society within which she was immersed. Charles Sinkler was now farming both Eutaw and Apsley Plantations, and so slave families were separated between the two. Cotton cultivation was hard work for everyone in the slave community. Eutaw and Apsley were cotton plantations with hundreds of acres of fertile, black, loamy topsoil. In fall the unpicked fields stretched antiseptic white against the gray earth.

Cotton did not always rule the hinterland of South Carolina. In 1793 Eli Whitney's invention of the cotton gin allowed seedpods to be extracted from short staple cotton. Cotton and the institution of slavery were synonymous. In 1780 South Carolina grew only one million pounds of cotton, mostly long staple Sea Island cotton, and had fewer than one hundred thousand slaves. By 1860 South Carolina had over four hundred thousand slaves, comprising 52 percent of the state's population. Over two billion pounds of cotton were exported worldwide but especially to Philadelphia, whose thriving textile industry used tons of cotton to make hosiery and cloth.

Cotton culture was back-breaking, hard work, all done by the hands of slave families. Late in the winter, the ground had to be prepared for the planting in early spring; throughout the summer, there was steady work thinning the plants and chopping out the grass; late in August, the bolls began to burst, announcing the start of a picking season that continued well into the winter. As picking progressed, the cotton had to be ginned, weighed, pressed into bales, wrapped in bagging, and then tied in preparation for its trip to Charleston, generally down the Santee Canal.

❧ ❧ ❧

Eutaw Feb 11th, 1843

Your letter arrived last night dear Mamma but what do you think of that wretched Taylor! Brother Seaman wrote last night that he had received Papa's letter the day before. He then went immediately to Mrs. Oates who told him she had never received any such package. Is it not too bad. I really am dreadfully disappointed and my jaundiced imagination pictures to itself the package as immensely large and containing long letters from every possible person. I am too sorry about Mr. Neville's letter.[26] What ought to be done to such a Taylor! But I cannot allow myself to dwell any longer on the subject except to say I hope the loss will be made up to me by new letters. I would not advise private opportunities however unless you are very sure of the person for indeed I think the mail is not so much to blame as you all seem to imagine. I am pretty sure I have received all the letters you have written and they always get here four or five days after they are written. Do in the future number your letters if it is not too much trouble and then I will know for certain.

I was very much amused at what you said about my cough in your letter. The fact was I had for a long while kept up a dead silence about it and would not let Eliza mention it for fear you might think it worse than it really was. But I hope now you don't feel the slightest uneasiness about me for it is I really think nearly well, so much so that I have on an average but three fits of whooping and coughing during the day and but two at night. I have regained my strength almost completely and I am able now to go out to the school room and teach the children for I cannot bear to be doing nothing.

I only wish I could teach the little blackeys. When Huger slept with me her little maid Serena, slept also in the room on the floor. I taught her a prayer which I made her say every night and gave her some general ideas. I found she had some previous ideas on the subject but as you can imagine it was a hard thing for me to preserve suitable gravity when listening to her answers. I believe there is a great deal more religion among them than you would think, for Mr. Dehon is coming very soon to give them instructions. They are certainly a most unaccountable race in some respects. With the exception of the house servants who are more like us they show a most lamentable want of feeling towards their own flesh and blood. Instances happen every day of their utter disregard of each other especially in sickness. They have to be forced to take care of the sick and if when they have charge of one he does not recover immediately, they would leave him to die if they were not made to stay and give the medicines, and then half the time they give all at once a dose that is to be given through the day! Even the death of their own children they view with the most philosophical indifference. It is nothing uncommon for a woman to come up to you and say with a most smiling and placid countenance, "oh Missy you know I jus bury dat lilly baby you 'mire todder day." When Mr. Sinkler bought Apsley all his servants were sent there and one day the mother of one of them came in my room. I told her I was very sorry, Bull had to leave her but that he would have very little to do and should come and see her every Sunday. She said for her part she was very glad he was gone, that she had too many children already in her house, that his Maussa's was the right place for him, and I had better give him plenty to do. One named Mollo came to see me on Sunday and I made some consolatory remark to him about his wife who is on this Plantation when he pretty plainly told me that he thought her a good riddance for she was continually fighting and scratching him. I feel very sorry (though it is the best thing for them) for their perfect indifference to their situation.

I have written on without thinking that you may find it rather a tiresome subject and I am sure I don't see how it has grown out of whooping cough. Do you not think it is a very good thing my having had it? For it certainly has not done me any harm for I am perfectly well so don't imagine me as I know you with your usual way will be sure to do, looking squalid and thin, on the contrary they all say I am looking remarkably fat and well. Every thing is going on here just the same. Mr. Sinkler sends his love. He went off this morning to spend a day or two with a friend of his about 20 miles from here and enjoy a deer hunt. He will write soon I know.

Eliza thinks of going down to Charleston to spend a short time. She is very anxious to go but I am afraid she will not be able to get off for her father cannot bear her to leave home and I really think her health requires it. She is not looking at all well and wants relaxation very much. She is kept continually on the go here for housekeeping is very different at the South from at the North, though I think one thing is, people here give themselves too much trouble about it and have a great many too many servants about the house which of course creates great confusion. For instance there are but four bedrooms to be attended to in the house and there are five chamber-maids to attend to them so of course that makes just five times as much confusion as is necessary.

I have finished your footstool. It really looks beautifully. I would like to send it on to you if I could hear of any one going to Philadelphia but even then I should almost be afraid to trust it after the trustlessness of that Taylor. Do you remember a man named Kidder who a long time ago took an album of mine to New York to be drawn in and never was heard of afterwards. Don't let any one make a pair of slippers for Papa. I am working him a very pretty pair. Give my love to him and tell him I wish I could send him one of the fine shad that are very plentiful here now. I have not heard anything about Grandma for a long time except through Aunt Hannah who wrote me a long letter the other day in which she copied a piece of verse Grandma had sent her at Christmas. I hope she will be in Philadelphia when we return. Dinner is ready dear Mamma so I must stop. With love to all, I am ever your affectionate daughter, Emily

I wrote to Frank last. Thank Papa for the *Punch.*

Eutaw, March 15, 1843

My Dear Papa,

As the mail which Mamma scolds so much may have failed this time and not have given my last letter to Mary, I will say again in this that your letter of the 1st of March containing the check arrived safely. I am very much obliged to you for it and have put it away safely. The London Papers have afforded much entertainment here for they are not to be got in Charleston, as indeed also have done the various Ladies' Magazines to the female part of the community. Leslie (Miss) has surpassed herself in her Home book. I hope Mary read it before it came here for there are some of the richest things from her pen I ever saw. I have been quite relieved to find you are all at last beginning to believe me about my cough being well. It is indeed so now I have not had any symptom of its returning for two weeks, so I think that now being out of the woods I can fairly cry. Are there any signs of Mary, Frank or Henry's breaking out with it? Everything is Spring like now and reminds me of May with us although it is very backward season owing to a cold spell which came on a couple of weeks ago and put everything back. We think of leaving here in the beginning of April and I shall try to make an arrangement with Mrs. Fisher about coming on with her. This is mail day and I hope our ebony courier will bring back with him letters for me. You are now in my debt and as I have written so lately I have not a great deal to say. When I return I will have quantities to tell about all I have seen which I know will amuse you all very much. I wrote to Aunt Hannah today and I hope and trust she will not show it about. Frank must prevent it for it strikes me it is a very trashy letter. She wrote me a very long letter sometime ago in which she says she sent to the church at Texas some of Franks' poetry about the dentist next door, his wives and Nancy to be the third. They must be exceedingly edified with it.

Brother Seaman brought up with him a few days ago a French book I think you would like very much and which the Philadelphia Library ought to get. It is called Mathilde on Les Memories d'une Jeune Femme, Par Eugene Sue. I don't know whether you would like it much for it is not in your line, but I know Mary would. It is not romantic and she could safely read it for it is highly proper. How does Frank make out now? I must confess I was rather at a loss what to make out of the Temperance Magazines he sent me a few days ago. Did he send them on account of the extraordinary pictures in them, or in a serious point of view? A Mr. Arthur has been writing some Temperance stories lately.[27] I saw the advertisement on the back of one of the Magazines you sent me which is called the wedding night or the story of a wife who tempted her husband to take a glass of wine on their wedding night. He became intoxicated from it and was a drunkard for four years after. Another is on the danger of a young lady's marrying any one who may become a drunkard. It is getting so near Post time dear Papa that I must finish this letter which I am almost ashamed to send, as it seems to me so poor. Give my best love to all and believe me your affectionate daughter, Emily

V

Summer Retreats—
Virginia and Flat Rock,
1844

WE DO NOT HEAR FROM Emily for eighteen months, during which time she undoubtedly returned for her usual summer visits to Philadelphia. Perhaps one of the reasons for the silence is the fact that Emily and Charles's first baby, Elizabeth Allen Sinkler, named for her aunt, was born on July 7, 1843. Philadelphia was a premier medical center in the antebellum years, and it is possible that Emily went home to Philadelphia to have Lizzie, as the new baby was quickly nicknamed. Undoubtedly Emily's routine of October through April at Eutaw Plantation continued. Because the plantations were so unhealthy from May to the end of September, Emily was forced to find other haunts where cooler weather prevailed. Thus we next find Emily and Lizzie on a trip to the springs and spas of the westernmost part of Virginia in her own barouche. She traveled there with her father-in-law, William Sinkler. They enjoyed the company of some of Charles's Navy friends, including the Trapiers, Mr. Beverly, and several other comrades.

Emily was traveling with her father-in-law and Eliza Sinkler, expecting to meet Charles, who was on orders in the Navy, in Flat Rock, North Carolina, in September. Flat Rock, even then, was the watering spot for Charlestonians. Charles Baring of England, whose manor house, Mountain Home, was a magnificent estate overlooking the Blue Ridge Mountains, founded Flat Rock in 1828. The Count de Choiseul followed in Baring's footsteps after having received letters in England concerning the salubrious situation in the mountains of western North Carolina. Choiseul was an emigré from revolutionary France and served on the board of Baring's bank before emigrating to North Carolina and building first Sans Soucie, a magnificent Victorian castle, and then Chanteloup, whose garden was to be designed by Frederic Law Olmsted. Thus the Flat Rock where Emily and Charles vacationed in 1844 was already becoming a preferred summer retreat for lowcountry South Carolinians as well as attracting the well-to-do from other states and abroad.

Salt Sulphur, August 28th, 1844
Francis Wharton Esque
150 Walnut Street, Philadelphia, Penna

Your letter today my dear Frank gave me the information I had been waiting for some time where to direct. I knew to direct to the White Mountains would be rather vague; indeed I have not the least idea whether you ever got there. So after receiving this letter you must sit down and give me an account of your perambulations—in a paternal mood—. The other day I told some gentlemen who were boasting of their walking exploits that they need not talk, that my brother had walked this summer from Philadelphia to the White Mountains and from there to Newport so you may suppose I am naturally anxious to know to what extent I have been romancing. If you have been there I suppose you have been as much delighted with mountain scenery as I am.

I like these Springs much better than the White although it was warm at first.[28] Now it is actually cold and has been so for several days. We cannot do at all without a large fire and two blankets at night. As you may imagine the weather makes it charming for walking and the walks about here cannot be surpassed. I have two acquaintances here who are always ready, Mr. Ogelby and Mr. Beverly. The latter is a Lieutenant in the Navy and you know all officers are noted for their attention to the consorts of their brothers in arms.

Yesterday morning we had almost an adventure. We made up a party to go and see a famous view about a few miles off. I invited the Trapiers to go in the barouche with me. Eliza and her father went on horse-back and three or four gentlemen preceded us on foot. The road was pretty bad up the mountain and we stopped at the house of the gentleman who owns the observatory we were going to. This observatory is built on the very top of the highest but one of the Alleghenies and we had a steep time in getting up to it— on foot of course. But when we reached the top of the observatory the view was splendid. There was one ridge after another of mountains like waves of the sea. Two Englishmen of the party said they had never seen anything to compare with it but we seemed at such a giddy height at the top of this very high building that I was glad to dismiss the picturesque and was quite contented with the view from the ground.

Mr. Ogelby then proposed our going home by way of the highest mountain and said the carriage could go. But such a road!! I hope never to see such another. It was almost perpendicular and one mass of rock piled one on top of another. Of course we got out and walked and when we were about a quarter of a mile from the carriage a regular mountain storm came up and we were forced to get in again with the addition of Eliza and then such a scene. All four curtained in and the carriage would bump first one side and then the other and the horses would rear and slip and Miss Hannah shrieked and Miss Sally shuddered. Miss Hannah would insist on peeping through the curtains. I told her not to. She would call out; "that horse fell then and now my side of the carriage is touching the ground." I could not help laughing but I was very glad to get home safe with only soreness from the jolt. The Trapiers did not enjoy themselves much here. They were here during the warm spell and until I came they never went out of their rooms and could not mix with any one.

I showed yours and Lizzie's letter to Mrs. Lowndes today as she was anxious to hear something about her sister Mrs. Allen Smith. Her father Judge Huger and I are great friends. He is a member of Congress from Charleston.[29] Mrs. Lowndes sent some message to you which I forgot about. You would like her much better than Mrs. Smith. We leave here on the last day of August (Saturday) for the Red Sulphur, stay there until Monday and then go to Abington, Virginia five days journey off, then to Greenville, Tennessee, three days, then to the Warm Springs of North Carolina near Asheville, and on the 16th of September expect to be at Flat Rock where Mr. Sinkler will meet us. We expect to stay in that region and in Greenville, S.C. until October. That is a delightful climate in the mountains and the favourite resort for Southerners who cannot come this far.

The Commodore has given Mr. Sinkler a months leave and at the end of that time if there is any case of sickness in Charleston he will leave me near Columbia at Mrs. Mannings or Col. Hamptons until the frost but I do not think there is the slightest chance.[30] It will then be October, and thus far which is quite late you know, they have had not a single case of fever and the average number of deaths has only been two whites and one black a week. Tell Mary I got number 6 today and on Sunday a *Recorder* and two *Ledgers*. The Recorder came very apropos. People talk here about he she until I am sick. A gentleman told me

that Mr. Tyng has just had offered him in Kentucky a church with a par-
sonage at $4,000 a year but declined and every one says he is using
every effort to be Bishop. Love to all, Ever yours, E. S.

The very next day Emily moved on to Red Sulphur Springs, where she
enjoyed the fine mountain venison and ice creams of a spa hotel. During the
nineteenth century, the "cure" was much in vogue all over Europe and America.
Fashionable spas grew up around sulphur springs, and a daily regime of bathing
and drinking sulphur waters began. Those with incurable diseases like tuberculosis, or consumption as it was then called, took the cure and exposed others, not
realizing that it was contagious. Little did Emily know that she was endangering
both her life and Lizzie's by sitting across from a consumptive at dinner.

Emily is asked in this letter about the "wars" going on in Philadelphia. All
during the 1840s there were race riots in Philadelphia as well as riots against the
new Irish Catholic immigrants. Philadelphia was a center of a militant anti-
Catholicism. Racism and anti-abolitionist activity were also rife in Philadelphia
in the 1840s. Philadelphia's African Americans occupied a separate world, segre-
gated by the color line. They had been disfranchised in 1838, and in 1842 a spectacular riot occurred when white hooligans attacked a parade of the Negro
Young Men's Vigilant Association, a temperance society. "In rioting that recurred
throughout the night . . . black men, women, and children were beaten, homes
were looted and the Smith Beneficial Hall, said to be an abolitionist meeting
place, and the Second Colored Presbyterian Church were burned to the ground.
Only the use of the militia on August 2 ended the riot."[31]

The Philadelphia of the 1840s also had over fifty-two street gangs of
teenagers and young men who fought each other "for territorial rights on street
corners, mauled and terrorized passersby and covered walls and fences with graf-
fiti." However, the most serious rioting of the decade, the riots of 1844, was
caused by "Philadelphia nativism and anti-Catholicism." "Many forces coalesced
in Philadelphia in the summer of 1844—Protestant clergy and laity, unchurched
masses, the popular press, politicians—to produce the worst mob violence that
had ever ravaged the city. The spark that set off the explosions was a letter written by Bishop [Francis Patrick] Kenrick on November 14, 1842 . . . asking that
Catholic children be allowed to use their own Bible and be excused from other
religious instruction while attending the public schools."[32] This request was
transformed by the anti-Catholic forces into a holy war or crusade. Riots, burning, and looting broke out in the Irish Catholic area of Kensington, perpetrated
by the Native American Party. "When it was all over three Catholic churches,
numbers of Irish Catholic homes, and a Female Seminary were burned, while a
total of 5,000 militia had been called in to quell the disturbance."[33] Undoubtedly

Emily was happy to be enjoying the spas and springs of Virginia, rather than being immersed in the "wars" and conflagration of Philadelphia, in the summer of 1844.

Emily gives a detailed description of how one went by carriage from Charleston to West Virginia. The C.H. in the designation of a town meant Court House. It is interesting to note that while Emily was voyaging across the South, her brother Frank was walking the White Mountains of New England. The Wharton family were all avid hikers.

ਣ‌ੴ ਣ‌ੴ ਣ‌ੴ

> *Red Sulphur Springs*
> *September 1st, 1844*

My dear Henry,

It is time that I should answer your letters or else I am afraid you will not be so prompt in writing again. We left the Salt Sulphur yesterday morning and got here just before dinner, a drive of seventeen miles. This is a very pretty place situated in a small valley with mountains rising on three sides like a triangle—very handsome buildings and an excellent table. But there is a great drawback to it. The water is thought to be very good for pulmonary complaints and consequently there are the greatest quantity of consumptives in the different stages of the disease, all about. At least every other man has a cough which as you may imagine makes the place very disagreeable and I am glad we are going away tomorrow.

The table is very nice. Delightful Charlotte Russes and ice cream with a regular bill of fare written out every day, but my opposite neighbour spoils all. Poor man he is evidently in the last stages of consumption and has an awful cough. When you go to watering places on your own responsibility you must be sure to come to The Virginia Springs. The White is the gayest and most fashionable but the Salt is decidedly my favorite. It is the nicest place I was ever at. You never saw such lovely walks and drives in all directions. I used to go out twice a day. There was a beautiful drive or walk to a little town called Union (where I bought this paper) which was a great favourite. It was a little more than three miles from the Salt and I walked there twice much to the surprise of the people who thought I would never get back.

I often wished Papa could have some of the nice mountain venison, which they had there in great abundance and which is thought to have a very fine flavour. There is a ball every night and plenty of the usual amusements. Little one used to go da-daing about the whole time but I did not let her drink any the sulphur water for it is bad for babies, notwithstanding her endeavours to get at it whenever she was at the Spring.

We leave here tomorrow morning on our journey. We sleep tomorrow night at Giles C.H. If you would like to look out our route on the map I will tell you the principal towns we passed through going on and which we will go through going back. Going on: Columbia, Winnsboro, Chester, York, S.C., Lincolnton N.C., Danville, Rocky Mount, Sweet Springs,Va. Going back: Giles C. H., Whythe C.H., Smyth C.H.,Abingdon Va., Greenville Tennessee, Warm Spgs N.C., Asheville, Flat Rock, N.C., Greenville, S.C. I don't know which route we will take from Greenville for Charleston but I know one thing and that is I shall be very glad to get settled. Traveling in your own conveyance is pleasant enough for a few days but I have had quite enough of it.

Tell Frank I received the Newspapers containing the account of his travels the day after I wrote to him and was delighted with them. I hope he has written some more of those letters. If he has he must be sure to send them to me. I could have told they were by him in a minute. I have sent on a little package to Mary by Mr. Beverly containing some hair and I will write to her next week and tell her what to do with it. Don't forget to tell her this in case the package should get to her before the letter. Mr. Beverly expects to be in Philadelphia about the 26th. Has Mr. Griffin made his appearance yet? I sat next to a gentleman at table today who seemed to come from the extreme Southwest. He struck up a conversation and asked me if I knew whether the wars in Philadelphia had ceased. What do you think of my cutting my first wisdom tooth today. It is quite funny to think of Lizzie and me cutting teeth at the same time. Lizzie is a very tricky little child, very full of little showing off ways and says papy and pretty very plainly. I must stop now for you must be getting tired of a crossed letter. Give my best love to all, Ever your affectionately, Emily

When Mr. Sinkler was on active duty in Charleston, as he was in the fall of 1844, Emily and Lizzie joined him at Stewarts Inn. In this next letter she has returned from her journeying to Virginia and North Carolina and tells of staying in Columbia on her way back to Charleston. Emily was surprised at the lowcountry custom of going and staying a week or more with friends. Mrs. Wade Hampton of Columbia was a special friend of Emily and Charles, and it is Mrs. Hampton's receipt for Charlotte Russe that Emily included in her receipt and remedy book.[34]

Charleston was a major commercial port in the antebellum years with barques, schooners, and steamships plying the coast trade, carrying cotton, timber, and naval stores to ports in the North. It also had a substantial navy yard where Charles Sinkler was the principal officer in charge. Emily mentions the difficulty of managing a port operation where many of the sailors were African American.

Charleston October 7th, 1844

My dear Papa,

I was just going to sit down to write to you when your letter containing the check arrived. I am very much obliged to you for it and have it carefully locked up. The Barque J. Patton Jr. has of course not yet arrived but I will write immediately when it does.[35] We got here safely on Friday the 4th and found everything waiting for us, and the city delightfully cool and perfectly healthy. There is not the slightest danger of my getting country fever. First place because I can't get it unless I go into the country and there has not been a single case of yellow fever or any other fever in Charleston the whole summer. Besides there have been two frosts in the country.

I spent a short time in Columbia most delightfully with Mrs. Manning. The people there are the most hospitable I ever saw and I have made all sorts of promises for visits this winter. People here think no more of asking you to spend a week with them than you would in Philadelphia of inviting to tea. I have promised to spend the time of the session with Mrs. Hampton. They are all a very generous family and just when I was there gave 15 thousand dollars to build a new Episcopal church in Columbia. Lizzie and I are very glad to be at the end of our journeying for some time and we are so pleasantly fixed here. James and William Sinklers family and ourselves all living together and Lizzie is enchanted with the children. She walks up and down the piazza as stiff as possible with them and you would be too much amused to see the cortege that accompanies her in her wagon, her four cousins pulling her and always at least four little blackeys holding on and all singing at the top of their voices Lizzie joining in. She has the most unbounded admiration for them and they for her.

Mrs. Middleton sent for me as soon as I got here and has been very kind in invitations. I was at a pleasant little party there. Tell Frank I received his letter at Columbia and will answer it next week. Also Aunt Hannah's which please tell her next Sunday I will answer very soon but I find very little time to write here to any but to those at home for my time is completely taken up with visits and family meetings. Those two letters are the only ones I have received of those which were directed here for Dr. Sinkler sent them to a place he thought we were to stop at so I will not get them until today when Eliza will bring them down.

Mr. Sinkler is at the Navy Yard today so he cannot send any message but he will write to you very soon. He is a great deal there and it is a very disagreeable place. He is the only official there and the sailors are all Negroes who are constantly in mutiny and he has the most unpleasant scenes. Indeed I never feel perfectly easy. The Commodore is never there and there is but one white man besides himself ever at the Yard. Almost every day he has to put some of them in irons and he hardly gets home before some one comes running for him to come there. I must stop now for I want this letter to go by today's mail. Excuse the hurry it has been written in and believe me your affectionate, E. S.

St. Philip's Episcopal Church, Charleston, South Carolina. Emily and Charles Sinkler attended St. Philip's, which she described as "the handsomest church I was ever in . . . All the pews, altar and pulpit . . . are walnut, and the church is filled with splendidly carved pillars, very elaborately done." (Courtesy of St. Phillip's Episcopal Church)

Epiphany Episcopal Church

EUTAWVILLE, SOUTH CAROLINA

Epiphany Episcopal Church, Eutawville, South Carolina. The church was constructed in 1849 as the chapel of ease for the Rocks Church; Charles Sinkler, Emily's husband, was a warden at both churches. (Courtesy of Epiphany Episcopal Church)

OLD ST. STEPHEN'S CHURCH ⋆ 1823

Old St. Stephen's Church, Philadelphia, Pennsylvania, the church attended by Thomas Isaac Wharton and his family. Located at 19 South Tenth Street, on the site where Benjamin Franklin flew his kite, the building was built in 1823. It was designed by William Strickland and decorated by Frank Furness and Louis Comfort Tiffany. (Courtesy of St. Stephen's Church)

St. John in the Wilderness, Flat Rock, North Carolina. Built in 1833 as a private chapel for Charles and Susan Baring, this historic and beautiful chapel was established as an Episcopal church in 1836. Emily and Charles spent many summer holidays in Flat Rock and would have attended St. John. (Courtesy of Historic Flat Rock)

Women's fashions from *Graham's Magazine,* circa 1848. Women of the 1840s kept up with the latest trends through such publications as *Graham's, Leslie's Fashion Monthly,* and *Godey's Lady's Book.* The French Second Empire mode depicted here featured gowns of silk accessorized with laces, ribbons, fringes, feathers, and flowers.

Women's fashions from *Godey's Lady's Book,* circa 1849. Note the lace cap with ribbons and flowers and the black mittens on the woman at left.

Women's fashions from *Godey's Lady's Book,* circa 1855. Note the jacket fastened by knots of satin ribbons and the collar and cuffs of lace on the woman at left, and the scarf mantel of embroidered lace and the bonnet of flowers on the woman at right.

Eutaw Plantation, oil by W. Russell Briscoe, 1976. Built in 1808 by William Sinkler on land abutting Eutaw Springs Battlefield, Eutaw was a cotton plantation. Emily Wharton Sinkler came there as the bride of Charles Sinkler in the fall of 1842. (Author's collection)

Eutaw Plantation. This photograph of Eutaw Plantation shows that the house stood fourteen feet off the ground on brick arches, so as to avoid Santee River freshets, and was constructed of unpainted cypress boards. (Author's collection)

Eutaw Plantation, rear elevation. This view of Eutaw shows some of the outbuild-
ings, including the churning shed, on the right, where butter and cream were
made, and the large stack of wood and kindling, on the left, for the many fireplaces.
(Author's collection)

The Lodge at Eutaw Plantation. This neoclassical building served as Seaman Deas
Sinkler's doctor's office when he was in residence at Eutaw. (Author's collection)

The weathervane from Eutaw Plantation as it is today. William Sinkler was famed for his racehorses, which often took first prize at the Washington Race Course in Charleston. (Author's collection)

Montage of Belvidere Plantation. Built in 1785 by Margaret Cantey, the widow of James Sinkler, Belvidere was a prosperous cotton plantation of several thousand acres on the banks of the Santee River. In 1847, when Charles resigned from the United States Navy and became a full-time cotton farmer, he and Emily made their permanent home at Belvidere. (Author's collection)

Belvidere Plantation, an etching from *Belvidere* by Anne Sinkler Fishburne, University of South Carolina Press, 1950. Rising fourteen feet off the ground on brick arches, Belvidere had a covered front porch and two large entry doors leading into the living room on the right and the dining room on the left. There were large elms in the front yard, which was grazed by sheep.

Belvidere Garden. Emily's garden had a long central allée planted with lavender, iris, and arbors of Cherokee roses. (Author's collection)

The Iris Walk at Belvidere, watercolor by Marty Whaley Adams Cornwall (top), and the iris walk as it was in Emily's day (bottom). (Top, courtesy of Marty Whaley Adams Cornwall; bottom, author's collection)

Garden Walk, Belvidere, circa 1910. Pictured are Emily Wharton Sinkler Roosevelt (left), the granddaughter of Emily and Charles Sinkler; and Elizabeth Allen Sinkler Coxe (right), Emily and Charles's oldest daughter. (Author's collection)

The front steps of Belvidere. With its canopy of Spanish moss and front porch entwined with Carolina jasmine, Belvidere was the epitome of an Upper St. John's cotton plantation. Note the tea olive trees Emily planted on either side of the steps. (Author's collection)

African American servants
at Belvidere, circa 1914.
(Author's collection)

African American children
in a cotton field at
Belvidere, circa 1914.
(Author's collection)

Maumer, a house servant at Belvidere Plantation, circa 1914. (From *Memories of a South Carolina Plantation during the War* [1912])

Bull, the butler at Belvidere Plantation, circa 1914. (From *Memories of a South Carolina Plantation during the War* [1912])

Old Bear William, the "Great Hunter," on the Belvidere lawn, circa 1914.
(Author's collection)

VI

Back to Eutaw Plantation, Fall 1844 and Spring 1845

OCTOBER FROST KILLED THE BUGS and mosquitoes along the Santee River. The fields turned yellow and white with goldenrod and Queen Anne's lace. Ducks began their southward migration, and their whistle could be heard over the Santee Swamps. Once again the Sinkler clan packed up and headed for Eutaw Plantation. It was during this pleasant time at Eutaw that Emily became pregnant with her second child, Wharton, who was born on August 7, 1845.

The excitement of Christmas preparations was in the air. The garden at Eutaw was a blur of pink, red, and white as the camellias came into full bloom. But country living brought with it isolation. Emily was again dependent on her family for such things as *Littell's Living Age* and Saturday Philadelphia newspapers for gossip and worldly events. It took over a month for elections to be finalized during this time before the telegraph, and so it is not surprising that Emily did not know that James K. Polk had defeated Martin Van Buren. Henry Clay had run as Van Buren's vice-president, and it is interesting to note that Henry Wharton was a Clay supporter, and that thus the Wharton family might have been Whigs.

Emily also refers to stock held by William Sinkler in the Bank of the United States. The Bank of the United States had failed after Pres. Andrew Jackson removed United States deposits in the bank in 1836. The ensuing inflation fostered a whirlwind of speculation that ended in panic, bankruptcy, and a long depression that lasted into the early 1840s. "The city [Philadelphia] plunged into profound depression, psychic as well as economic, in February when the Bank of the United States closed its doors for the last time [in 1841]."[36]

~ ~ ~

28th
Eutaw December 7th 1844

My dear Papa,

I saw the name of Mr. Dulles in the paper as having arrived in Charleston and was in hopes he might have brought me a package from you but as there was an opportunity up from town today and none came I suppose he brought none. Tell Mama I received her letter on last Monday and am very much obliged to her for it. She has written to me several times lately at the expense of her eyes, I am afraid. I wonder whether you are having the same weather in Philadelphia as we are having here. It is really as warm as May. The garden is full of flowers. Camellias in full bloom. I hope it will get colder before Christmas for it would seem very incongruous to have open windows on Christmas day. Every one here is looking forward to great doings then especially the Negroes although they are in much anxiety about one of the fiddlers who has joined the church lately and does not approve of dancing.

After Church last Sunday Mr. Dehon came home with us to stay until the next day so as to have church for the servants in the afternoon. They behaved remarkably well, the women sitting on one side and the men on the other. There is something very wild in their tunes. It always makes me feel melancholy but they persist in curtseying after every thing.

Lizzie is very well and improving very much. She is seventeen months old to day. She says a great many words and can point out the men horses, etc. in a picture book very well. She will call me nothing but Emily or Emmy and her father Chaly. As for Papa or Mama she never thinks of saying either. It is certainly very disrespectful. It would amuse you to see her patronizing airs to her little cousin Henry. She trots into his room and says "baby" in the most contemptuous tone. When she is allowed to have him on her lap she is as careful as possible. Washes his face with her apron and several other little nursery acts.

What new books have been lately imported by the city library? I am afraid you would think me sadly behind the age for I have not seen a new book since I left Philadelphia six months ago. I intended subscribing for the *Living Age* in Charleston but I quite forgot it as we were coming off. If you ever buy any of the numbers do keep them for me. Also any Saturday paper, anything of that kind is an excessive treat in the country.

I suppose Henry is very much mortified at Mr. Clay's defeat. Is it true that Mr. Van Buren is to be president instead of Mr. Polk? I saw something of the kind in the Charleston paper although I don't know how they can manage it. Henry owes me a letter for a long while and so do Frank and Mary. Mary said she meant to write to me once a week but I have not heard from her for three weeks which is not at all encouraging. Have the things arrived yet in the schooner? *Le beau-père* wants me to ask you something about the United States Bank. I believe it is whether there is any chance of selling the stock. I must stop now and will conclude with the sentiment that the smallest favours in the way of letters and papers will be most thankfully received, Ever affectionately, Emily

It is three months before we hear from Emily again, and she is now enjoying spring at Eutaw Plantation. Emily loved spring with its return of green peas, asparagus, and, most of all, strawberries. She ate their luscious, red fruit fresh with clotted cream and preserved them for winter to eat with wheat toast. She is again anticipating her return to Philadelphia in the summer, even contemplating bringing some of the Eutaw prize hams to her father.

Eutaw, March 15th, 1845

Thank you my dear Papa for the money. It arrived safely night before last. Your letter also was very acceptable. I only wish you would write oftener. You see how punctual I am in answering them. You said that you sent two *Ledgers* at the same time but they did not come although I suppose they will on next post-day. But it shows how little dependence is to be placed in the mail. I only hope that letters do not take the same liberty. When is the new post-office bill to go into operation? *A propos le beau-père* has received the Willmer and Smith papers and was much gratified by the attention as he also is by the notice you took of the hams. If you like them still I will bring some for you when I come on. You must not think because I do not come as early this year as I did last time that it is because I am not anxious. On the contrary I want to see you all ten times more now than I did then but I know that it will be impossible for me to do so this year because Mr. Sinkler is very busy at this season and if he leaves too soon every thing will be ruined. You know it is perfectly healthy on the Plantation until the 20th of May and the family then go to the pine land until they arrange their plans for the Summer. One thing you may be sure of and that is the *beau-père* will not let me stay one minute later than it would be perfectly safe for he is constantly uneasy for fear you and Mama will be uneasy.

I am thinking the whole time about seeing you and what you will think of Lizzie. She will be sure to disgrace herself for she sees so few strangers that she is very shy. She was very much pleased with spelling over your letter which is one of her latest accomplishments. She came to me the other day and said g–I–p, pig. I don't know who taught her but she knows a great many letters. She is just now very much pleased at having her little cousins in the house and she enters fully into all their games.

Brother James and his family are paying a visit here before Eliza goes so we have quite a large family—four married couples. The bride and groom are behaving in the orthodox style, very amiable and tender to each other. They go in three or four days but I don't think it much of a separation for their home is only 30 miles from here. To be sure they have a river to cross in a flat and a long swamp but it is nothing to 800 miles.[37]

The stamp is beautiful and has been very much admired. I had not an idea that it could be done in this country. It is a very nice thing to have your own paper. I don't recognize the seal; you have used it several times. Is it the shield to the coat of arms, but then I don't see the motto.

Are there any signs of spring in Philadelphia? After having three weeks of warm weather, no fires and doors open, there has come a sudden change which if it continues will blight every thing, I am afraid. We are all shivering over the fire and having asparagus for dinner two things which seem to me rather dissonant. Do you still take the *Recorder*? If so I would be very much obliged if either you or Frank would send it on when it is convenient for Eliza has ordered hers to be sent to her post office and we will be entirely destitute of news. If Mama wants them kept I will put them carefully away and bring them on with me. If you do not take them will Frank subscribe to it for me and ask them to send it to Vances Ferry until further notice. I am very glad to see Frank is making out so well. I will write to him next week and to Henry the next after. The little one calls you all and knows who have given her different presents. Party Warty, Panky (Frank) and Henry Warty. When I ask her where you are she points up the avenue and says "yonder" with a very unconcerned face. Her grandfather thinks her a prodigy but I am happy to say I see no signs of it. I have seen no new books for ten months and am now reading over Irving's works but he is such a favourite of mine that I never get tired of reading his books.[38] Give my best love to all and tell them to write regularly.

Your affectionate, E.S.

VII

Eutaw Plantation, Fall 1845

IT IS EIGHT MONTHS BEFORE we hear from Emily again, and in the interim she has probably returned for her summer trip to Philadelphia. On August 7, 1845, Emily and Charles's little family increased with the birth of Wharton Sinkler, whom they affectionately called "Bud." Emily has also come back from Philadelphia with an Irish maid for the children, Catherine O'Rourke.

Emily was beginning to grow accustomed to South Carolina culinary ways. She refers here to hominy, or grits, and tells her family how to prepare it. She also sends fat lighter, which is from the heart of the long-leaf pine tree stump and excellent for starting fires, or for making gun powder.

∂▲ ∂▲ ∂▲

Eutaw, November 15th, 1845

My dear Papa,

    I dare say by this time you have received a letter from Mr. Huger telling you of a box and à barrel which we have sent on to you. The barrel contains sweet potatoes of two sorts, yams and Spanish. The box has in it quite a mixture, four hams for you from *le beau-père* (by the bye he thought it was a great deal too few to send), a little bag of fresh hominy, one of rice and one of ground-nuts and some light wood. Don't think you ever saw this latter. It is the dead part of the pine tree and is used here for lighting fires. I have sent you a little to see how very nice it is [and if] it will light coal fires instead of charcoal. All of these are this years products of the place and I intended also sending you some pecan-nuts but they came after the box was packed. The potatoes I am afraid will not be good. They went down to Charleston in the wagon and must have been very much jolted. So as soon as they come to you, you had better open them and take out the good ones. I only hope they will not be frost-bitten. A very nice way to cook them is first parboil them and then slice and fry them. Slice them about the thickness you do egg-plants and lengthwise. I have just sent enough hominy and rice for two dishes of each. The hominy must be washed well in three waters and then boiled in enough water to cover it for fifteen or twenty minutes.

The boxes were sent to the care of Chapman Huger, *le beau-père* and Mr. Sinkler's Factor with directions to ship them to you by first vessel with a bill of lading. In future when you have any package or papers to send to me I wish you would direct them to the care of J. Chapman Huger and you will be sure of its reaching me directly for Seaman is very often out of town and a Factor is expected to do every thing of the sort. By the bye this neigh-bourhood is making excellent crops of cotton and our little place with only 10 hands to work it makes 900 dollars. The *beau-père* has just put up four thousand bushels of corn, six thousand bushels of potatoes, and 600 of oats.

Lizzie and the baby are both well and looking remarkably well. Lizzie talks incessantly of all of you and I am sorry to say is not near as friendly with all the family here as I could wish. She is very amusing and occupies herself principally by reading stories from a book about going to Tiladelty next Summer. She has learnt several new expressions which she makes use of on all occasions such as I b'lieve and I spec. The baby is as good as it is possible for a child to be and really gives no trouble. It is quite touching sometimes to see how he puts himself to sleep while Catherine attends to Lizzie. Catherine is quite happy and is out of doors nearly all day. She came in just this minute to tell me she put the baby in his crib wide awake while she went to do something and when she went back for him he had put himself fast asleep. Well, good-bye dear Papa; do give my best love to all. I want to write a postscript to Mary so I must stop. Ever affectionately, Emily S.

Anna and Emily entertained the family with music each night after supper. The living room would glow with soft candle- and firelight as Emily and Anna sang the operas of the day. Seaman Sinkler knew their musical abilities and kept them supplied with popular operas. Mary, likewise in the cultural mecca of Philadelphia, was sent on buying expeditions to Carey and Harts, one of Philadelphia's top publishers, for new sheet music.

Eutaw December 6th, 1845

My dear Papa,

Seaman came up on Thursday and brought with him the Dulles package. I gave the papers to Catherine who was delighted to get them.

One of them was called "Old Ireland." I told her what you said about the writing on them which struck her very much. She certainly is an excellent creature and every one is very much pleased with her. I have no idea of parting with her as long as she will stay with me.

I am glad the hams etc have arrived safe. If I had only delayed sending them a little while I could have sent you some of the finest lemons I ever saw. They are the size of a large orange and from a place south of Charleston. The *beau-père* is much pleased at the paper you sent him. Indeed, with so much awe did he regard it that he would neither open it himself nor allow any of us to do it for two or three days. I receive the Ledgers regularly and tell Mama that notwithstanding her folding I got the papers safe.

I enclose ten dollars which as you are always kind enough to attend to little business transactions I will get you to lay out for William. He wants a foot warmer. I have seen them in the fur shops in Philadelphia and Mrs. Cowell had one of them. They are lined with fur. If one and the box does not exceed the sum, Anna wants with the money that is left one of the opera books such as I bought at Carey and Harts. Mary knows the sort and can get it. She must get either Anna Bolena Puritani—La Muette di Portici or Otello, and if neither of these are to be had Mary can choose what she thinks best with the exception of Norma and Somnambula. William is very modest about the trouble he is giving but the foot warmer is not to be got in Charleston and he has taken a great fancy for one. Will you have the still greater kindness to put them in a box and send them to Charleston directed to W. H. Sinkler care of J. Chapman Huger—(his factor—) At the same time you send it will you ask Mary to put in it a pair of white woolen stockings that I was knitting and which I left in her work stand drawer.

We are coming on very well. We intended going back with Eliza when she goes next week to pay her a visit but Tom Kinloch wrote on Thursday to say he would be up on Monday so we will defer our visit until after Christmas. All the family are assembled here for the first time since last year. Seaman brought a gentleman up with him and I see a carriage full of company coming down the avenue now.

I always read your messages to Lizzie and she says, "tell Party me no forgotten him and me come back again next summer." She told her father this morning when he told her this was her home—"No where me Party and MARTY is my home" and talked it out with him. If any one asks her where she wants to go to she always points up the avenue and says "Way younder to Tiladelphia."[39] The baby is getting quite a distinctive character of his own. He is constantly trying all sorts of little artifices to get to suck his thumb which Catherine has waged war against. When is the Wistar Party to be? You must keep the answers for me. Well goodbye dear Papa, I must stop now for I know you don't like crossed letters. I will write to Mama next week. With love to all, I am ever affectionately, yours, Emily S.

In her next letter Emily hints at some inter-family squabbling but states that she is not involved in it. However, she is obviously upset by the fact that Eliza is so "wrapped up" in Mr. Manning, her new husband, that she spends much less time at Eutaw. Probably with Eliza gone, Anna became the lady in charge of Eutaw, and this transition may have caused some friction amongst the family members.

Eutaw, December 13th, 1845

My dear Mamma,

I really am very sorry to hear from Mary that your eyes are so bad this winter. I had been expecting a letter from you for some time but you must not think of writing until they are better. I had no letter for the last two post days but tell Papa I got the Ledgers. We are all very well and every thing is coming on perfectly harmoniously. I am on the best terms with every body and so is every body with me and I am happy to say I have nothing to do with any little discontents that may arise now and then.

I do wish you could see my baby now for I am sure you would agree with me that there never was such a perfect little fellow. He is as fat and good as it is possible for him to be and has always on his face the most serene and happy expression and if you give him the slightest encouragement he will roar with laughter. I have real comfort out of him and every day I wish that you could hold him while he is going to sleep for I know you would enjoy it. When I have to hold him I always take the opportunity to make him do so. He takes his thumb and in about the time you could count 30 he is sound asleep. Every one in the house is glad to hold him when he comes in the room. Catherine is invaluable to me and seems so far quite happy and contented. She does up my collars beautifully and while we were in Charleston the last time she bought some chocolate for the express purpose of surprising me with a cup now and then on going to bed.

Mr. Kinloch is up here now and I suppose will stay an indefinite time. He makes himself very pleasant and agreeable and is quite an addition to our little circle. In the evening we have some very good music.

Anna and I have some nice new duets and Tom Kinloch has brought up his flute. To be sure he will harp on the heart's affections and the forsaken and twilight dews but every one is so used to his singing them that it would not seem natural for him not to sing them every evening. He brought me up a beautiful present.

Seaman has given Anna and myself each an opera (the music I mean) and I am determined this winter to practice so that when I come on I will surprise you. The *beau-père* has promised us a new piano this winter but I am afraid we will not get it for Seaman says he must buy one which he has seen in town and which costs $580 and the *beau-père* says that $400 is quite enough.

By the bye when you see Ellen McIlvaine will you be kind enough to give her a message for me. She wrote to me about Frances and Sarah who she said had gone on to Charleston and who she wanted me to interest myself about but as she did not give me either their last names or their directions of course when I was in Charleston I could not find them. But when Seaman came up the other day he said that the night before about 11 o'clock a man came to his office and said he wanted him to go to see a sick person. He went and found a woman very ill with an abscess in her throat. She told him that she knew me in Philadelphia at Mrs. Cadwaladers.[40] It turned out to be Sarah. He says he did not think she would live through the night but the abscess broke before morning and she was quite relieved. He has promised to get work for them.

Eliza is here now but is going up on Monday. Nothing can persuade her to stay to Christmas, because Mr. Manning has to go back. She is so completely wrapped up in him that she is quite altered and is very provoking to her friends. It is too bad she will not stay to Christmas. When it is the custom for all the family to be together at a set time she ought to keep it up.

Lizzie is very well and talks incessantly of you all and is very fond of boasting of what her Party and MARTY do and very often she will say "ah ha me MARTY has chocolate drops." And when she sees pictures of boats she will say, "ah that's me Party's boat." No matter now what she is asked she always answers Party and MARTY gave it to me. You would laugh at the queer little dirty letters she writes. Well goodby dearest Mother, Ever thine, E.S.

The following jingle to Mary Coré Griffith expresses Emily's delight in Plantation Christmas at Eutaw. She notes that Eliza and Seaman are absent. Eliza gave birth to Elisabeth Peyre Manning on December 21, 1845. Emily notes in her poem that none of the Sinkler family knew that Eliza was expecting a baby.

One good turn deserves another
So I think my dear Grandmother
I will, without any more delay
Answer your rhyming letter to-day.
A merry Christmas a happy New Year
May those have, who are to me so dear
My friends I've often thought of them all
And wished for them with me in the Hall.
On Christmas Morning bright and early
Oh what a noisy hurly burly
It was not very long after four
When the fiddlers were playing at my door.[41]
And all the Negroes on the place
With a smirk a bow and smiling face
Were wishing the compliments of the season
And many things more without rhyme or reason.
Catherine was very much amused
(For she has heard the planters oft abused)
To see the very funny ways
In which they've passed these last three days.
I'm sure the presents they have had
Were enough to make any one glad.
The men had every one a cap
And of tobacco many a nice scrap
The women had each a handkerchief
And then all had a piece of beef
On the piazza they've danced from morning till night
There's no doubt you'd have thought it a wonderful sight.
We have passed a very jovial time
But I'm afraid I can't tell it all in rhyme
The only thing to make us sad
Was that Seaman and Eliza were not to be had.
Poor Seaman could not get away
He has enough to keep him for many a day
He has just begun a journal to edit
And I'm sure he will do it with great deal of credit
He means to send it on he says
I hope you will think it deserving of praise.
His present to me was a beautiful thing
And besides he sent me two operas to sing
What do you think little Lizzie received?

The number I'm sure will be hardly believed.
A sweet little handkerchief marked with her name
A thimble, three dolls and a beautiful game.
A bag and a box some books and besides
A lady to know who in Charleston resides
Sent the prettiest thing I ever did see
Out of it you and I, I am sure could take tea.
It's a set of french china beautifully flowered
On Lizzie presents have always showered.
Do tell Mama I wish every night
She was here to see the sight.
The music we've she'd like I know
The guitar, the flute and the piano.
Mr. Kinloch, Anna and I do play
How well it passes the evening away.
But now I must tell you the wonderful news
And it I am sure will you much amuse.
We heard on Monday from over the water
That Eliza Manning has a fine little daughter.
Never were people more amazed
And her father is like to any one crazed
The poor little thing had not a stitch to its name
Now don't you think 'twas a crying shame
They have called the child Eliza Peyre
After Eliza's kind belle mere.
But now I will stop and you must be glad
For never yet were rhymes so bad.
Goodbye dear Marty think always of me
As your very affectionate Emily.

VIII

The Mexican-American War, 1846

THE ALL-ABSORBING TOPIC of the day became the question of the threat of attack on Texas by Mexico if Texas joined the Union. From July of 1845 the Philadelphia papers were full of discussion about the threat of war with Mexico. Zachary Taylor was ordered to march to the frontier of Texas with fifteen hundred troops.[42] By November of 1846 President Polk was calling for fifteen additional regiments of volunteers to serve in the war against Mexico. Those troops were to march with General Taylor toward Saltillo.[43] The Whig Party opposed the war and felt Democrat Pres. James K. Polk's ambition to annex Mexico was behind the war. Indeed, the *Philadelphia Pennsylvanian* reported the Whigs believed President Polk was interested in "reveling in the halls of Montezuma and annexing Mexico to the United States."[44] Charles served in the war, and so it is not surprising that Emily read every paper for any account of the war.

Eutaw, January 1st, 1846

A happy New Year my dear Mary to all of you. It is some days before my usual writing day but I must wish the compliments of the season. I had quite a treat on last mail night. Three letters and the *Ledgers*. Henry's was very amusing tho' he was rather severe on some of the peculiarities of the age. Tell Papa I will answer his letter very soon. I have heard nothing as yet of the Schooner Harp but I dare say we will get a letter tonight from Mr. Huger with some news about it. As you can imagine I am all anxiety to see the contents of the box and Lizzie is the same, having been duly apprized of it and understanding fully all about it.

You do not say which opera you got. We are a little fearful that it may be one we have already. You know I have Il Barbure di Siviglia and Seaman has given us Otello and Don Giovanni and has sent for

Puritani. However, if you have got the last it can be easily counter-manded by him and changed for another.[45]

You are much mistaken if you think Lizzie has forgotten any of you. Last night she was kneeling down to her prayers (which she says regularly every night and morning) and as it was rather late I curtailed the long string of relations she generally prays for by saying, "and every-body else." When she got up she looked at me most reproachfully and said, "you forgot Henry Wharton tonight." Yesterday her Grandfather was promising to buy her when he went to town a frock, silk stockings, shoes and a long list of things, and then said now who do you love best in the world. She hesitated a minute and then with a judicious arrange-ment said, I love Grandpa and Party Sinkler. She is looking very well now. I wish you could see little Wharton before he loses his fat. He has out grown all his clothes much to my annoyance, as I have to make new bodies to everything. Shoes and stockings that Lizzie wore when she was 18 months old barely fit him now and he is only 4 months. Catherine I am sorry to say insists on giving him meat to suck and almost every day after dinner when I go up stairs I find him with a bone in his hand. You said you like to hear anecdotes of them but I think you have had enough of it now.

You must write me a long account of how you have spent Christmas—what presents you have received, etc. We have a round of company staying in the house but all are gone now except Mr. Kinloch. We have however not had so many as most of our neighbours. Some have had 30 and 40 in the house all the holidays. At the South all the members of the family spend their Christmas with the head of the fam-ily and no one stays in town who has a place to go to.

Owing to Eliza not being here we were not so amusing as usual. What do you think of her having a baby? We were very much surprised to hear of it for everything was done in the most Eve-like manner pos-sible. I am going up there as soon as she is well enough. The baby is called Elizabeth Peyre Manning and her father who went up immedi-ately to see her says it is a very pretty little thing. It is his ninth grand-child. Your last letter was Capital!!! By the bye I had almost forgotten Mr. Sinkler wants Henry to subscribe ten dollars for the Cultivator at Ziebers for this year 1846 and have it sent to Vances Ferry, P.O. Papa has some money of his. How could you make such a mistake about the unfortunate plough? I wrote distinctly Mr. Newton's Stall 41 between 7th and 8th. Well good bye—I dreamed last night that mama was here; everything was as natural as possible but I often dream that. Henry (one of the servants) says he thinks I have a very shabby family never to come to see me. Ever yours, Emily Sinkler.

In her next letter Emily notes that Mr. Sinkler is awaiting orders, or yellow papers, for the Mexican War from Secretary of the Navy Mr. Bancroft. Mr. Sinkler's ship, *Ploughing the Main,* is still awaiting orders. She also is happy that the ploughs that the Sinklers had ordered from Philadelphia have arrived.

ই৯ ই৯ ই৯

Eutaw, Feb 28th, 1846

My dear Papa

I received your letter and the money last mail night for which I return sincere thanks. Mr. Sinkler is very much obliged to you for the trouble you have taken about the ploughs and has heard from Mr. Huger that the Schooner North Carolina is arrived and has delivered to him the ploughs which will come up by the first opportunity. By the bye I wonder how many vessels we have had in service during the last three years? As to Mr. Sinkler's *Ploughing the Main* he has been "waiting orders" since the first of last November but has heard nothing from the Department since, which has been the case with all his friends. I suppose Mr. Bancroft has been waiting to see how the war question is to end.[46] All the family in the mean time rushing to the mail bag twice a week to see if there is any yellow paper in it. I have been rather mortified to find that the Northerners are the ones who are so anxious for war. All here are opposed to it and lay all the blame on the North.[47]

Lizzie was delighted with your message to her which I read to her. When I came to the part about "soon they'll be ripe, etc." she repeated it off by herself. When we were in Charleston she called all the boats Party's. The little man is getting quite a character of his own and fights for everything he sees without any discrimination of course. He considers Lizzie the most important character in the world and is rather too engrossing in his attentions, pulling her hair being his favourite amusement.

The country is again flourishing as people have come back from the races. From being entirely alone one day the next day we had ten arrivals making it of course quite gay. Spring has set in some respects tho I am afraid the cold weather we have had the last week will destroy all the blossoms. You would like, I know, to see the quantity of robins there are about the house. The *beau-père* does not allow them killed in the grounds and their little red breasts make the trees look quite lively.

Has Bishop Potter dined with you yet? I see from your letter that he is not at all averse to parties—two in one evening is doing very well for a Bishop. How has Mrs. Major Biddle left her money? In Southern or Northern property? When you are done with the [*Illustrated*] *London News* do send them on. They are a great treat and go the rounds of the neighbourhood. By the bye it is a strange thing that our Postmaster never marks any postage on newspapers.[48] I am looking for his bill to see if he charges any for some one said he does not. Did Mrs. Elizabeth Dorsey receive the letter Catherine wrote her? I directed it but it was unfortunately sealed or I should have been very much tempted to take a peep. It must be capital. Tell Mary if she sees it to send some extracts to me. Did I tell you that she received a letter with no other direction but Miss Catherine O'Rourke, care of Mr. Sinkler, P.O. South Carolina. What was the point of the P.O. I can't imagine. If it had not been that the Postmaster Mr. Alfred Huger knew the *beau-père* I suppose it would never have reached her.

I see by the papers that the storm we felt in Charleston extended to the North and the worthy Wardel (I never rightly knew if he is Tickler Wardel or not) has a letter about it from Long Branch. Tell Aunt I received her letter and will answer it. I puzzled for a long time over something she said about Willy Smith coming to see her. I could not think it possible that we had a new cousin at last. I was relieved by remembering Miss 8th street Wilhelmina. Don't tell her this tho for she would not like it. Becky must have come out quite a genius from all accounts. I suppose she is recovering from the fall she had on board ship. Give my love to all, Your loving child, E. S.

Both Frank and Henry worked in the Philadelphia prosecutor's office, and there was frequent mention of this office in the local newspaper, as Emily's reference indicates. She is always hopeful that they will visit come spring. During this time Charles was away in the Gulf of Mexico near Vera Cruz with the Navy, and so Emily was reliant on her Eutaw family for companionship.

Eutaw, March 21st, 1846

My dear Frank

Perhaps it will not be unpleasing to you to receive a letter from me although you will have the trouble of answering it. You must expect a very dull epistle as there is nothing going on here that would interest you. My sole object in writing is to get your answer. En passant I see that one of the Hulpsh duos is defunct. I believe it is the one that came

so near being named after me. I look in every *Ledger* that comes for
something about you and am often rewarded by such a piece as "owing
to the energy of our prosecuting attorneys" which I never fail to show
round the family.

Is it impossible for you to spare the time to come on here this
Spring? You would have time enough to pay a nice visit and I am sure
the benefit you would derive from change of scene and rest to your eyes
would compensate for loss of time. I really don't ask this as a matter of
course sort of thing but because I really feel it and I wish you to consider it in a serious way.

Your God-son it will gratify you to learn is quite well and well
grown for his age. His acquisitions are not numerous but highly
respectable. But it is not expected that he will equal his worthy God-
sire in walking up and down stairs at eight months (as you did you
know). Lizzie has some extraordinary remembrances of you for whenever she takes anything that does not belong to her she always says
Uncle Frank gave it to me. She was pleased to inform me this afternoon
in the carriage that when she goes to Philadelphia she means to buy
Uncle Frank a black coat with white buttons.

I must tell you something but you must promise not to let it get to
his ears or I will never trust you again. Catherine got a letter a short
time ago from Joshua Molliston![49] The most perfect thing I ever read.
She was very loath to let me see it at first but I insisted on it. His style
is very affectionate and extremely patronizing such as "I always thought
you was an amiable girl" and "my pen cannot express my feelings but
when we meet we will tell each other our thoughts face to face and I
shall have much pleasure in making you a cup of tea; enquiring friends
is well." I wish I could remember more of it for it was a real treat. Now
don't talk of the letter at the table before him I beg.

Delancy Izard has returned from Europe and is now in Charleston.
I did not see him when I was last there but they say he is very much
elated with his acquisitions. He has just given an extravagant price for a
pair of horses. Tom Kinlochs' mother who has always been thought a
perfectly sane person has been doing some very queer things lately.
Some would amuse you very much if they were "faut" for a letter. One
thing was unexceptionable so I will tell it. Mrs. Powell McCrea (a lady
from Washington, Miss May who married a nephew of Mr. Singletons)
was staying a short time ago at Mrs. Robertsons' where I was in
Charleston. Mrs. Kinloch came to see her and took a great deal of
notice of her little girls, told them that before they went she would send

them a present. So the day before they were to go her servant arrived with a silver waiter covered with a damask napkin. On opening it there was one baked potato in it. Another time lately while Mr. Singleton's son in law was with her he invited some friends to dinner by her request. All she had for nine people was a wild turkey that Mr. Singleton had brought down with him and a little piece of corn beef. When this was removed all the dessert she had was a small dish of baked sweet potatoes. Mr. Robertson who was there and told me of it said she did the honours as if it were a sumptuous repast. Poor old Mr. Kinloch is pretty sane now but looks very miserable and neglected. Did you ever hear of the time he spanked an old lady about as fat as Miss Peggy Read from one end of King Street to the other? It was 3 o'clock and very few people in the street. Of course he was quite cracked at the time.

When you see Sarah Coleman give my love to her, and tell me when you write if she has had any admirers this winter. Do write soon an agreeable letter. Mr. Sinkler sends his love to you. Give mine most affectionately to all, Ever yours, Emily S.

There are but three "replies" to Emily's letters in existence. The following letter to her by William Sinkler, her father-in-law, shows the intimate nature of their relationship. Emily is in Philadelphia spending the summer with her parents while Charles is serving in the Mexican War. It reveals the predicament faced by plantation owners in finding healthy habitats during the summer months. Eliza had moved to Homesley in the sandhills, not far from Stateburg, South Carolina. The rest of the Sinkler family now began to spend time here. Its high sand hills and piney dry air were thought to be relatively free from summer diseases. Mr. Sinkler's views on the Mexican War show that he believed in loyalty to the United States government above all.

Eutaw, 29th June, 1846

My dear Emily

I came this morning to make my final arrangements for the summer. As I expect to leave tomorrow, I will embrace the few moments that are allowed to acknowledge your letters of the 5th and 16th. Your attention was never better timed, for I have never been as dull, or desponding. It is now years since I have been accustomed to having my children from me and then it was while obtaining their education and at no great distance from me. But at present all my children are from me except Anna and William and soon they will be. James was to have gone to Virginia by the way of New York and Philadelphia. It seems his disease became so serious that after he got to the City his physicians deemed it all important to secure a return of health, that he should take a trip across the Atlantic. So soon as I heard it I went down (Charleston) to see him. He was adverse at first to follow the advice but his physician pressed it in such terms that he reluctantly consented. He sailed in the ship Catherine on Saturday week. Heaven grant every benefit may result. I would have gone with him but time nor circumstances would admit. A great deal has devolved on me in consequence of the absence of my sons. It causes me to leave with great reluctance. I only wish I could have remained until August and then to have gone immediately to Philadelphia. Anna and William and their child will soon go to the Sand-Hills. I have arranged to go tomorrow and will remain in the Sand-Hills about ten days when I will leave for Virginia.

You must have had a pleasant summer of it thus far and no doubt have enjoyed yourself. I often think of you and the dear little ones. I am pleased to hear that Lizzie so frequently speaks of me. It shows that she has not forgotten me.

I am glad to find that all difficulties have been amicably settled with G. Britain relative to Oregon. I hope the war will soon terminate with Mexico and that my dear Charles will soon be permitted to return in health after a useful and pleasant cruise, having discharged his duties faithfully, which I trust may lead to his promotion. I do not wonder that Mr. Beverly should be reluctant to go to Sea.[50] But that he should make any excuse about the War being iniquitous is preposterous. Who are to be the Judge. It is enough to know that our country has declared War. Be it just or unjust every individual ought to feel that he is willing to render his support much less an officer in the Navy. I am sorry to find that Gen. Scott has been so imprudent. I consider his fate now sealed, whether as an officer of the Navy or as a candidate for the Presidency. I fear too that Gen. Gaines imprudence will be attended with unpleasant results. I am called off my dear Emily and will have to carry this unfinished letter to the Sand-Hills.

Sand Hills, July 2nd

I arrived here after a very hot ride on Tuesday, found all friends quite well. Eliza is well and her child quite a picture. She is the emblem of innocence. The best tempered little thing I ever saw. She is as you will suppose a great pet with everybody. I dined yesterday with John

Manning.[51] His house is magnificent and splendidly furnished (Milford, sometimes called Manning's Folly, on account of the masses of money spent upon it).[52] After ten days I expect to leave here for Virginia. I dread the journey by land. I might yet go by the Wilmington route. I wish you were here to accompany me. I think a trip to the mountains would only have prepared you to enjoy the pleasures of Philadelphia in greater degree. Certainly your company would have rendered my time pleasant and comfortable. What a life mine has become: every child from me. It requires much real philosophy to support my situation. If nothing occurs to prevent, I will certainly pay you and the children a visit. If it be only a short one. Remember me most affectionately to your Father and Mother and all the family for me. Kiss your children tenderly for me. I love them much and hope Lizzie will be quite glad to see me. May heaven bless you my dear Emily. Your fond father, W. Sinkler

IX

The Death of Seaman;
the Birth of Arabella, 1847

WE DO NOT HEAR AGAIN from Emily for eight months. Emily, as we know from the *beau-père*'s letter, made her usual trip to Philadelphia for the summer, returning to Charleston and then to Eutaw Plantation by October. When we hear from Emily it would appear that Frank has been to visit in the fall of 1846, as she refers to a book he has left behind. Charles also resigned from the Navy in February of 1847 and so is now home at Eutaw with his family.

The year 1847 was one of immense emotional ups and downs for Emily. Seaman Deas Sinkler had been Emily's "soul mate" from the moment she arrived in Charleston. Seaman had studied medicine in Paris for three years. His love of music and literature were in tune with Emily's own passion for both. Life sparkled when Seaman came to Eutaw, as he did almost every weekend. He had given Emily a guitar with mother of pearl inlay that she hung around her neck with a beautiful blue velvet strap. He had arranged to have a Steinway piano that cost $500 sent to Eutaw for her use. He provided her opera music. He sent her books. Seaman tested her French with riddles and word games. His flawless French was a delightful change of pace from the lowcountry drawl. He had showed her how to make French bonbons using the delicate, marshmallow-like Guimauve. When Emily was sick with whooping cough, he did his best to ease her pain with the best remedies of the day.

Seaman Deas Sinkler was beloved by Emily, the whole Sinkler family, and the Charleston community. His death from consumption saddened them all.

            ðŸ•®   ðŸ•®   ðŸ•®

Eutaw, Dec. 17th, 1846

My dear Frank,

Make your mind easy about your book for if Henry Drayton has not already left Charleston you will get it by him. Some one is going down from here tomorrow who will take a letter to Mr. Lesesne asking him to give the book to him. Mr. Sinkler means also to write tonight to Henry Drayton asking him to come up and pay us a visit. We are all very well now and I am very glad to say that Lizzie is quite recovered. It is a great relief to me for I was very uneasy about her. Bud or Wharton as every one calls him here is perfectly monstrous in size. I could not have believed he could have grown so much as he has done lately. Both he and Lizzie eat hominy and rice as heartily as if they never knew potatoes. As yet I have heard nothing of any movement on Cassidys part but I should not be at all surprised to see him prancing down some day soon. Richard Manning says his brother gives him $300 a year and that he has laid up at least two thousand dollars, so he is quite a speck.

The whole of the Sinkler family is now together and will continue so until after Christmas. Last evening it was quite amusing to see eight children under 11 dancing and playing together in the parlour.

Seaman we thought a great deal better until day before yesterday when he was taken with spitting of blood. He is well again to day but there is every reason for him to be careful of himself. Why does not Mary write? If I don't get a letter tonight I shall think her very negligent. I received Papa's note last mail night. Give my best love to Mama and tell her I will write to her next week. It is so much later than I thought that I must conclude as I must labour through a letter to Aunt Hannah, Yours ever, E.S.

Eutaw, January 7th, 1847

My dear Mary

For fear you should feel at all revengeful towards the Post Office department I will inform you that I have received three letters from you and expect to get your fourth by the mail tonight. We are all very well except poor Seaman who gets worse every day. He came up here about four weeks ago and for the first three or four days improved very much. But he took cold and for three weeks has been gradually declining, until last week he refused either to see a physician or take any medicine since he has seen three. They all speak in the most serious way of his case. Dr. Huger very kindly came up to see him day before yesterday and his opinion is of more importance than any one else's as he has great experience and is an elderly man. All concur in saying that it is consumption and that his only chance of recovery is in going to Cuba. There would be no hesitation at all about it if it were not for the fatigue of the journey from here to Charleston. But as he seems anxious to go himself, I think he will be able to make the exertion—as he can go by steamboat thirty miles of the way and the other thirty can be divided into two days. He has chosen Mr. Sinkler to go with him which I am very sorry for but of course he must be gratified. William says he will go also as he thinks two of his brothers ought to be with him. I think it is dreadful for one so very ill to go away from home but as the physicians say it is the only hope and there have been instances of wonderful cures in Havana.

They at first fixed on tomorrow (Friday) for him to leave so as to be in town on Monday in time for a steamer which is to stop in Charleston on its way to Havana but today is a rainy day looking like rain tomorrow in which case he would not be able to move. If so he will probably leave in a vessel of the 15th. If Philadelphia was only in any decent distance what a nice time this would be for me to come on and pay you a visit while Mr. Sinkler is away.

Tell Hen it would be a very pretty thing if he could come on. This is a very dull letter but you must excuse it for poor Seaman's state is such that we can think of nothing else. Until today he has been able to lie on the sofa part of the time but he is still in bed now. He does not cough much nor spit much blood but it seems like a general decay. Dr. Huger says he is a complete martyr to his profession. I enclose a note from Lil which I dare say will amuse you. I have written verbatim just what she told me direction and all. Love to all, In much haste, ever yours, E.S.

Eutaw, January 21st, 1847

My dear Mary,

Our poor dear Seaman is gone. He died on Tuesday night at 11 o'clock after great suffering. They were to go to Cuba and every preparation was made but the steamer arrived on Friday or Saturday in a disabled state which was a great mercy for he would have gone in her and then died at sea. For three days and nights before he died he was not able to lie down a minute but sat up with his head bent over on his breast suffering most acutely, principally from suffocation. On Tuesday night at 9 his father left him to go to Mr. Alfred Hugers where he stayed as the physicians said there was no likelihood of an immediate termination. Brother James and William also left him leaving Charles and Dr.

Stoney, an intimate friend of Seamans, to sit up. At a little before 11 Dr. Stoney observed that his head had fallen back on the back of the chair and on feeling his pulse found it was going! Charles took his hand and found that his pulse was going—he kept his hand in his until the breath was gone and prayed all the time most earnestly that God would take his soul at the last. He died exactly at 11 without a single groan or struggle.

The scene was most awful when they called his father for although he knew Seaman was in danger, yet he had no idea that death could come so soon. The next day (yesterday) Brother James brought his father home by the Rail Road and Charles and William set out with the body in a carriage to take it to the family burying ground. Think what an awful time they must have had—the most pouring rain you ever saw, cold as possible and very dark. They had to travel night and day for the burying ground is 40 miles from Charleston and they would walk the horses the whole way.[53] The funeral party left here this morning to meet the body. They have to go thirty miles. His poor father would go, he said he did not see why he should not see the last of his child. You never saw deeper grief than every one, servants and all feel.

His father says he is completely broken up for the rest of his life. It is a great comfort to him to think how devoted Seaman's brothers were to him. For the last six weeks Charles and William have taken it by turns to sit up every night with him. He spoke very little for the last three weeks as it caused him great pain, but called on Charles constantly. It is a great pleasure to Charles and myself to know that a servant of ours, a very nice boy you may have heard me speak of, was devoted to him through all his sickness, never left him for a second until he died and anticipated every wish.

It is a great pity that Seaman was not able to talk more. He spoke very little of death and did not seem to imagine that it was so near, tho the day he died he told Brother James he thought he would never get well. I don't understand his disease. The physicians said it was galloping consumption but they gave him no remedies. He spit very little blood, hardly coughed and seemed nothing but a wasting away. It is a most severe blow to his father for he was so proud of Seaman, and I often have heard him say that in all his life Seaman had never said a disrespectful thing to him nor done one thing against his will.

I received your letter and Henry's by the last mail. I cannot imagine why you have not heard from me regularly. I have never omitted a single Thursday to write. Since the 1st of January I have written three times to you. Tell Mama I wrote to her some time ago. In the letter I asked you to get Liz a pair of Glove knots. Tell Hen I will answer his very soon. How I wish he could come on this winter. The children are both very well and hearty. Lizzie goes to Sunday School to me every Sunday and gets a ticket with "good" marked on it which she keeps in a little box. I asked her about the visit to little Barker and she appeared to remember it perfectly. How I should love to see Mr. Smith's collection. Tell Papa I am in earnest and if there is any chance to send it on please do it, and I will take the greatest care of it. Any thing you send by opportunity, direct to J. Chapman Huger. Did you observe in one of the last *Records* an account of Mr. [William] Keble's church near Winchester and the spring or fountain near it?

Eutaw, February 11th, 1847

My dear Mary,

We got safely home day before yesterday and found your letter and Papa's awaiting me. I spent a very pleasant time in Charleston very busy as you know country people always are in town; my list was really a curiosity. What with commissions, etc., it was very long.

Poor Seaman I missed him extremely, for this was the first time I have ever been in Charleston without his being with me the greatest part of every day. He died at his cousins Mrs. Frosts and as she was with him constantly I was in hopes she could have told me some things about him that I had not heard before, but she could not. One thing made me feel very sorry. She says that the first time she saw him they were alone and he took her hand and said very distinctly—I have something to say to you that I must say. I must tell you one thing. But while he spoke his whole frame seemed so agitated that she was afraid that any more conversation might lead to serious results. So she told him that he had better defer it. He seemed very unwilling at first but gave up. After that she never got an opportunity. At first there was always some one in the room and then his mind wandered, but she never came near him but he looked most meaningfully at her and then at whoever was in the room. I would give anything to know what it was. I often thought before he left us that he had something he wished to say but we were all so afraid of bringing on Hemorrhage.

The Convention you know was sitting while we were in town and Charles was there the whole time and much interested in what was going on.[54] There was some discussion about the trustees but I believe it ended in none being elected who were favourable to B T O—I mean the trustees to the New York Seminary. A resolution of Henry Lesesne's also created a great deal of talk. It was to have a church or churches exclusively for the coloured population. Now all are together.[55]

The Lesesnes all desired their love to be sent to you and Mama. We dined there one day and had a very nice dinner. I saw the Middletons every day, both Lizzie and Mary Lowndes are at home now. I never saw such an improvement in any one as in Harriet Middleton. She has grown extremely pretty and lively. Lizzie and Buddy were very much admired and looked very nicely as their things were perfectly fresh. Bud especially attracted universal attention—his hat and feathers being something quite new in Charleston and the great round face and red cheeks were also a rarity. Tell Mama he does not look so much like Mr. Ingraham since he has got the rest of his teeth. A very funny thing about him is that no matter what you say to him he always answers. Lizzie got a great many presents in town being a general favourite. She has seven winter frocks. Mrs. Frost's eldest son, a little boy of seven, fell desperately in love with Lizzie and told his mother she was the sweetest little girl he had ever seen and said he must marry her when he was old enough. It was very droll to see them together.

It seemed very natural to meet Mr. Spear in the Street. His church is not yet built, but he preaches in the College Chapel. He says now he means to live and die in Charleston.[56]

En passant how very cutting you are about my literary tastes! I would have you to know that I am rather more cultivated and enlightened in my tastes than you think. My scale is rather above Leslie, etc. Life in Earnest I have read with a great deal of pleasure and have lent it to several persons. Fitzsimmons liked it so much that he got a copy for his Mother. Tell Mama Peranzabuloe is delightful.[57] If I ever get to England I would go a great deal out of the way to see the old church in Cornwall.

We stayed at Mrs. Robertson's in town and she was all kindness as usual. They are to build on the Battery[58] in a few weeks and she has arranged a room and dressing room especially for me. She gave me the most beautiful Prayer book I have ever seen, quite a new style by Appleton. I must stop now for I want to add a few lines to Papa. Tell Hen I will write to him next week. Yours as ever, E.S.

Emily's trek across the Santee River and the Santee Swamp took most of a full day. She boarded the ferry at Vance's Ferry. She was journeying to the Santee High Hills, where she stayed en route with her cousins the Richardsons and the Mannings.

❧ ❧ ❧

Eutaw, March 18th, 1847

My dear Mary,

I really felt quite unfinished last week for it was the first week I have ever omitted writing and I will not let it happen again. This time it was owing to being away from home and not knowing the mail day in Clarendon. We set out on the 9th to go up to see Eliza, crossed the River at Nelsons Ferry and as it was a long Ferry went the whole way over the Swamp in a flat. We got over very well and reached Aunt Richardsons at 2 o'clock. We stayed there that night and the next day went to Mrs. Mannings which is about nine miles further on.

We found Eliza and the baby both perfectly well.[59] The little fellow is the image of Richard, quite plump and with a pretty little crop of thick short jet black hair. Eliza is just as satisfied with her two babies as possible and thinks it is all as it should be. She takes such things better than anyone I ever heard of. We stayed at Mrs. Mannings several days very pleasantly. Then spent a day and night at Richard Richardsons and on our way home spent a day and night at Mr. William Richardsons. The children were everywhere admired. Lizzie was thought the most obedient and intelligent little girl they had ever seen and Bud even among the children there who are uncommonly large was regarded as a noble fellow. He is very unsociable to strangers, however. You would have been amused to hear something Lizzie said to a lady who was staying at Mrs. Mannings. It came out so quickly that everybody laughed. This lady asked her if she would not come to see her at Camden (in this state). Oh said Liz, Party Wharton takes me to Camden and we go and we go in a steamboat and get ice cream there, and once I cried for my tea there and Party Wharton got me tea and crackers.[60]

Coming back we found the water extremely high in fact a regular freshet, so we had a great time getting across the Swamp and river and did not get over until 10 o'clock. The head boatman of the flat was a regular specimen of the tribe set forth by travelers. He talked incessantly and kept up the spirits of the rest wonderfully. We were nearly four hours crossing the Swamp, and whenever the spirits of the other boatmen flagged he would call out, "Come daughter Jane, put on the Kettle, we're a coming." One of the men he called "my Brudder" another "my heart" another Doctor and Sonny, etc. He kept me laughing the whole time at this queer sayings. One of his oddities was that he wore two of his back teeth on a string round his neck and said he always heard they were too faithful companions to throw away.

As the Irishman said the best part of the journey with me was the coming home for I found a whole collection of letters—yours and Papas were especially interesting on account of the news of the box. I am looking for it with the greatest anxiety. It had not arrived when the last mail arrived but I hope tonight to hear that the vessel is in Charleston and if so there will be an opportunity for it to come up in a few days. As soon as it does come I will write. The wagon had come from town while I was away and brought me several silk pocket handkerchiefs. Mrs. Robertson sent Charles some English cheese which had been sent to an English gentleman in Charleston. Charles has put it up to send it on to Papa and I hope he will find it good. Thank Hen for the "Battle of Life."[61] I had not read it before but I am very much disappointed in it. I think it is the poorest of Dickens' works. As soon as the box comes I will write to Papa as I have not time today.

I wish I could write you some funny things about Catherine and Cassidy, but I am pressed for time. I have no doubt but that it will be a match. She breakfasted and dined with him in the freest way. Love to all, Yours ever, E.S.

In Emily's next letter we see again some of the sibling rivalry evident between Emily and Mary. Emily obviously took her writing responsibility seriously, working to tell anecdotes of people and places that she thought would amuse. She bridled at Mary referring to her letters as "circulars," a term implying a sense of boredom and sameness.

Eutaw, April 8th, 1847

My dear Mary,

I have received your letters by the two last mails. I was quite startled when I saw the last for you had written so recently that I was afraid someone was sick. Before going any further I want to know what you mean by calling my letters circulars. If you only knew how little I have to write about you would think it wonderful that I get through a letter at all. You who live in a city could have no trouble in writing but situated as you are when you know that the slightest thing about the family, the house and my friends and acquaintances affords me matter of speculation and wonder for a whole week, why you ought to write pages. What have I under the sun to write about! You are of course aware that nothing changes in the country but the seasons and one cannot be like Thomson for ever writing about them. Then if you did know the neighbours I would not be much better off for with the exception of our family we see the others but twice a year when on a formal visit. But enough. I trust I have vindicated myself.

Now as to James Smith. I was thinking about him the very day your letter came and as I thought it probable he might be in Charleston I wrote to him begging him to come up and appointing the ways and means. I enclosed the letter to Mr. Henry Lesesne as I did not know where he would stay. After the Post Boy had gone I heard that Mr. Lesesne was out of town and soon after your letter came. It was evening and too late to send the boy eighteen miles with another letter so I had to wait until the next day when fortunately Daniel Lesesne went to town and I wrote another pressing letter to James and Mr. Lesesne promised to go to every hotel until he found him. I hope tonight to get a letter from him fixing a day to come up. I told him particularly to write for if he does not we will not know when to send the horses to the Station. I don't know what more to do. We have written five letters to him, and I asked Frank when he went to Smiths to tell them to tell James to direct to Vances Ferry as soon as he got to Charleston.

Eliza arrived yesterday with her whole family on a visit. Mr. Manning and his brother and sister, the two babies, the two babies two nurses, the last baby's nurses baby with its nurse and the coloured babys nurses sister—what a cortege! Of course, they could not all come in one vehicle. It is very inconvenient for Eliza that her head nurse has several young children. Susan Manning is a very nice girl, about 20, and the most beautiful amateur hair dresser you ever saw. You would not know my pate when it issues from her hands.

We had a collection in our church last Sunday for the Irish.[62] But as most of the gentlemen had sent their contributions to town before, it was not very large. The *beau-père* got up to forty dollars but stopped there. I was quite amused at receiving on Monday an epistle from one of our neighbours asking me to subscribe to a Library for Nashotah.[63] She evidently thought I knew nothing about the Mission. She sent one of Breck's letters thinking I had never seen one before. I subscribed although Charles was very anxious I should first ask some very searching questions about the theology of the books and the character of the agent of Prot Epis S.C. Union who is to buy them.

Mrs. Holbrook is a Southern Becky Fisher. She is a sister in law of a lady of the same name who Mama met once but a very different sort of person. She has no children and is perfectly devoted to the cause. She favours me with numerous calls for subscriptions and generally to very dry things. She informed me that she was making up a box of winter clothing for the Nashotah people and expected me to help but I really could not make waistcoats and pants for the celibates.

From very wintry weather we have gone into summer, the thermometer at 85 at 3 o'clock, children in summer clothes, the trees in full
leaf, strawberries and peas expected in a week. Etc., etc. I hope Hen has
written by the box. In your next say when James Smith is to be in
Charleston on his way home so that I can have a letter for him when
he arrives.

The invention of the magnetic telegraph in 1845 had a dramatic impact on
news reporting. In June of 1846 Philadelphia was connected to New York and
Washington by telegraph. It was noted in the *Philadelphia Gazette* that the print-
ing telegraph was a "most ingenious wonderful thing as it makes the ordinary letters, arranges them in words, and can be governed by any person who can
spell."[64] The arrival of the magnetic telegraph also meant that the results of the
next presidential election, which would be held in all the states on the same day,
would be known the very next morning. As Emily indicated in this next letter,
she is longing for instantaneous communication between Charleston and
Philadelphia. She is also excited about the invention of gaslights for both street
and home use. Charles resigned from the Navy in February of 1847 and by spring
was back at Eutaw. The much-mentioned James Smith has apparently arrived and
is happily ensconced at Eutaw smoking choice cigars.

Eutaw, April 28th, 1847

My dear Henry,

Your favour of the 21st ultimo is to hand and I proceed duly to
answer it by return mail. As I dare say you have before this discovered it
is a hard thing to begin a letter by acknowledging the receipt of one
without using very small talk such as I have begun this with. I could not
imagine from the size of the envelope what it contained and was very
much amused to find the ribbon. Thank Mary for it and tell her it is
exactly right.

I say now that I do my shopping in Philadelphia and the papers
which came by the same mail were a great treat. I am sure I read more
in them than any of you do and was particularly interested and tri-
umphant over the illumination—be sure and tell me in your next if our
house was lighted or not.[65] I observed that "our citizens" with the
exception of friends and those in mourning all testified their patriotism
not excepting Mrs. S. Davis whose [. . .] is particularly noticed.
Apropos, I suppose you have seen long before this of Mr. Hunter's
exploits at Alvarado, etc. It was a very brave thing in him and I suppose

Com. Perry will honourably acquit him. I always wish when the Mexican news arrives that there was a telegraph from Charleston to Philadelphia. There is great talk of having one between Charleston and Columbia.

What an enchanting friend C. Marshall must have been and how I should like to excruciate myself over his work. Books, as the worthy would probably remark, is exceeding scarce in these parts (Friends you know never use good grammar). You did send the last number of *Dombey & Son*[66] but you need not send any more numbers as a paper which we take publishes an extra with it as soon as out.

Lizzie was very chatty when I told her you had sent her a kiss and brought out a great many reminiscences of you some of them rather apocryphal. I hear her talk of the doings of Party Whartons house. You could not imagine anything short of Buckingham Palace. Yesterday she came running into my room with her face crimson with agitation and her eyes like saucers exclaiming that she had found her ring which she had lost ever since she came to the South. Her delight was unbounded. It seems she was looking into something that had not been opened since we left Philadelphia. There she found the long lost and never forgotten ring, and then came the long account of each member of the family, of poor Uncle Frank taking her to the beautiful shop, etc. etc.

Her education is regularly going on. She comes to me for a half hour every day and spells in words of three letters, besides saying moral and religious lessons from a book I have just got for her called *The Peep of Day*. Bud although a low child has, I hope, –some aspirations. For instance he frequently drops down on his knees calling out Lizzie and mutters something like prayers. Also he takes up a book and tries to imitate her. He calls himself Bubbo which is decidedly coarse. What do you think of a lady who was staying here last night saying that he has the finest face she ever saw!

James Smith has a box of cigars for you which Charles sends you and hopes they will be good. They are Chapman Huger's choice. I suppose you have cool weather now as it has been quite so here. What is in season now? Choice shad I suppose. I ate blackberries several days ago but only a few. Strawberries are plentiful and so are green peas but nothing else. I have heard nothing about the new waiter yet not even his name. Tell me something next time and if you have heard anything about the amiable but erring John I suppose nothing but an eating house would take him in.

I must stop now although I feel as if I had much more to say but it is late at night and I have to get up early as I am going to spend the day with Mrs. Dehon.[67] What do you think of driving 20 miles to dinner and back the same evening. Tell Mary she owes me. Love to all, both great and small. Your loving Sister, ES.

With summer's arrival, the Sinkler clan was again faced with the prospect of hot weather and epidemics. Emily was excited to be making plans to take the four-day cruise on the *Southerner,* landing this time in New York and coming by train to Philadelphia. However, the *beau-père,* Anna, and William Henry were headed for Pineland, a mile and a half from Eutaw, where the family had summer houses. It was between Eutawville and the two plantations. Emily's room at her home on 150 Walnut Street was on the fourth floor, quite a walk-up, but typical of Philadelphia row houses.

Eutaw, May 13th, 1847

My dear Mary,

I have good news to communicate and that is that we have determined to leave on the 29th of this month. Charles wrote to Chapman Huger by last mail to engage our passage in the next trip but one of the Southerner which will be the 29th and I hope we will hear tonight that he has been successful. I think it is very probable that he had no difficulty in getting a state room as when he wrote it was nearly three weeks before the time. Our plans are thus—we all leave the Plantation on next Tuesday the 18th (the *beau-père* thinking it necessary to move a whole week before the rest of the neighbours) for the Pineland where we will stay until the 27th when we will go to Charleston, sail on the 29th and be in New York I trust on the morning of the 1st of June and come on to Philadelphia by the afternoons line. I will write you once more from here and also from Charleston and you will have time to write to me once more but you had better direct to the care of J. C. Huger, Charleston.

Lizzie is delighted with the prospect and says she is sure she knows everybody in Philadelphia. Wharton you must be prepared to find a very rude little boy. There are very few persons he loves and he is particularly rude to men. Catherine is trying in vain to raise some recollections in his mind. Mama will, I know, be touched by the neat little frocks I am making up for them. Give my love to her and tell her I will be too glad to see her and I would rather have the same room I had last summer if no one is in it and if so any place will do for me but I had rather be in the fourth story.

I am sorry that in the time of my visit comes your annual trip for I have had quite enough of green trees and roosters and am panting for brick walls and noise. Give my love to Eustatia and tell her I shall certainly expect to see her. It will be too bad if she can't wait until the lst of June for me.

Eliza left us a few days ago. She will now not move again until she comes to see her father again next winter. He and William and Anna are perfectly undecided as to their plans but will I suppose stay in the Pineland until late, probably August. I have been engaged in making preserves and jelly for next winter which I hope will turn out well. The strawberry seems so nice that I must bring on a jar with me. The *beau-père* has given me some hams for Papa which we will send on by the first opportunity.

Your last came by Monday's mail. I was quite amused with the account of the fancy ball. Why did you not knowing my weak mind send me on a copy of the Herald? We got our 7th *Dombey* on the 3rd of May which I dare say was only a few days later than you got it. Of course *Dombey* means to marry Mrs. Grainger and I hope she will lead him the life he deserves. Joey B is a sweet creature.

I suppose you have seen James Smith by this time. When you do next thank him for me for the handsome book he sent me. How did he like the Southerner? Mrs. Middleton is going to New York in her on the 15th to see her children at school.

We have had two men at work this week with whom you would have been delighted. They came to show some new plan of making manure and stayed several days. They were Frenchmen and from the part near Switzerland. One was a hussar in Napoleons army for many years and served four years in Germany, Battle of Austerlitz, etc. He is a real character and says he left France the day Louis Bonaparte was exiled and will never return until he is on the throne. I talked French and German to him. I suppose you will raise your eyes and say what sort? But at any rate he thought it wonderful.

I must stop now. Love to all. I only hope you will all be half as glad to see me as I will be to see you. The *beau-père* gets very animated when he compares himself with Papa and Mama. You loving sister, ES. Tell Aunt I am coming so soon that I will answer her letter in person.

In this next letter, summer in Philadelphia was only a memory for Emily, Lizzie, and Wharton. They would have enjoyed outings to the suburbs, including Germantown and Camden, taken rides on the omnibuses, shopped on Chestnut Street for new music at Carey and Harts and at L. J. Levy for new dry goods. She would have attended church with the family at St. Stephen's Episcopal Church.

She may have seen performances at either the Chestnut Street Theatre or the Walnut Street Theatre. She may have shopped for seeds at Robert Buist's City Nursery & Greenhouses at 140 South Twelfth Street. She may have visited Lemon Hill or the Spring Garden Water Works with its parklike setting. Emily would then have returned by ship in September either on the *Southerner* or the *Emma.* By October she was back again in Charleston, and, as she was seven months pregnant, the family decided to spend the time of her confinement in Charleston. Emily, Charles, Lizzie, and Wharton stayed at Stewarts Inn. It is interesting to note that Emily and Charles have just purchased a new Philadelphia-made carriage, probably one from G. W. Watson's.

Charleston, October 24th, 1847

My dear Henry

In the first place is not this most delightful letter paper? You ought to congratulate yourself as well as me on it for you stand a much better chance than usual of getting a pleasant letter owing to the good humour which I experience in writing on it. (After this announcement I feel a total check of ideas and words so don't be too sanguine as to the brilliancy of the production.) In the second place I have received your very entertaining letter and if promptness in answering will prove to you how much I should like to have just such another very soon my purpose will be answered.

How much I wished on last Tuesday that there was a private Telegraph between Charleston and Philadelphia. I would have sent you the last Mexican News immediately for it arrived after the Wilmington boat left on Monday afternoon and had to wait until Tuesday afternoon. I did not see the names of any I knew killed in the Pennsylvania regiment but several of our acquaintances here have been victims. Mr. Sinkler sent the news of two deaths— (Mr. Col. Dickinson and Willis Cantey) to Richard Manning as soon as it arrived to take on to his Aunt. By the bye I saw the names of Major Twiggs as being killed in this last battle and Decatur Twiggs in a former. Are they the same who were at the Navy Yard once? I see that a steamer has come in with fourteen days later news (this dishing up to you must be highly gratifying) and suppose there is a new *Dombey.* If so will you send it to me when every one is quite finished with it. If you will also send me *Neal* (oh call it weak not low) I shall be very grateful.

We have succeeded in having a share in the Charleston Library which has slumbered in the family since it was founded transferred to us and I can get as many books out as I want.[68] The Librarian told Mr. Sinkler that he would find the Library a pleasant lounge in the morning which he was not particularly gratified to hear as you know he likes to sit in a corner with a book and neither speak to nor look at any one. Who do you think was one of the first presidents? No less a person than Lord Charles Montague—not a very active one, however, I imagine.

Did Papa get a letter enclosing 200 dollars to pay for the carriage? Tell Mary that Baratet, notwithstanding my earnest solicitations, would not send in the bill for making my dress before I went but I suppose has done it by this time so as there will be a little money left after the carriage is paid for I wish it appropriated to that purpose.

25th. I was interrupted yesterday in my letter writing and of course today do not feel the same ardour about it. Lizzie and Wharton often talk of you. Lizzie went twice to church yesterday and behaved very creditably. Bud is decidedly improving in mental qualities but I have not time to dilate. Do write very soon. Give my love to all and tell Mary I will answer her letter which came yesterday, next week. With love, Yours, ES

Charleston, Nov. 7th, 1847

My dear Mary,

Your last came duly to hand and was as usual a source of much entertainment besides relief as to the money for Papa is always so punctual about such things that we were afraid from not having heard before that it had not arrived. The Trapiers have not yet arrived. Are they to come by sea or land? I am looking with interest for their names to be mentioned in the Newspaper. Did I tell you that Mr. Sinkler got a very affectionate letter from Richard Trapier asking him to be Godfather to his baby and saying that he knew of no one to whom in case of his own death he would as willingly confide the spiritual education of his child.

We are very comfortably fixed here (Stewarts). We have good rooms and a private piazza in front of them, and as we have our own servants it seems more like our own house than a boarding house. Rachel attends to the rooms and washes; Maid Lucy has a supervision over everything and Edward attends to the eating department. He was poor Seaman's servant and is a very gentlemanly boy. Buddy is of course devoted to him and thinks it the greatest of honours if Edward will go out with him.

By the bye I must tell you one of Bud's exploits that caused me quite a fright. One day last week Katey was to take the children out but

Bud refused positively to go and after a great deal of coaxing she and Liz set out without him. For some time he kicked about in a very sulky way and then came to me and said: "Has Katey gone and left Buddy at Home?" I said yes Sir, you were a naughty boy and would not go. He said nothing but I observed him snatch up his hat and go out of the room. Supposing he had only gone to the Piazza I thought nothing of it for a few minutes but then very fortunately I got up to look after him and could see nothing of him. One of the waiters of the house was going past and I sent him to look for him and where do you think he found him? Trudging as fast as his legs could carry him up the street and saying he was going after Katey and Lizzie! Just think of his finding his way down to the street door and setting off on his own hook. I can assure it is a lesson never to trust him out of sight.

Lizzie is a great favourite with everybody in the house and especially with a little boy of 10 with whom she flirts terribly. It amuses me very much to see how old she is growing in one respect. She will go out to breakfast or dinner alone (of course I mean after being taken by some one to the house) and I always hear a good account of her. She and Katey are the best of friends. Liz is willing to sit by her and sew all the morning and goes regularly to church with her as Katey says she feels more comfortable about going into a pew when she has Lizzie with her.

While you, I suppose, are freezing over large fires, the weather here is very warm, open windows and no attempt at a fire. I have not seen Lily McEuen for several days and suppose she has gone in the country with her Aunt Mrs. Izard Middleton who sent her love to you the other day.

The last *Dombey* is just published here and I have read it. There is very little in it don't you think? So much sameness in all the characters. They are so extremely true to themselves the whole time that it is quite tiresome.

I have been asked lately when Heyward Drayton is to be married, the lady insisting that he is engaged. Is it so? I wonder that Maria Cox does not write to me about her engagement. Is it regularly announced? You must gape over these stupid letters I write you so different from yours. I wish I could change places with you for a while to show you that I have brains too. If you only knew the people here I could tell you plenty of amusing things. But as I am not Mme de Sevigné,[69] I can not think of telling you anecdotes about people whose names you don't even know. Goodbye now, love to all, Yours ever, ES.

❧ ❧ ❧

Charleston, Nov. 14th, 1847

My dear Mary,

The Trapiers have arrived at last and safely delivered the package which was very acceptable. They are staying in this house and have rooms next to ours, but I have not seen much of them for they have a great many friends and are out nearly all the time. They go in the country tomorrow. They made me very envious by their account of the delightful cold weather in Philadelphia for here it is exactly like May, no frost whatever so that people feel very doubtful about going on their plantations and with the exception of two showers of 15 minutes duration there has not been a drop of rain for eleven weeks.

Lizzie is actually beginning to read and is deeply interested in it. She is as good as it is possible for a child to be and is also beginning to have some idea of sewing. Her great ambition is to learn to write so as to write letters to you. Bud is well and very boyish. I never saw a child display so young his contempt of the female sex. He cares for nothing but boys and mens society and I would have given anything if you could have seen him this morning going off with two boys of 12 who stay in the house and have holiday today.

Thank Papa for the address. It has arrived safely and I am going to send it to Dr. Frost to read today. The papers mentioning it have arrived and I said so in one of my last letters. Betsey's scissors shall be returned as soon as I have an opportunity. Unfortunately they are nailed up in a box to go in the country but she may rely on their safety. It is best to encourage such feelings towards her husband [as] it may keep off flirtations.[70]

Did you see the letter from Bishop Ives in which he says it is very doubtful whether Bishop Potter would have voted against B.T.O? Why was not Bishop Potter present? Bishop Gadsden asked one of the Lesesnes the other day if Mr. George Wharton was any relation to me for he said his speech was decidedly the best that was made in the Convention during the whole session.[71] Mr. Campbell has improved wonderfully in looks and preaching. He is a stout, quite handsome man now and some of his sermons are excellent. I have not seen Mrs. Shubrick since her return but hear that she is delighted with the attention she received in Philadelphia. Mr. Sinkler was delighted with a sermon he heard last Sunday from Bishop Otey. Did you ever hear him?

Dr. Huger came to see me a few days ago. He is expecting two consumptives to spend the winter with him, one from New York and the other a brother in law of Mr. Gordon's who he has never seen but is taking in out of friendship to Dr. Chapman. Lily McEuen is enjoying herself very much and is exceedingly admired by her Mother's relations. Her playing on the piano is thought charming. As soon as there is a frost she is going in the country.

Delancey Izard is in a miserable state, so ill last week that it was thought he must have died but they say it will take two or three more such attacks to kill him. Mama always said he would turn out badly.

Tell Mama there is a plant that I mean to try my best to get for her, the sweet olive. The perfume is enchanting and it will stay out the whole winter here in flower not at all affected by frost so it must be hardy enough to be planted in her garden.[72]

Eliza desired her love to be sent to you when I next wrote so I have executed her wish. She leaves town in a day or two after a very unusual stay away from home for anyone of the name of Manning. However her Aunt Mary has been in so precarious a state that she could not leave her before. She is no better now but the Dr. says she may continue in this way for a year so Eliza cannot of course stay any longer. Aunt Mary suffers dreadfully with Neuralgia and has been now for a year in bed.

I must stop now having exhausted every topic and touched on I am afraid very little to interest you. Tell Hen to write, Yours ever, ES.

Between November 14 and December 10, Emily, who was now twenty-four, gave birth to Arabella Wharton Sinkler. Dr. Huger probably assisted with the birth. Pregnancy and birth were not discussed in polite society, and so it is not surprising that Emily refers to herself as being "sick." She refers to the kindness of Mrs. Frost, undoubtedly the same individual in whose house Seaman Deas Sinkler died. The new baby was christened in St. Philip's on December 22, 1847, and named Arabella Wharton Sinkler, for Emily's mother.

Charleston, December 10th 1847

My dear Mary,

You see I have again resumed the pen and you may look for my usual weekly lucubrations. I am happy to say we are all quite well. As for myself I feel as if I had taken a new lease of life. You can't think how kind every one has been since I have been sick in coming to see me and sending nice things. Not one day has passed without something being sent to me. Mrs. Frost regularly every morning sends me breakfast and has been as attentive as possible. Lizzie Middleton comes every day and sits with me so I have been as comfortable as it was possible for me to be away from home.

I suppose you don't care about hearing much about the baby and the fact is there is very little to tell except that I have often heard people talk of good babies but I never saw one before. She literally never cries during the whole 24 hours but once and that is when her head is washed. No colic and she sleeps in bed.[73]

I have been excessively amused in drawing out Mrs. Campbell's character. Some one ought to write the Natural History of Nurses for I am delighted to see how closely they resemble each other. For instance you remember Coppinger's peculiar views of religion. Well I asked Mrs. Campbell what church she belonged to. "I attend the Methodists said she and I suppose I've joined them for Brother came to me and asked me why I never came to the Altar." But to make a long story short for I can't give it in her words, she has a strong objection to "class" and "class leaders" tho' she acknowledges she can't do without Methodist preaching. So it was arranged that she should only be obliged to attend class once a month and then never tell her experiences and if you could only see her toss her head and say, she tell her experiences, indeed! You remember an unfortunate grandson in law for whom pop could never find a bitter enough word. Campbell is equally savage about a daughter in law. She says she told her son when he was going to be married . . .

Tell Mama her letter was so sweet it made me cry. I am expecting one today from you. Tell Mama I wish she would let me know immediately whether the baby shall have a middle name, whether she shall be christened simply Arabella or if the middle name shall be Griffith or Wharton. Don't forget to let me know this immediately for she is to be christened on the 22nd.

Take Papa down to Langenheims with all possible secrecy and have his Daguerre taken exactly like yours for me.[74] Be sure to do this for then I will have the whole family except Hen and he I expect soon to see in propria persona. That will be $16.75. Then I want you to ask Papa if it will not be possible to get me a small box of real Burlington Herring, the real roe fish.[75] They cannot be got here and no matter how small a box. If the campstool is done you had better put it in the box. I want it very much to fill the room at the first go off. Tell Hen he owes me, I think. Yours affectionately, ES

X

Moving to Belvidere, 1848, 1849

IN JANUARY OF 1848 Emily and Charles Sinkler moved the short, one-mile distance across Eutaw Springs to Belvidere. They referred to Belvidere as being "over crik" from Eutaw. Belvidere, like Eutaw, was in Upper St. John's Parish. They moved, probably, because the Sinkler family of Lizzie (Elizabeth Allen), Bud (Wharton), and Arabella (Ella) had grown too large for the Eutaw house. Also, since Charles had resigned from the Navy, he was ready to take up cotton farming on a full-time basis.

Belvidere was located on the cypress- and oak-lined Santee River. Capt. James Sinkler, son of a Scotch immigrant, secured a land grant to Belvidere in 1770. James Sinkler died on November 20, 1800. He had been married three times, first to Miss Cahusac, then to Sarah Cantey, and finally to Sarah's sister, Margaret Cantey. In 1803 Margaret Cantey Sinkler built the Belvidere house. She lived there until her death on December 4, 1821. Belvidere remained uninhabited from 1821 until Emily and Charles moved there in 1848. At Belvidere Emily was the mistress of a large house and an extended family of over one hundred slaves.

Charles and Emily would eventually own over one thousand acres, all called Belvidere but consisting of individually named tracts: Dorshee, Black Jack, Brackee, Belvidere, and a small piece of the Eutaw. Belvidere was shaped like a huge piece of pie, with the north rim running along the Santee River, the southwest boundary along Eutaw Creek, and the southeast boundary marked by the River Road. Nelson's Ferry Road bisected the plantation.

Belvidere was built on an arched foundation so that the first floor was ten feet off the ground. Its broad piazza had two side-by-side entry doors, one into a living room and the other into a dining room. There was no central hall. Both front rooms had large fireplaces. There was a library off the living room. The front yard was grazed year-round by a flock of sheep. Towering elm trees and white oaks shaded the lawn, and the pink and red blossoms of crabapple trees flowered there in spring.

Emily developed lovely gardens on either side of the high brick front steps. She established the family tradition of planting tea olive trees on either side of the front steps. The perfume of their waxy, white blossoms lingered on the cold December air. Emily also laid out a beautiful garden. The Belvidere garden was designed with a long central allée. The allée was covered with Lady Bankshire and Cherokee roses, intertwined with wisteria. On one side were flower beds and paths lined with lilacs and crabapple trees. On the other side was a rich kitchen garden full of asparagus, spring peas, mushrooms, and spinach. Emily writes home that it had been forty years since the garden had been maintained. She talks of foraging all through the country for roots and cuttings. Several friends provided her with cuttings of iris from their gardens. She also planted old-fashioned roses, such as the Glory of France, Harrisonian de Brunnius, Cloth of Gold, and Souvenir de Malmaison. Emily's beautiful iris walk, framed by rose hedges, became a family legacy. Her annual beds of mignonette and heart's-ease were bright with the colors of blue and pink.

During the spring months Emily was delighted by a visit from her brother Henry. Henry arrived in early February and left on April 8 on the steamship *Southerner.* The first successful steamship service between Charleston and Philadelphia began in 1846 with the *Southerner.* During his visit Henry was treated to the usual Belvidere and Eutaw hunting routine: deer, duck, quail, dove, even wildcat. There were visits to Charleston for the February races, as well as family fun, reading and playing games. The months of March and April were very special for the new mother. Emily and Charles reveled in baby Ella's winning ways. Lizzie and Wharton were out of doors in lovely spring days, creating a playhouse under the watchful eye of their Irish nanny, Katey. Emily, as was her way, was reading current literature, enjoying Charlotte Brontë's *Jane Eyre.*

Eutaw, January 3rd 1848

My dear Papa,

A happy New Year to you and many many returns. I received your letter enclosing the bill of lading by last mail and have sent the latter to T. B. Huger in order to have the box up as soon as possible. I am very much disappointed about the daguerreotype and do not believe it is as ugly as you say. I therefore beg that you will send it on by Henry unless a "conseil de famille" decides that it is too disfiguring. You know a person is never able to judge of the merits of their own likeness especially of a daguerreotype.

Everything is coming on rapidly at Belvidere and we expect to move next week. The furniture is all unpacked and wonderful to relate is neither wet by salt water or rain or bruised which I was very apprehensive of, for some was packed very carelessly.[76] Between some of the boards there were spaces of a foot wide extending from one side to the other. Fortunately there was not one shower during the whole transportation which was not to have been expected as they came from Philadelphia in separate detachments, then came up the Santee in an open Canal boat and were then waggoned 13 miles.[77]

Of course I am now employed in the most congenial manner to my tastes, i.e. arranging everything. It is too hard that after giving everything you and Mamma can not see how handsome all looks. Mary speaks discouragingly in her letter about her coming but I cannot bear to think of her giving it up for it would be such a good opportunity for her to come with Henry. The children are quite well and you never saw them look so hearty as they do now. The little body is very good and quiet and as Catherine says "takes notice dreadfully for one so young." Tell Mary I shall attempt cutting off a little lock of hair but I am sorry to say the boasted hair is not only all rubbing off but is turning light. Her eyelashes however are jet black.

I enclose Mary some extracts from the *Home Journal* (Morris & Willis paper) which are too absurd for me to enjoy alone. I also enclose for your special edification a picture I cut out of the *Brother Jonathan* you sent me and which I hope escaped your observation.[78] Please twigg the expression, the genuine New York expression of the man and also of the woman who is rocking herself in the rocking chair. I also enclose the length of Lizzie's stockings and will be much obliged if Baker will get me three pair at a Stocking store in Second Street on the opposite side of the Alley that is next to Townsend & Sharpless' (between Walnut and Chestnut). I believe you said there was still some money remaining so please give some to Baker of it and tell Hen to bring the stockings on with him. If still some remains (money) I will be much obliged if Henry will subscribe to the *Recorder*[79] for another year immediately as I think it must be almost a year since he subscribed last for us and tell the man to direct to Vances Ferry, again. While we were away we had it directed to Charleston·

I hope Henry will not let it be long before he comes on. I would advise his coming the Washington route. The expense (if he comes on direct) is 27 dollars and he had better stay as short a time as possible in Charleston now (as nothing to interest a stranger occurs until February) so he must write when he intends leaving Philadelphia so that we can tell the exact day he will be in Charleston so as to have the carriage waiting at the station. He can then pay a visit to Charleston during the races with William.

It is late so I must bid goodbye with love to all. I will write to Mary next week so tell her to continue writing. Lizzie's amazement has been great on hearing of Undine's late performances.[80]

❧ ❧ ❧

Belvidere, January 17ᵗʰ 1848

My dear Papa,

You see I am going to inflict another epistle on you to day and I hope that this together with the other I wrote you lately will meet with their reward in the shape of an old fashioned letter from you, not five or six lines on a sheet of note paper. You see by my date that we have at last moved home and are regularly fixed (by the bye you could not see the last by the date). We came over on last Wednesday and tho' at first there were some laughable incidents yet now things are going on as decently and in order as if we had lived here for a twelve month. We dined at Eutaw and came over immediately after dinner and you never saw two such little crazy creatures as Lizzie and Wharton were. They were perfectly beside themselves with the novelty of the thing.

One occurrence I must relate tho' it savours a little of life in the backwoods. The servants consist of Bull, waiter and coachman, Rachel, chambermaid and washerwoman, and Chloe, cook. The first two have been with us for a long while and are quite au fait to everything, but the latter has only been learning to cook for a short time and knows very little of "genteel manners." I gave her one of the Delaware herring by way of a treat to cook for tea but to my horror three or four minutes after I gave it to her I heard a tramp approaching and enter Chloe smiling with the fish broiled, it being then 5 in the afternoon. I gave her some partridges, which she inquired were to be thrown out. I am happy to say that she is fast becoming civilized and bids fair to be an excellent cook.

We have had company rather sooner than I wanted. For the next afternoon when we were by no means settled I was upstairs arranging some things, having left Mr. Sinkler arranging the books in the bookcase and gloating over the Encyclopedias. After a while I chanced to look out of the window when my eyes were greeted by the sight of a long peddlars waggon and several gentlemen standing in front of the house, one with a law book in his hand. Two of them came to supper afterwards and spent the evening. It appears that peddling is against the law of the State and this waggon they had been on the hunt for until they saw it come through our gate.

I believe I have never told you how delightful the potatoes have turned out. We have not yet taken any out of our barrel as we have some few left from our own growing and are keeping yours for great occasions, but the *beau-père* has had his constantly and they are pronounced the finest ever seen in this latitude.[81]

The box has arrived safely with everything in good order. The children are delighted with the toys. One box is not yet opened (the largest) being kept for the day on which they are to have company to spend the day with them. They have two little cousins (Marion and Francis Lesesne) of corresponding ages who live 4 miles off and of whom they are very fond. Last Tuesday was Francis' birthday and they spent a very happy day at Pond Bluff.[82]

Did Mary get a letter from me? I ask because several letters which by this day week's mail directed to Charleston have not been received there. Tell Frank and Henry I received their letters by Thursday's mail. I was very much disappointed that Hen fixed no time for coming on. What does he mean by it? I mentioned to some gentlemen who were at Eutaw last week that I expected one of my brothers on and they told Mr. Sinkler he must certainly bring him to their house and they promised a fine deer hunt. Tell Frank his account of his horse was capital. I will propose a name which if he does not like he must tell me and I will think of another—Robin Gray—after the old man in the song (the auld can be dropped as not very complimentary). I think he said the horse was a whitish gray. Tell Hen [letter stops here]

ই❧ ই❧ ই❧

Belvidere, January 31ˢᵗ 1848

I hope my sweet blessed Mother knows that why I don't write to her oftener is because I mean all my letters for her as well as for the person each one is directed to. The chief object of my thoughts at present is Henry's expected arrival. I suppose he is to leave tomorrow and by the time this reaches you he will be almost at his journey's end. We got his letter on last mail night but I wish he had been a little more explicit about his movements. He says he will stay a day or two in Washington and be in Charleston about Saturday but will write from Washington. It will be impossible for us to receive the letter in time so we have made the best arrangements we could think of. Mr. Huger will be at the wharf on Saturday morning as the boat arrives to meet him and to tell him that he must go direct to the Rail Road as we will have the Carriage waiting at the Station.[83] In case he does not arrive on Saturday the Carriage will wait at the Station until he does come. I think he had best come directly up as it will be an unnecessary expense for him to stay in Charleston now for William expects him to go down to the Races with him in about 3 weeks.[84] Lizzie is enchanted about Henry's coming. When I told her about it she danced about until she almost dropped. The next morning at breakfast she exclaimed, "One thing I can tell you all—I mean to go back to Philadelphia with Uncle Henry when he goes." Wharton is too young to feel much on the subject tho' he professes great enthusiasm and desires to see Uncy Henry. His coming makes me feel very grasping about the rest of you coming and now that Hen has broken the ice I hope he will show others that it is possible for them to follow. The baby is quite well but of course does not participate in the predominant feeling at present tho' if you give her the least encouragement she smiles continually. She is very forward for two months, can sit very straight, etc. etc. I feel all the time I am writing that this is a most shabby letter but I must say I think I am quite excusable as *imprimis,* the Carriage has gone for Miss Lesesne and I expect her every minute to spend a week, and *secundum* Buddy is alongside of me chattering like a crow and writing with ink pictures of Party and Marty.

We have had a good deal of company lately to dinner and tea including Fitzsimons who is much improved by moustache, imperial etc.! and who is to go to Europe in six weeks. Tell Papa I got his note and wish he would send the 100 he spoke of by check as before. If there is any left of the 21 after paying for the things I sent for last I wish he would keep it as very often I want some little thing in Philadelphia. In the list of things paid for he forgot the brown linen so he must deduct it. Did I ever tell you how much I thought of the tablecloth? It is beautiful. I think I shall never attempt again writing in the day time for I am so much called off that I hardly know what I am about. I am writing now with the baby in my arms so I must reserve all I had to say until my next. Tell Mary write on. Yours ever, E.S.

Belvidere, February 14, 1848

Thank you my dear Frank for the many pretty things you sent by Henry. To begin at the scarf and end at the Gaiters every thing was appreciated. Bud and the belts are inseparable and when they came I was just thinking of sending to town for one for him. Lizzie thinks of the muff as only a little girl can who has never had one before. The scarf was worn by Charles to the convention and excited much admiration being the first ever worn here. My tooth pick case ornaments the etagere now, being reserved for choice dinner company. The baby sends her love to you and says she has lent the Gaiters to Buddy until she is old enough to wear them. Tell Party the books were most acceptable and will supply us with light reading for a long while as well as the family at Pond Bluff. It was very considerate in him to send the Wistar Answers. He knows my weak turn of mind. You can think how delighted we are to have Hen with us and only regret that all of you are not here. Last evening we wished particularly for you for we had a cheerful supper of fresh fried trout and brim. Hen is every thing he ought to be and great company for me. Last week Charles had to be away for three days at the Convention and Hen and I had a most cosy time. I make him repeat every day the anecdote in Blackstone about the Pope, in Norman French interspersed with original comments (by me) on the Popes and Cardinals. Give my love to Mama and tell her I will answer her letter next week. The other day I was standing before the looking glass with a cap on beginning to dress and Buddy came in the room and saw me only in the glass and immediately exclaimed, "oh there's Marty," but directly he saw me and came up to me and turned me all around looking very puzzled, saying, "no you are not Marty." It shows that he must not only see the likeness but also remember Mama. Have you read Jane Eyre or are you too much immersed in the manufacture of law books to read anything else? I don't know when I have read anything I liked so much. There are two such beautiful characters in it. When are you going to finish your last letter? If you knew how I enjoyed your letters you would write oftener. This I am conscious is a very shabby specimen but I violated a rule about writing at night and consequently have been called off from the time I sat down. Yours most affably, E.S.

In this next letter we see something of Emily's punctual, orderly nature. Her life is closely organized so that communication with her northern family is no happenstance matter. There was great excitement for her in anticipating and receiving the mail. She wrote at night and had set writing days for each member of her family.

Belvidere, Wednesday Evening, February 16th 1848

My dear Papa,

I was much gratified at receiving a regular letter from you on last mail night for which I return thanks as also for the money which arrived safely and is as safely put away until needed. As you make some queries as to our mail arrangements I will proceed to inform you of them. There is a mail from Vances Ferry twice a week. A boy leaves the Eutaw every Monday and Thursday at 3 p.m. for the Post Office with letters and returns the same evening with letters etc. that have come up that day from Charleston. The letters we send down to the office leave Vances Ferry early on the mornings of Tuesday and Friday and arrive in Charleston in time to go on the same afternoon in the Wilmington boat. Consequently the letters we send to the P O on Monday ought to arrive in Philadelphia on Friday afternoon and those we send on Thursday on Monday afternoon. I always write on Monday, this is an extra and will go to Vances Ferry tomorrow (Thursday). On Monday evening I received your letter also one from Mary also the *Ladies Newspaper* which you kindly sent and which is duly appreciated (N B a *Ledger* is always acceptable). A letter to come by Mondays mail ought to be mailed in Pa in time for the afternoon Southern line on Thursday, one for Thursday's on Sunday, however there are so many detentions etc. about Weldon and Petersburg that one can never tell.

Henry's visit is affording us the greatest pleasure. He is amiable, agreeable, gentlemanly, handsome, intelligent—in fine all he should be. I hope he is enjoying himself. He is to spend two or three days in Charleston next week under the *beau-père*'s wing. Do not be alarmed about his going to the races. It is an entirely different affair from the Northern Races—no gambling etc. and all the ladies go. The *beau-père* has a horse to run for whom he was offered the other day $2,500.[85]

Have you read *Now and Then* by Warren?[86] It is miserable, I think. Such a sickly old goose as that Dr. Hylton is and so maudlin too. Hen has been reading his law book all the morning on the strength of its being a rainy day and this afternoon as it cleared off he amused himself by cutting wood, coming in at dark very red and virtuous. Lizzie was delighted with her Valentine which arrived on the very day and which is carefully put away. She is beginning to read very well. This morning in four pages she only missed eight words. To be sure she is only reading in a book of words in one syllable. You are much mistaken if you think the children do not remember you all. Sometimes Lizzie will be recounting the manifold delights of "Party's house" not forgetting the going to market, riding in omnibuses etc to Buddy and he will get so excited on the subject that he will stride off to the door saying he is going to Philadelphy right away now.[87] He grows stouter every day.

I thought I mentioned how very nice the Herring are. We have them constantly and they are much admired by all. The Encyclopedia are very useful. Hardly a day passes but we refer to them for something. You would be surprised to see how many valuable books we have—nearly 600 books. Some we had before but the most valuable belonged to poor Seaman. And some are beautifully bound. We have nearly all the standard works.

It is getting late at night so I must conclude with the hope that you will write soon again. Believe me dear Papa, ever yours most affectionately, E.S. Tell Mary I will write to her next Monday. Tell Aunt ditto.

Emily loved to have company. She enjoyed the excitement of preparing a lavish country dinner. She always ended a multi-course feast with three desserts. In this next letter she describes hosting Elizabeth Huger and Margaret Sinkler. The three delicious desserts served at this party were faithfully recorded by Emily in her receipt and remedy book and were amongst the missing pages noted in *An Antebellum Plantation Household,* published by University of South Carolina Press in 1996. In May 1999 those missing pages were discovered and are presented here for the first time.

Charlotte Russe. Put 1 oz. Coopers Isinglass previously soaked in cold water into 1/2 pt milk with a vanilla bean. Then over a slow fire and when the Isinglass is dissolved strain and when luke warm add 4 eggs well beaten. Add 1/2 lb sugar. Take 3 pts. Sweet cream, whip very light, add to the eggs and Isinglass stirring all the time. Put in mounds heaped with sponge cake as soon as mixed. [One package of gelatin soaked in cold water equals 1 oz Isinglass.]

Epergne of Custard. Sweeten with whole sugar 1–qt milk. Flavor to your taste. Put in a large flat saucepan to boil. Beat very light the whites of 8 eggs and when the milk boils lay them on it in spoonfuls till they harden a little. Skim off carefully and lay in a dish. Then beat up the yolks and stir them into the boiling milk until it thickens. Turn this over the whites, which you may ornament with bits of jelly or marmalade.

Apple Snow. Peel and core 8 apples. Grate a good many bread crumbs, and put either jelly or brown sugar in the cores. Place the apples in a dish and fill round and cover with breadcrumbs interspersed with pieces of butter. Sprinkle brown sugar, a little cinnamon and a little wine over the top. Bake in hot oven for 1 hour. Make meringue with 4 egg whites beaten up with 4 tablespoons sugar. Put on meringue while Apple Snow is hot and put back in oven for few minutes to brown.

Belvidere, February 26, 1848

My dear Mary,

This letter will go to you once more on the usual day, there having been several little episodes lately to interrupt the usual train. I expect Henry up this afternoon from town and hope he has had a pleasant time. He is I am afraid finding it rather dull in the country. It is so different from Philadelphia that it must seem monotonous to him. Last Sunday as there was no service in our church I made him read a sermon to me. He first began one of Hugh Whites but was so disputatious and critical that I had to tell him to stop and got Melville's beautiful sermon of St. Paul, a tentmaker which he of course admired. I am enjoying his visit very much and hope that next winter I will have you the whole winter. If steamships succeed between Charleston and Philadelphia it will be nothing of a trip. I am looking with some anxiety to see how the *Columbus* performs on her first trip.

Lizzie has worked with much pains and interest a book marker for Minny Wilcocks which you must send to her. It was Lizzie's idea so although there is nothing very wonderful about it except that she made it herself entirely I must send it. I leave the note unsealed so that if Mama on looking at it thinks it not fit to send, "it is of no consequence at all" as Toots says. Lizzie is getting very useful. In the morning she wipes all the tea cups and saucers and puts them away and reads really very well. A book that Papa sent her called Little Lessons for Little Learners she can read in by herself. Thank Papa for the Ladies Newspaper. The last number came on Thursday night and I like it very much. I know you will be amused to hear that I began a knitted oval D'Oyley and wished for your assistance very much in a troublesome part. I hope you noticed an advertisement of a new accomplishment which was entirely to supersede the sometimes tedious Berlin work and which informed those ladies who intended coming to look at it that those who did not mean to be pupils would be expected to buy something.

Since I wrote we have had another dinner party tho' not large. Elizabeth Huger has been getting married and came up to pay Sister Margaret a bridal visit so we dined them. We had soup, boiled Turkey and celery sauce, roasted haunch of venison and tongue for first course, Charlotte Russe, epergne of custard and apple snow. I can see your incredulous look when you come to the Charlotte Russe but you may spare it for it was perfectly successful. I have Mrs. Hampton's receipt which she paid 10 dollars for and every thing was right about it even to the ladies fingers around it. To be sure I had a very accomplished servant from the Eutaw to help me who has been accustomed to making them. You would have been amused I know at the style in which everything was conducted, a roll at each plate, napkins folded fan shape, finger glasses each with a piece of lemon.

Have I ever told you how beautiful I think Jane Eyre? How much superiour to Dombey? Did you notice in the book some of the new style of spelling in center, theater? I must stop now hoping I shall hear from you tonight. Love to all, yours ever, E.S.

Emily's obvious excitement at the arrival of a Wharton present box is wonderfully explicit in this next letter. However, its contents, including such everyday necessities as coffee, raisins, apples, stockings, boots, etc., shows the scarcity of everyday items in the South.

Belvidere March 27th 1848

My dear Mary,

Having a good deal to communicate today I have taken a long sheet of paper—to proceed the box has come! We had heard of its being sent to the canal so on Friday the *beau-père* sent for it. I dined at Eutaw and at 6 when Anna and I came back from a drive we found the box arrived. You can imagine we speedily had a wheelbarrow brought and the box conveyed to Belivdere whither Anna and I sped as fast as possible (such was the enthusiasm among the small coloured population as to the arrival and probable contents of the box that one boy not much taller than Lizzie offered to carry it over on his head). Imagine us now arrived at Belvidere and the lid of the box off—expectation on tip toe—and all crowding round the box. Every thing arrived safe and in good order. The chair is beautiful, the admiration of all who have seen it and matches the furniture exactly. You can't think what a relief one thing about it was to me. From you saying the strap was half work and half velvet I imagined it was so—E.S. velours—which you know would have been frightful. As it is it is beautiful. I am much obliged to you for it and hope that next winter nothing will prevent your sitting in it yourself. Tell Papa the raisins are delightful, like Jack Abbotts breakfast of ham and eggs, full, firm and plump. They are kept for great occasions and some are to be sent to Pond Bluff as also some of the ginger cakes which are as fresh as the day they were made and pronounced by the *beau-père* excellent. The apples with the exception of two or three kept perfectly and were much relished by the children who have had none for a long while. But the opening of the white box of bonbons was the thing. I imagined the box was cream candy so passed it over until the last. How beautifully it was packed. I must tell you of the arrangement I have made of them. William came from town the day before and brought me a beautiful vase into which I have fitted a piece of pasteboard and placed on it all the tall bonbons. You can't think how pretty the effect is. Then I got a little rustic basket which was given me lately and filled it with pretty strawberry leaves and among them laid the strawberries. You never saw anything so natural. I called poor Robin in to hear his remarks. He said he was fair scared to think of things coming so fresh all the way from Philadelphy and begged me to keep the seeds of the strawberries for him (he thought both the flowers and strawberries real). He said my people were a heavy people. When I showed him the chair he could not believe you had made it. The Gaiter boots fit me very well and are just such as I wanted. Ditto the stockings, ditto the boots, ditto the Potters clay and Mount eagle, ditto the Napkin rings. Tell Papa we have not yet opened the coffee, but it is what Charles had been trying to get in Charleston all winter. The drinking chocolate is pronounced the best ever drank. William and Anna drank tea here on Saturday to taste it. I need not say how much the sugar plums were appreciated. The table cloth is a beauty. Bud is delighted with his toys and has them fixed in the play house of which more anon.

I wish you would mention to M. Cardeza[88] that I have written to her about the purses and directed to the care of Mme. Greland. Don't forget this. Of course Miss you did not send the letter by Henry. The only drawback to the opening was that Hen and C.S. were not here having gone up to Clarendon from whence I expect them back today.[89]

I know Chs will like his Almanack. It is a very great disappointment to me that Henry goes so soon. I have done everything in my power to beg him to stay but in vain. He says he always meant to go on that day and he does not like to change. It makes us afraid that he has not enjoyed himself and that he is tired. I know the country is duller than town but he ought to reflect on how much pleasure it gives us to have him with us and how seldom, we have such treats. Has Papa received my letter? I hardly dare to hope that he will come and yet cannot help it. But if he cannot I really cannot see why Frank could not give me only two weeks.

This is the time to see the South. I am sitting now with the door open and a crab apple tree directly in front is laden with blossoms diffusing the most delightful fragrance through the whole air. The only spring thing we have is asparagus as yet but our green peas tho' not in blossom are a foot high. Tell Frank we were much amused with the papers which came last Mail night. Neither Hen or I could imagine what he meant by sending the *John Donkey* unless to show that he was in Harrisburg.[90] The first thing I did on opening the *Ledger* was to look among the lost and found. Poor Shelah!! Of course he put in the part "answers to the name of Shelah" for the amusement of his family. Apropos, did you see in the last *Ledger* Papa sent the advertisement of a lady wishing to engage with a Southern family to go South as childs nurse in a place where she can practice music. "N B the lady has never lived out before" I should think not indeed! What are we coming to—imagine my engaging her. Item to Papa, a letter is always acceptable.

Lizzie says I must tell you about her playhouse. It is on our lawn, under the shade of some elm trees and is made by Katey. First there is the parlour which is on the grass large enough to hold her chair and Buds. There are little benches made of wood covered with moss, also tables of the same and a fireplace. Then there is a stable which Bud mostly frequents. Then a grape vine swing and a spring with a tin cup and an avenue around which small fir trees are planted. It all looks very pretty. Uncovered of course, [and] a small paling being all that constitutes the walls. They all go out soon after breakfast and stay nearly all day, little Ella sleeping in the basket wagon. That child is the sweetest creature you can imagine, very much like Lizzie both in size and face. She has now and then a little meek look out of her eyes that would kill you. Her father perfectly dotes on her. She is decidedly his pet. Lizzie would amuse you very much now. She is quite companionable being very sensible and I only wish I had room to write some of her remarks. She went to church twice yesterday and gave a very good account of the sermon in the afternoon. She is quite au fait to the prominent scripture worthies and could hardly contain herself in the afternoon when Mr. Gadsden mentioned Daniel and the Lions Den.[91] Wharton also went but left before the sermon. The service was for the blacks so as Rachel was there I ventured to take him. He behaved very well until he saw Henry Sinkler get up and go out and then he trotted after him. His amens after every prayer were rather more than I could stand. I must bring this long letter to a conclusion as I have some Lemon Syrup to make. Yours ever affly, E.S.

Read Bud's note to Papa. He was very much hurt because Lizzie laughed vociferously at his telling me to write B. P. Lizzie is very much pleased with the little Hymn book you sent her and is learning the Hymns. I have not had such comfort in writing for many a day owing to the delightful new pens.

Belvidere, April 3rd 1848

My dear Papa,

I received your letter on last Thursday it being just 10 days since I wrote to you. I am very much disappointed at the result of my letter for notwithstanding all Henry's dampers I could not help expecting you. Remember if I come to Philadelphia this summer I have a written promise from you that you will come to Belvidere next winter and you may depend upon it I will hold you to it. You know of course that I would infinitely prefer spending the summer in Philadelphia to anywhere else especially as in June it will be nine months since I have seen any of you and if it is possible we will come some time in the summer. Mr. Sinkler says he begs leave to enter his protest against one thing which he says has been going on for now almost six years and that is a sentence which is always put in your letters about his disliking Philadelphia, a charge which he solemnly denies.

Henry has fixed on Thursday for leaving here but says he will write from Charleston. He expects to leave in the *Southerner* of the 8th. I am almost hurt at him for insisting on going but it is very natural he should want to get back. I shall miss him very much and wish he could have had as pleasant a time as my inclination prompted. The shades of Belvidere were amazed last week at an attempt at a tea party which I gave in honour of Henry. It was a small affair but I enjoyed myself and so I hope the others did. We played Frank's game of rhyming answers some of which were quite good tho' not equal to Franks.

The children are perfectly well. There has been but one dose of medicine given among the three since we have been in the house and that was for a cold. Lizzie is expecting your note with much anxiety. You would be amused to hear her talk baby talk to little Ella, such as this. The other day I overheard her apostrophizing a little cough the baby gave as "that blessing coughey" and those "angel slobberings!!" Ask Mama what she thinks of a girl who is laid wide awake and laughing on the same bed with Bud at 7 o'clock, puts herself to sleep, [and] at 10 is brought up to my room and laid in her crib and never awakens once until sun light the next morning.

This letter was begun with the best intentions in the world as to its length and quality. But when on the first page company came in so I have to resume it now with the feelings one has on hurrying down to the boat at 5 minutes before the time — it wanting now but a very short time of the Post hour. We drink tea at Eutaw tonight so as to be at the opening of the [mail] bag. When you have all quite done with the last *London News* I should like to see them very much. I have spelled through those in the box having been duly edified with the Kissings etc. of the sage of Ashland. There seemed to be very little sage for so many geese!! (original), the young ladies being the geese.

Tell Mary I have had a letter from M. Cardeza containing a valuable piece of family information which I had not heard before. I shall be pleased to see the Professor. I have tried the chocolate pudding with success. Tell Mary to send me some more German recipes. I must stop now in great haste. With love to all. Yours every affly, E.S.

The Sinklers have left the plantations and are residing in Pineland, a summer village thought to be a bit healthier than the lowland plantations. Emily is planning one of her summer trips to Philadelphia, this time traveling on the *Southerner.* Her fear of rough voyages is palpable, such that she requests prayers in St. Philip's for the family's safety.

Pineland, May 25, 1848

My dear Henry,

I have only time to say that we received a letter from Mr. Huger by Mondays mail saying that he had engaged passage for us in the Southerner of the 3rd of June. So I hope you will see us all on next Tuesday week at about 9 or 10 in the evening (which day will be the 6th). The number of our state-room is 3. Mr. Huger did not mention the number of the berths, but I hope one will be 49. I feel rather qualmish about the voyage and hope it will be smooth. How anyone about to undertake a 6 months voyage to India would laugh at me. But we live in a world of comparisons. Some one must have prayers offered in the Philadelphia St. Philip's for a family gone to sea. We will have it done in the Charleston St. Philip's.

I received your letter and Mary's on Monday for which mille grazie Mio Signor. This I don't pretend to call a letter. You can load it with all the opprobrious terms you choose. I am fully conscious of it delinquencies. I will write a decent letter by Monday Mail. We expect to leave here on Thursday the 1st with much love to all, Your loving sister, ES P.S. All well here.

Emily's next letter is in the fall of 1848. In the interim she has spent the summer in Philadelphia. Arabella Wharton Sinkler died in the cholera epidemic during the summer in Philadelphia.[92] There are no letters mentioning Arabella's death, and the only hint of the event is Emily's mention that mourning dress is unbearably hot. It is interesting to note that she is in mourning five months after the death. Emily did not have another child for five years, until October 1853 when she gave birth to Charles St. George Sinkler, whom she nicknamed Charlie.

Emily had now been in lowcountry South Carolina for eight years. She and Charles struggled with the problem of finding a habitable place to spend summer months. The Sinklers had tried Virginia, Flat Rock, North Carolina, and Philadelphia. Finally, after Arabella's death, they decided to build a house in the Santee High Hills also known as the Sand Hills. Summer weather in the Sand Hills, though hot, was not known for the sickness of the Santee River plantations. Emily and Charles named their new house Woodford after a Wharton family place in Pennsylvania.

A peculiarity of the following letter is that the transcribed copy has two different endings: ending one is signed to "mother," and ending two is signed to "dear sister." Perhaps she sent the same letter with different endings. Both endings are reproduced and identified as ending one and ending two.

Belvidere November 30th, 1848

My dear Mary,

You are an example of fidelity in letter writing and I wish that other members of the family who shall be nameless would take pattern by you. Your last was duly received on Monday evening. I was so certain that I would get a letter from you that although the Postboy was detained much beyond the usual hour I sat up in bed until he came and was rewarded by the letter. I am very sorry to hear that Mama is still in bed and am looking anxiously for the next letter to say how she is. If I only had her here I could make her well I am sure.

Why have you not said anything in your last letters about coming? I am making preparations for you in the preserving line this very day and Anna and I are practicing two new duets for your especial edification. I hope you are getting ready some pieces which will suit the tastes of persons who are not quite au fait to intricate music. La coup I know will be liked, also a piece of which I do not remember the name. By the bye did you get the music book I sent you by Dr. Huger and did you see him? I enclose 12 ½ cents in this letter and wish you would buy me a paper of the best mignonette seed and also a paper of Hearts-ease seed of the large dark purple sort. There is a variety in which the petals are large and dark and there is only a small spot of bright yellow in the middle. I would like that variety and if that is not to be had get the next best the man has.[93] In my last but one I enclosed a note to you asking you to see about some furniture chintz for me. On second thoughts I think brown holland or grey linen would be best as it always looks well after washing. Ask Mama what she thinks. Of course it is not needful that it should be very fine. It is to be got in Charleston very good for the purpose at 18 3/4 cent a yard. I wish you would inquire the price in Philadelphia and let me know in your next letter. Don't forget this. I enclose a few Birds feathers for Mama feeling at the same time that I have been very shabby about feathers for her. Some are Doves and others Partridge.

Tell Frank, Charles says he wishes he would come soon for there are some very fine horses at Eutaw now which are to run at the Pineville Races on the 16th of January and Charles is anxious that Frank should see them before.[94] There are private races at Eutaw once a week which perhaps you might like to see. At any rate there is a very nice little pony here which will be the very thing for you to ride on. One feels so much safer on a pony than on a tall horse, for if a pony should fancy to throw you off your chance of being hurt is half as great. However, neither ponies nor tall horses have such fancies here. (This last is meant for Mama.)

I suppose Papa got my letters in which I tell him about the new place. This is an additional reason for your coming this Winter for you will see this part of the country this Winter and of course you will come next Winter to see how you like Woodford. The *beau-père* is to live with us half the year there and Brother James is thinking of buying a place very near for a Summer residence. So the Sinkler family have made up their minds to be no wanderers and pilgrims for six months of the year. The *beau-père* has been trying for 15 years to settle himself in the Summer and has at last succeeded.

[Ending one]

Eliza is here now but is going up on Monday. Nothing can persuade her to stay to Christmas because Mr. Manning has to go back. She is so completely wrapped up in him that she is quite altered and is very provoking to her friends. It is too bad she will not stay to Christmas when it is the custom for all the family to be together at a set time, she might keep it up.

Lizzie is very well and talks incessantly of you all and is very fond of boasting of what her Party and Marty do and have. Very often she will say, ah me Marty has chocolate drops. And when she sees pictures of boats she will say, ah that's me Party's boat. No matter now what she is asked she always answers Party and Marty gave it to me. You would laugh at the queer little duty letters she writes.

Well good-bye dear Mother, Ever thine, E.S.

[Ending two]

Lizzie sends her love to you and "asks you" how all are. Where she learnt the latter form of enquiry I don't know. You will I think be struck with how well both she and Wharton look and how much he has improved in morale as well as physique. Never a day passes but they talk of you all and so much so that Henry Sinkler and Lizzie Manning talk and play continually of Partys house, Germantown etc.

Kate sends some fern for Mama and also some Poppinacks, a flower which the Natives here think a great deal of. Was it not too bad about the sausages. However, I hope to get them off yet. I enclose you a quarter and wish you would send me in your next letter two yards of black ribbon, I got it at Moores on 8th Street near Chestnut some to trim my bonnet. You may remember it, a stripe. If they have not that pattern get any they have for 12 ½ cents. I only want it to go under a collar. I have got a very pretty black barege. There were not plaids to be got in Charleston so I had to get a plain one but as it is fine I hope it will wear well. If I had only known you were going to send the box I would have asked you to get me one just like yours. How sick I am of mourning. It is the hottest dress in the world. Lizzie was delighted with your little note and is constantly writing to you. I wish you could see Bud. He is in summer clothes and is the fattest little dumpling you ever saw. His forehead is exactly like Papa's. I am sure you will say so and his hair grows just in the same way. I must stop now and hope you think this letter long enough. Has there been any obituary of Helen Cox? If so I wish you would send it to me. Adieu, your loving sister, E.S.

Belvidere, Feb. 21st, 1849

My dear Henry,

A letter arrived by Monday's mail from Mr. Lesesne announcing that he had received a dispatch from Philadelphia to the effect that Mary and Frank were to leave on next Saturday. It seems hardly possible that after expecting them so long that they are actually coming and that this day week they will be in Charleston. Perhaps it is best that Mary should make her first sea voyage in the Southerner as persons who have been on her and on the Columbus say that there is much more motion on the latter than on the former owing to her machinery being underneath the vessel. I have no doubt but that Mary will be sick![95] How anxiously we shall watch the clouds! It reminds me so much of last winter when we were expecting you and of the almost sleepless night I passed when I knew you were at sea and when the wind howled in these old trees as if it were an evil spirit. This winter has been very free from stormy weather. Indeed there has been so little rain that the country is suffering very much. It is much milder today than for the last week. We have had really cold weather, snow one day and every morning thick ice. Water froze in the house in the children's room when there was a fire until 10 at night. I hope to be able to meet them in Charleston. At all events Charles will. I am very anxious to go and think that I can manage it.

Susan Manning has been staying with me for the last 4 or 5 days. She came down with Eliza thinking that Mary would have arrived by this time and she will be obliged to go back before she comes after all. However Susan will come again if possible. We have been riding a good deal on horse back and I hope when Mary comes to give her "great sport" in that line. Do you remember William's horse Blue Dick? A sort of iron grey horse which he rode constantly. Well the poor creature is dead and from an extremely small splinter which he ran in his foot. He died in spasms from lock-jaw. It is a great loss to William.

Your last letter was extremely entertaining and I am looking very anxiously for another. Tell me if you think Ellen is engaged to Lamae? I am sorry there is no prospect of my letter rivaling yours as I can hardly snatch a minute now and then to write and when I do write I have the feeling of hurry constantly on my mind. Besides having company in the house I am very busy in making preparations to go to town and getting the house ready for our return. I mean today to convert the room back of the dining room into a bed room.

I am sorry to see by Mary's letter that you still have inclinations to cold. Now why can't you run down in the Columbus to us and be perfectly cured? Charles would have written to you to day about it but he was obliged to leave home to go up to Woodford to see about something or other. He has also not written a letter in answer to a Naval friend who kindly wrote to tell him that two Lieutenants would be in Charleston very soon who he wished Charles would be attentive to. The *beau-père* has been unsuccessful at the Races this year but bears it very well. He got no pity from some members of the family who would rather see him running a different Race.

I will write next week from Charleston. Now I feel so ashamed of this that I would not send it if I did not think it would be thought that something had happened if no letter arrived. Best love, your fond, ES

Belvidere March 29, 1849

My dear Henry,

It is some time since I have written to you but as I know your clear and reasonable mind has understood why it has happened, I will not waste time and paper in making excuses. Your letter and Mama's arrived by last mail. Tell Mama I was inexpressibly touched by her writing so long a letter and telling different pieces of news in it too! I will write to her next week. Our young neighbour Julius Porcher has gone to Charleston to proceed from thence to Philadelphia on next Monday and has been favoured with taking on some grape cuttings for Papa which Mr. Manning sent me. I hope they will arrive in good order. Papa had best consult the gardener about setting them out. I said in my note to him that I had sent him some Mexican garden seeds but in making up the parcel I entirely forgot it. I will do so however by Mr. Agassiz.[96] Talking of that worthy we are having much amusement in planning his reception here—how we are all to be in attitudes in the Piazza and how we are to talk broken English to him, ec, ec. We still go on with Macauley and our thirst for useful knowledge is surprising. The whole of last evening was spent in looking out words in the Encyclopedia and Classical Dictionary. Apropos to this last work, I hear that there was a report in a certain house that shall be nameless that a copy of said Classical Dictionary was feloniously abstracted from the aforementioned house by me, which report I am happy to be able to contradict and to deny. I have invited Mary to make a tour of discovery through our books and if she finds one which is not lawfully ours to seize upon it. It belonged to Dr. Sinkler.

Mary wishes you to be informed that yesterday she rode 16 miles and came home too, hardly at all fatigued. She has become excessively fond of it of which I am of course glad. Our ductile friend rides with her and enters with enthusiasm into all our pursuits. We have reduced him very much to the state to which Aunt Mary brought Uncle Wharton's dog Point. Mama will tell you the story. Mary is capital company as you well know. She is not quite as much annoyed by the fleas as at first and a doubt arises in her mind as to whether all the hives under which she has suffered in former country places have not been also fleas.[97]

Anna and I are learning Lucia with great energy and the duet at which we now are is pronounced our chef d'oeuvre. I am learning for Mama the last song in it which Mary says she used to like to hear Mrs. Cueste sing. I am reading Goethe aloud every day to Mary so you see our time passes in a most virtuous and instructive manner. Our motto is "Mirth and Innocence." Mary declines having Milk and Water added.

What induced the Leamings to come to Charleston at this season of the year? I suppose business. This is the time when every one who can leaves town so they will see it to disadvantage. We have heard nothing more of Mary Ingraham. I invited her to come up to see me and gave her the address but I suppose she will not do so. How often we wish for you here dear Hen. If I had hold of a string which was attached to you by the other end (like those pictures of birds on seals with the motto *le plus loin, le plus sine* above them) how soon would I draw you here. Would you join in our evenings? Or would you think it a bore? I hope Margaret Wharton is better and that we shall hear something about her by tonight's mail. I send you by this mail an album containing a story about a song which I liked very much. Try to find out what the song is for your attached sisters. Love to all, I have put the seal on the letter I referred to, ES

Cholera was an acute, often fatal, infectious epidemic disease that was much feared in the nineteenth century. Arabella Wharton Sinkler undoubtedly died of a cholera epidemic in Philadelphia in the summer of 1848. In this next letter we see Emily's frustration and anxiety about returning to Philadelphia if there were still any possibility of cholera. Amongst Emily's remedies in *An Antebellum Plantation Household* is one for using copperas, a hydrated ferrous sulfate used in water purification, to disinfect cesspools, sinks, and other filthy places. A microorganism prevalent in contaminated water spread the disease. Emily refers here to the steamship the *Osprey*. She traveled in many of the different coastal steamers, including the *Emma,* the *Southerner,* the *Columbus,* and the *Osprey.*

The letter is torn at the seams, causing the noted omissions.

Woodford August 25ᵗʰ, 1849

My dear Henry,

I do not know that you deserve to have your single letter answered [. . .] I will to night address my epistle to you. I am in some perplexity now as to our movements. We intended going to Philadelphia in September as you heard in the spring and had fixed on the middle of the month as the best time and the time which suited leaving here best. Well here is September fast coming upon us in a few days will be the 1ˢᵗ and I have heard hardly anything since we came here three months ago about our coming. I conclude that the cholera perhaps will make it unsafe for us to come. At all events I feel naturally in some perplexity as to what to do. As you may imagine in leaving home for such a distance there are many things to be done which render it impossible to pack up and leave at a moments notice. For instance a man is to be hired to look after the crops, arrangements have to be made with a person for painting the house if we are to go away which if we are to remain I will not have done until later in the season. Now there are many other things too tedious to enumerate but which I am sure you can understand about. I have looked in vain in every letter for some idea that we are expected, that it will be agreeable for us to come or that it will not, but in vain. In but 2 letters for more than three months has there been any allusion to our coming. In those two letters it was in a very indefinite way. Now I know you would be all glad to see us yet it is pleasant to hear so and you may remember that when I expected you all to see me I never omitted in a single letter to say something about it. I have asked in several letters for some account of the cholera, and also for information on which is considered the best of two steamers for if we are going it is important for us to know. I prefer the Osprey but I do not know what she is thought of in Philadelphia. Another thing is if we do not leave here in the middle of September we cannot come at all for if we put it off it will make the time we have to stay so short that it would not be worth while to take such a journey. Now I hope someone will write immediately and say what is the true state of the case about the cholera, whether it will be safe for us to come and above all whether we are expected and desired. I hope the letter will be written soon for even then I will not get it until the 5th or 6th of September, too late to make arrangements to go off in the middle of the month. I do not wish you to take by anything I have said that I wish to compare my anxiety to have you all with me to yours to have me for I know it is a different thing. You with so many externals to constitute enjoyment cannot consequently be so dependent on the company of those you love. You all living in a city with all your friends about you are as a natural consequence a lot more independent for your happiness on having me with you as I am on having you. I hope that what I have said will not prevent a true statement of the case about Cholera. If it is thought unsafe for us to come I think it is perfectly natural that nothing should have been said about our coming. Because you may think I am hurt about the matter don't urge me to come and say nothing about the risk for we of course would not dream of coming if the Cholera was still in the city.

We are all perfectly well. I feel quite convinced now that this place has the great recommendation of health if nothing else. I am glad to say also that the crops are considered to look remarkably well. Especially so as there will be everywhere a great short coming in the cotton crop.

News I have very little to tell. Our life is passed very quietly. Tell Frank William is talking a great deal of a [...] he thinks he will like. He came up to see us in a very stylish equipage and looked very well with of course a great outfit of handsome clothes. He says he would like to go to Philadelphia for a few days but cannot arrange it on account of Anna who thinks it would be too much trouble for her to go. The children would send their love if they knew of my writing but they are both tucked away soundly in bed. Lizzie is deep now in Miss Edgeworth's Frank Rosamond. After she had gone to bed this evening she came running out to ask me if the Miss Leslie who wrote a story she had read today in *Parley's Magazine* was the same who wrote Leslies Receipt and that she would like to see her so much.[98]

Emily's desire to see her Philadelphia family overcame her anxiety about the possibility of a cholera epidemic. She followed her customary pattern and visited Philadelphia during the months of September and October, returning to the lowcountry and Eutaw Plantation for the Christmas season. Her voyage home was an extraordinary feat of fortitude and included several train trips, a steamboat passage, and finally a horse-drawn conveyance from the Branchville railroad station to Eutaw.

Eutaw, November 12ᵗʰ, 1849

My dear Mama,

I hope by this time the Telegraphic dispatch has safely arrived. It has really been impossible for me to write before as you will see from my account of our journey. I wrote to Papa from Washington on Tuesday evening. On Wednesday morning at 9 we got on board of the Potomac steamboat and went down the river until 1 o'clock. The only incident was passing Mount Vernon. It was pointed out to the children who were duly gratified. On board the boat we met with Mr. Russell Middleton and two of his sons who were our compagnons de voyage for the rest of the way and with whom we were extremely pleased. I don't know when I have ever met with anyone who made such an impression of goodness, virtue, religion, morality, intelligence, etc. Mrs. Middleton was detained by Arthur's sickness with mumps but was to follow as soon as he was better. At 1 we got into the cars. Stopped to dinner at 3 and got to Richmond at 6 with one or two stoppings to change cars, take meals, etc. We journeyed on in the most monotonous manner until 4 o'clock on Thursday when we arrived at Wilmington

N.C. having been in the cars for 27 hours. Henry can imagine from experience how often I exclaimed "oh the dreary dreary moorland! Oh the barren barren shore!" Mr. Middleton however was a great relief. We got directly on board the steamboat and then our usual aquatic fate awaited us. As we were going down the Cape Fear at 6 o'clock just after leaving Wilmington we got aground on the mud and there remained until 6 the next morning! And consequently instead of arriving by daylight on Friday morning we were detained until ½ past 11 on Friday night. This was owing to our having fallen on the slowest boat on the line in addition to the running aground. We also were favoured with quite a rough sea. Still the weather was beautifully bright and cold and there was not the slightest cause for alarm. As the Captain insisted on going directly back to Wilmington to make up for lost time we were obliged to land nolens volens. We went to Charles Grandmother's and found them not yet asleep, and right glad we were to get into comfortable beds, tho' we were not as tired as you might suppose for we had a thorough rest on board the boat. And now for the children. It would be almost impossible to say enough of their good behaviour on the journey. They were the amusement of every body in the cars and there was not the slightest crying or fretting. Mr. Middleton told me and also Mr. Henry Lesesne that he had never traveled with such children. Lizzie's cold is almost well. Indeed I might say quite so. Change of air has done wonders for her. She would send many messages to you if she were here. She is playing out of doors in a very healthy childlike way and has quite recovered her spirits. We left Charleston directly after breakfast the morning after we arrived so there was no time to write. Met the James Sinklers in the cars and had a delightful drive up. It was one of the loveliest days I ever saw. We arrived at Eutaw at 5 and found them all delighted to see us. Don't be the least uneasy about the night we stayed in Charleston. There had been ice two days before and the fever had entirely disappeared. We were there so short a time and saw no one which I was sorry for as I should have liked to see Lizzie Middleton. I heard that she and her husband were confirmed last week and that he had become very religious. Tell Hen that "Jones" traveled all the way on with us, was very grand, gloomy peculiar, spoke to no one, never raised his eyes from the ground, so of course I had no opportunity to speak to him.

We will be here in all probability about two weeks at present as the paint on the house at Woodford is not dry. Do direct the next to Vances Ferry. In my next I will tell more particularly. I hope some one will send me the two last *Neals*. Tell Papa I have not heard of the arrival of the steamer as yet but we intend sending to the RR today to see if the boxes have come. I feel in some trepidation about the outcome. This letter is a sort of gathering of all our doings since we left Washington which I have put down without any method. Against my next I hope my mind will be more settled. Tell Mary write and write on foolscap crossed. Anna sends a great deal of love to you and says she hopes to pay you a visit. Lizzie has come in and says tell Marty and Party I will write to them soon and to Aunt Mary too. Goodbye now, Yours ever, ES.

XI

Life at Woodford in the High Hills of Santee, 1850

FOR SOME UNKNOWN REASON Emily and Charles did not spend the winter of 1849–50 at Belvidere Plantation. A letter dated January 31, 1850, is postmarked from Woodford, the Sinkler place in the High Hills of the Santee. While it was purchased as a summer home, it apparently quickly became a year-round home.[99]

Emily and Charles turned to the Santee High Hills for a summer retreat away from the malaria of the Santee Swamp. Woodford was located at Bradford Springs, which was south of Camden and north of Stateburg. There was a railroad line connecting Branchville to Stateburg, so Emily and her family may have gone between Belvidere and Bradford Springs by train. They also traveled there by ferry, crossing the Santee Swamp. Emily was happy to be nearer to her favorite sister-in-law, Elizabeth Allen Sinkler Manning, who lived nearby at Homesley Plantation. Anna and William Henry Sinkler also purchased a home in the area. Charles had a substantial plantation at Woodford, growing both cotton and corn.

Life in the Santee High Hills seemed fast-paced compared to the lonely and quiet life of the plantations. Emily's Manning and Richardson in-laws were known for their dances, parties, and grand occasions. Cousin Dick Richardson owned two plantations, the Ruins and Big Home. His house, DeVeaux, in Stateburg was described as baronial.[100]

There are fourteen letters from 1850. Together they form a cohesive record of events and happenings. In these letters we see Emily's close relationship with her brother Henry. Henry was a Philadelphia lawyer who worked in the prosecutor's office. He was fun-loving and enjoyed games such as charades, backgammon, and a game of rhyming answers. He visited Emily in the winter of 1850. Emily called Henry "Hen" for short, and he fit in as though he had always lived in the country. Evenings did not seem so long when Hen was around to play charades and a game of rhyming answers. Henry's friend Winthrop Sargent visited

Emily for a lengthy stay in the spring of 1850, hoping to improve his health by the piney dry air of the Santee High Hills. Emily became warm friends with WS, as she referred to him, and missed him when he was gone.

Emily remained in the Santee High Hills at Bradford Springs through the summer of 1850, the hottest summer on record, according to her. At the end of the summer, on September 15, Emily and her children set out for a voyage on board the *Osprey* for her annual trip to Philadelphia. She was anxious again to avoid a hurricane, realizing that she was traveling late in the season. However, she was looking forward, as were the children, to trips with her father, Thomas Isaac Wharton, to Germantown in the "cars" and to the fairs and other events that enlivened Philadelphia.

❧ ❧ ❧

> *Number 18*
> *Henry Wharton Esq*
> *150 Walnut Street*
> *Philadelphia*
> *Pennsylvania*
> *Woodford*[101] *Jan 31st 1850*

My dear Henry

We have heard nothing since your letter of Winthrop Sargent, tho I have looked carefully in the newspaper at the daily list of arrivals both by the Wilmington boat and the Steamers and also at the list of arrivals at the Charleston Hotel. Charles has written two letters to him and Mr. Simons has also promised to see him.[102] We had a letter from him yesterday in which he says he has been to the Charleston Hotel but heard that Mr. Sargent had not arrived there.[103] I have an idea that he will come by the *Philadelphia* which I see was to leave on the 30th.[104] I hope there will be no difficulty about his getting up to us for it will be a great disappointment to Charles and myself if he does not come, and altho this is a very dull and ugly place yet the climate is considered excellent for colds and coughs from the extreme dryness and Pineyness of the atmosphere.[105] We will do our utmost to make his visit pleasant and intend to keep him a long while with us. Richard Manning has sent a very pressing and kind invitation to him to pay a visit to Clarendon. The Mannings are certainly very kind friends of ours.[106]

The packages arrived on Tuesday. Who could have sent me the four beautiful and expensive pieces of music?[107] I strongly suspect you dear Hen. I am extremely obliged to the anonymous donor whoever he or she be. Who sent the German newspapers, and who sent *Shirley*?

There was no note or line with any of the bundles. *Shirley,* I have begun and like the little I have read much better than I expected although the meat is very strong and the Radicalism rather *trop fort* for me. Pray what means "mit die Publicationes" written on the Title Page?[108]

I am reading now *Bartram's* memoirs and I assure you it is choice.[109] I fairly doat on the work and wish I had you here to read certain passages with. Only fancy how the RG's[110] would look if I read aloud to them extracts. It is very "pretty" to see how the ancient worthies of Philadelphia are spoken of in the work. There is frequent mention of Israel Pemberton "a pretty and ingenious lad." And the freshness and simplicity with which they speak of the insect and floral world is truly edifying and instructing to our blase minds. No young lady of the present day could speak with more raptures of the contents of Bailey's or Levy's stores[111] than P. Collinson in the extract which I am about to give you speaks of moths, ec.: "It is with great concern I see so many curious insects spoiled. Pray keep the Butterflies by themselves; and then no danger can happen. Some of the last are extravagantly fine. The white long tailed moth is amazing. Now and then when a fine one happens in thy way, take home being always provided with a box in thy pocket when thee walks abroad for these insects are seen accidentally. If thee was to go on purpose it is a query if thee finds one." In some future letters I may give some more extracts quite as delightful as the above. Let it not be supposed that I read to laugh, far otherwise.

I wish I could have Telegraphed to Mama the beautiful bunch of violets I got at church at Stateburg on Sunday.[112] It was nearly as large as my head and my parlor is now delightfully perfumed by it. I have just heard that the son of a neighbor of ours Dr. Anderson is engaged to a daughter of Judge Gibson. I did not know that the chief had an unmarried daughter. The Andersons are very nice people and live very nicely.

A few days ago Lizzie came running in exclaiming, "a great thing for men and boys has just happened," and went on to tell me that as she and her Father and Bud were in the Garden they heard the noise of dogs in full cry and immediately afterward saw two foxes running full speed through the fields pursued by dogs and hunters. This would be thought a strange sight near Philadelphia for I suppose a fox would be considered as much of a rare bird there as an elephant would be here.

You remember Robert, otherwise known as Roberty Bob, I suppose. Well he has taken a stand and says he does not like waiting in the house and wishes to work in the fields where he can have his afternoons, evenings and Sundays to himself.[113] He announces that he does not even wish to go behind the carriage. Just as I have had a nice suit of grey cloth clothes made for him too. Now then you must write to me very soon and a really long letter too. Tell me all the amusing things you said in your last you had to tell me. Tell the dear Mother I will write to her next week. Tell the well appreciated Mary to write on. Tell Frank he is in debt to me. Yours ever affectionately, Emily Sinkler

P.S. Tell Papa if there is any good opportunity I wish he would send me all his Wistar Answers. And I would like also all the party invitations and answers that are lying about the house.

ઢ ઢ ઢ

Number 17
Mary Wharton
150 Walnut Street
Philadelphia
Pennsylvania
39 Society Street
February 21st, 1850

My dear Mary,

Although this is my regular day for writing yet I suppose you will get the letter much earlier than usual as it will be mailed directly from Charleston. Now for an account of the past week. On Saturday we received our neighbors the RG's at dinner, this I mention as I wish Henry to know that his old *bete noire* the turkey Gobbler was on that day sacrificed at the domestic altar. Of course he remembers the old patriarch at Belvidere. Well, he had become so insolent and chivalrous and bullying (the last two words by the bye are pretty much synonymous) attacking even Josey, that I resolved to have him cooped up and a week before the dinner he was killed and hung up. And what a monster he was. Such a breast. He could have dined 13 people. Rachel made the dessert entirely and we had the best Omelette Souffle we ever had, owing I suppose to our new oven.[114] Your maternal feelings towards the dish which used to be quite scandalized at Belvidere would have been appeased on Saturday.

On Sunday morning arrived your letter and Hen's. Tell the latter his was charming, and I will answer it next week. I have not yours which was as agreeable as usual with me, so cannot notice the points in it this time. We went to church at Stateburg and after service went on to the Mannings it being very little longer than to go back home. On Monday morning at ½ past 11 we left and owing to the water in the

Swamp being very high we had to be ferried all through, and what is very creditable in this age of magnetic Telegraphs and Atmospheric Rail Roads we accomplished the distance of three miles in three hours.[115] Consequently it was very late when we got to the River and we had a good deal of difficulty in crossing. The wind rose very high when we were in the middle of the river and the boatmen could not put us at the landing. So we landed at a bank and had quite enough of the adventurous about the affair to satisfy my moderate aspirations of scenes. Lizzie said to me afterwards, "I prayed to God that the wind might kease and it did kease." She had read cease and imagined the c was pronounced as a k. Tell papa that Wharton made his first pun on the Occasion. Some one called out to Mr. Childers (the man who has charge of the Ferry Flat) and he turned to me in a very droll way and said, "Is that man Chilly that they call him Childers."

We got safely to Eutaw and the next morning before daybreak set off, Lizzie expatiating very amusingly on the beauties of the morning star, sunrise, etc. We arrived in Charleston between 1 and 2 and went to "Grandmothers" where we found them all exactly as you saw them a year ago.[116] The old lady is certainly most wonderful for 88. Her faculties and mind are the same as they were 40 years ago with the exception of her hearing which is not quite as good. The same evening I received the packages by Winthrop Sargent quite safely. I have been in such a bustle and excitement ever since I have been here that I have only just peeped at the contents meaning to do full justice to them as soon as we leave town, so in my next letter you will find thanks and comments. W. Sargent goes up with us on Saturday.

I am enjoying myself very much. A great many persons have called to see me and my time is so much taken up that I can hardly spare a moment for writing. But I knew that it would be thought better for me to write a disjointed letter than to omit writing entirely for a week. I forgot to mention that the day before we left home the ill-fated box arrived. The dress was very much tumbled but perfectly uninjured and fits me beautifully, better than any dress Clem ever made for me.[117] The trimming is very pretty too. The papers, etc I am much obliged to Papa for they look very Choice. I forgot to mention that at Eutaw I rec'd your missing letter which had been kept there for me. The children are delighted with their trip. They are on the Battery constantly with Kitty who I have brought down with me. Today there is to be a great parade of Savannah and Charleston Companies and they have gone off in great glee to Harriet Ravenel's house to see it.[118] Of course you remember

Harriet Huger.[119] I drank tea with her last evening in her beautiful new house on the Battery. She has a very nice husband. I am sorry that our visit is so short we will not be able to go to see the Russell Middletons.[120] He was here yesterday with a very pressing invitation for us to go to their place but we will not be able to do so. I was just coming away from Mrs. Henry Middleton's day before yesterday when I met Mrs. R. M. coming, so of course I could exchange but a few words with her. She sent most particular love to Mama and you and wants to know if you got her letter. I am rather ashamed to say that Charles has done all the Convention and Church doings.[121] He says nothing of any importance is going on. Tell Frank that he may shortly expect a package. William had the Gaiters made by the measure he sent but they were so small that they would barely fit a boy of 12 so another pair is in preparation which will be sent as soon as finished together with a gold pen and pencil, a memento from the Ladies Benevolent Society, very pretty it is too. I have a great deal more to say which I must defer and I know you will excuse it. With best love to all, Yours as ever, E. S.

Emily and her family were avid game players. They invented charades for evening enjoyment and her letters are full of charades being exchanged between Upper St. John's and Philadelphia. She even invented musical charades. The Sinklers and Whartons were partaking of a national pastime. For example, in the *Germantown (Pa.) Telegraph* of August 7, 1850, there is this charade: Upon my first the mother mild, Will soothe to rest her forward child, My second is possess'd, you'll see, Alike by drone and humble bee, My whole friend Buffon sure would place, Amongst the little Feathere'd race." The answer is in the August 14 paper and is a "lapwing." In this next letter Emily talks of exchanging charades with Henry, who was apparently a master charade maker.

Number 18
Henry Wharton, Esq.
150 Walnut Street
Philadelphia
Pennsylvania
Woodford March 1st, 1850

My dear Hen,

    This letter will arrive a few days later than it ought as I found it impossible to write on my regular day (Thursday) from reasons which will be apparent as you proceed in my epistle. I wrote last to Mary from

Charleston. Now I will try to take up the thread of my narrative. On Thursday and Friday Winthrop Sargent and myself amused ourselves by walking and driving about and paying visits, among others to a Mrs. Della Torre [wife of Peter Della Torre] from whom I received a letter from Mrs. Gordon introducing her to me and about whom more anon. I passed a very pleasant evening out on Friday and altogether had a delightful visit to Charleston.

On Saturday morning we repaired to the Depot where we found W. S. awaiting us.[122] To avoid too many details I will proceed to remark that we stayed at Eutaw from Saturday until Wednesday, at the Mannings from Wednesday until Friday (to day) and we have been here now about three hours.[123] You will be surprised at my writing so soon after our arrival but if I do not write to night I will miss the chance of tomorrow's mail and will be obliged to defer writing until nearly a week. We passed a very pleasant time at Eutaw. W. S. expressed himself as perfectly delighted with the place and its hospitality. He dined out and birded and rode and went through the usual Eutaw Routine. In the house we had Singing, Charades, and Games. One morning at breakfast it was proposed that every one should produce a charade before dinner. I enclose you the only two that were made merely remarking that the subject of mine had been talked about a great deal the Evening before.

We had also a very pleasant time at the Mannings but such difficulty in getting away you never saw. It really made us feel quite uncomfortable. We took there a delicious ride on horseback. I on the little pony I wrote about before and which is the very perfection of a Pony, Susan Manning on one of the tallest carriage horses I ever saw, and Eliza on the white horse Mary used to ride. We were gone nearly four hours. W.S. has improved wonderfully since his arrival. I never saw such a change in so short a time. He does not cough at all and I do not see anything the matter with him. He speaks of leaving on Tuesday for Jones.

Now for the contents of the boxes he brought. Tell the sweetest of all sweet creatures that the children have not yet seen the globe but I know they will be delighted with it for Liz is intensely interested in Geography. I intended getting one for her to relieve her of the anxiety about the Chinese who she pictured to herself as walking on their heads. Tell her also it was too sweet in her to subscribe to the *Recorder* for me. I could not imagine why it came so regularly and intended speaking of it in every letter but always forgot until afterwards. Accept my thanks for the beautiful books you sent. You know my weakness for More[124] and that delicious picture, and then the French book is so handsome that I am afraid you gave more money for it than was convenient. Tell Frank the book he sent has been exceedingly admired. It is by far the most beautiful edition of Watt I ever saw and will be a great ornament to my table. Thank Papa for the very nice envelopes which he so kindly sent as also for the newspapers, and the Wistar Answers are very relishing. Tell Mary I have received all her letters and mean to write her a real answer in a few days. The song she sent me I have learnt and think extremely pretty.

I am fully aware of the vileness of this letter but there are times when these things must occur, so you can well understand that just coming home with talking all around me and servants coming in constantly for orders. Just now Prayers caused a cessation. That was a delightful letter you wrote me and I wish you would write me another as soon as possible. The length of it was charming. I must come now with all humility to a conclusion but shall make no more excuses. W. S. sends his love to you and says he means to write to you very soon. I enclose only one of the Charades this time as I wish to copy the other. The children send their best love to all. Believe me dear Hen, Yours ever affectionately, Emily Sinkler

I will write to you very soon again to make up for this.

Number 22
Woodford, March 28ᵗʰ 1850

My dear Frank,

Again do I take up the reproachful pen to address you after the lapse of eleven weeks during which time I have in vain looked for an answer from you. Pray do not let such a lapse occur again. I get a glimpse of you occasionally through Mary's letters and now and then an anecdote of you reaches my ears through other mediums. For instance I was told lately that you were seen walking in the street with two young ladies one morning, whereupon ensued much amazement here among citizens. I was also told lately that you stood among the very first of the younger members of the bar. All this is very gratifying to me.

Charles received lately the newspaper you sent him and perused it carefully and then sent it to a gentleman who is a delegate to the Southern Convention. Nothing however comes up I think to Webster's speech.[125] It is the only congressional speech or debate I have read regularly as I have given up politics for the present, finding them not conducive to peace of mind or good temper. The newspapers however I read with great pleasure. What is generally thought about Prof. Webster's guilt in Philadelphia?[126]

I suppose Mama will be shocked but I must confess to reading the report of the trial with the greatest interest. I am afraid the evidence is conclusive against him but will they hang him on circumstantial evidence?

We have had the most extraordinary weather all this month. Nothing but rain varied by sleet and hail, and this morning snow. One is generally reduced very low for a topic when one falls on the weather, but when the weather falls on us so incessantly there is no help for it. It is before me in such a prominent way today that I cannot help referring to it, especially as through its means, I have been out of the house but once since my last letter, and then to church. I have of course paid no visits nor received any; indeed for the last three weeks such has been the continual rain and clouds that the only person who has been under our roof has been Mr. Welch, the teacher. Neither have I paid a visit in all that time. How would you manage under such circumstances? Dr. Johnson often speaks of any man as a fool who would live in the country and if he thought that of a country life in England what would he think of it in America!

Mr. Welch is one of the best men I ever knew. Before he became religious he was in very humble life, employed on the R Road, but for the last 5 or 6 years he has devoted himself to the religious instruction of the Negroes. He comes to us on every other Monday morning and stays until the next day, during which time he instructs the people in various class, first an infant class, then an adult class. He goes in this way from one Plantation to another, each gentleman paying him a certain sum. His worth, simplicity and piety exceed anything I ever met with. He has done a great deal of good here and every where. Lizzie informed me the other day that Rachel had given up "sin and dancing" but that Bull said he had not given up sin yet. Notwithstanding, Lizzie averred that she thought he would give up sin soon for she heard him crying quite loud when Mr. Welch was talking to him about his planting beans on Sunday. The children have just finished their lessons and Wharton wishes you to be informed that he is now in spelling and reading which is the fact of course. He reads in very small words but he still feels it a great promotion to be able to read at all and passes the principal part of his time in spelling to himself. He is in the full tide of learning Dr. Watt's Divine Song which he repeats with distended eyes. Lizzie who keeps a strict guard upon his words and actions, thinks him very much improved in the past six months and has only had to report one speech for a long time, namely that once when he was very cold he ejaculated "Oh dear Lord." Lizzie is the best child I ever saw. A word or look from her father or myself is quite sufficient and I cannot remember when I last punished her in the slightest way. You would be surprised to hear her talk about Pompei, Volcanoes, the World.

I have now I think said quite enough about the children and must turn to something else. Have you received yet the pencil and gaiters from Charleston. If you have tell me how you like them. I have heard nothing of the box I sent to Charleston to go to W. Sargent. I am afraid it is lost or destined not to arrive in Philadelphia as I have seen or heard nothing of WS's arrival in Charleston on his way back and suppose he must either be sick or have gone by some other way. Where are the gloves? I feel naturally a great interest in their whereabouts. Tell me in your letter (which now you cannot avoid writing) how Henry Drayton looks since his return and how he liked Paris, and if he is still attentive to Miss Chapman.

I have planted what I had remaining of your flower seeds and hope I will be more successful than I was last year, for then they were planted so late that they came to nothing. I am rather doubtful now if seeds planted the second year will come up.

Could you not possibly contrive to take a run to Charleston this spring? Have I not some slight claim on You? I shall not say much on the subject for you know what I feel about it well enough. Proper self-respect prevents me from pressing the subject. I shall only say that if you could come we could arrange your time pleasantly by your meeting us at Eutaw and coming up here afterwards. I think you might be afforded a pleasant visit. I wish the family to be informed that it is our intention to leave here on a visit to Eutaw on the 8th or 9th of April. I mention this this early as it will be best after the receipt of this letter for all letters and papers intended for me to be directed to Vances Ferry PO until further notice. I enclose two notes from the children to Mary and Hen and one from me to Mary. Tell Hen his is from Lizzie which he might not be quite certain about as she requested me to sign it "from a friend." I am really sorry to hear of poor Governor Wharton's death and poor Miss Kelly too. Give my love to all and believe me yours ever, ES. Charles sends his love to you. Tell Mary the answer to W. Sargent's charade is Eutaw.

Number 23
Henry Wharton, Esq
150 Walnut Street
Philadelphia
Pennsylvania
Woodford, April 4th, 1850

Oh my brother shallow hearted!
Oh my Henry mine no More!

Oh the dreary dreary Moorland!

Oh the barren barren Shore!

These lines are called forth by your omission to answer my last letter and by your allowing twelve weeks to elapse without writing to me!!
I am tired of mentally exclaiming as I open the Post Bag "She only said"
etc. "It cometh not she said" etc. I expected better things of you. Now
I hope I have made you feel sufficiently your delinquency and I shall
change the subject.

I wrote last Thursday to Frank and since then we have had another
week of dull gloomy rainy cloudy weather and I suspect I shall have
hard work to collect events that have transpired during it sufficient to
fill the sheet or make a tolerably interesting letter. Let me try if writing
in the manner of a journal will help me. On Friday afternoon we took
a long ride on Horseback on a road we had never yet taken and about
5 miles from home in a deep Pine wood we saw a small log house very
poor looking but extremely neat. A man was standing at the gate
employed in mending it and we stopped to ask him if he had any
Poultry for sale. He turned out to be a Bavarian who had come to this
country and after many wanderings had settled in this out of the way
place. I talked to him in German with which he professed to be very
much delighted. To tell the truth I could not understand much of what
he said. Of course I flatter myself that the reason was that he spoke in a
Bavarian dialect. On Friday we received an invitation to a wedding
which is to take place this evening. Mr. Harris Simons' daughter is to be
married to a Mr. Lucas of Charleston. The invitation was enclosed in a
very pressing letter from Mr. Simons but we declined as it would be too
much trouble to go so far.

Saturday, uneventful. Our neighbor Mr. Gaillard staying with us, his
family being absent. Easter Sunday dawned very gloomily, much too
much so to think of Church. A letter from the faithful Mary however
serves as a very healing Panacea. I was very sorry to see by it that Papa
was sick. Give my love to him and tell him I hope he is much better
and will soon write to me. On account of his sickness I have missed 2
weeks of *Neal* which he has regularly sent me of late.[127]

Easter Sunday was marked in our small family by an amusing incident. We have had a Pigeon House put up and Mr. Gaillard sent us over
some 23 or 24 young ones. As they were very young only 2 or 3 were
let out and as we were sitting at breakfast with the door ajar in walks a
very plump Pigeon, perfectly self possessed and at ease. This was great
fun to the children who immediately began feeding "Tommy" as they

called him with crumbs, etc. Tommy became shortly so delighted with his quarters that he hopped out of the room and in a few minutes returned with a companion and they both became as friendly as flies. We were obliged on Monday to turn them out of the room which they resented very much and are constantly now pecking and moving their heads against the window Panes in the fiercest way. I expect before long to see them dashing through the windows.

I must mention here an anecdote of Wharton which I mean for Mama. On Easter Sunday morning I told him what had happened on that day a great many years ago. He immediately said, "And I suppose the reason we keep it now is that we want to have Jesus all the time in our Memories."

On Monday I did nothing out of the way but put up a large box of cake and fresh butter to go to Charleston by Mr. Gaillard. On Tuesday I took a ride on the pony to the school to invite Mrs. Hummel, the German Teacher there, to dine with me on Saturday.[128] The poor thing who is very lonely here accepted most joyfully. I forgot to mention that on Monday evening we finished *Johnson* "clasum et venerabile women!!" On Tuesday we began *Southey.*[129] I must say I think the beginning rather egotistically minute. If the 2d volume is out yet do let me know. I am reading Chateaubriand's *Itineraire,*[130] which would be interesting enough were it not for his tiresome discourses on the ancient Greeks and mythology, a subject which most Frenchmen are demented upon.

On Wednesday I received by mail two packages which from the handwriting I should judge to be from Winthrop Sargent. One was a Tract giving an account of the *Perry* Shipwreck.[131] How W.S. came to send this I can't imagine. Do enlighten me about it. Charles and I have, of course, been very much interested in this narrative. It is without doubt by Mr. Trapier. I suppose you have all seen it; if not you must read it. Tell Mary I wish she would get me 8 or 10 copies and send it on by the first opportunity. I want to give them away. The other package contained a piece of Music (Instrumental), a Spanish dance by Tureck. I would like you to find out privately why he sent me this piece. I wish you would present my remembrances to W.S. and tell him I have received these and am much indebted to him. Tell him also that Charles received his letter and that I was extremely entertained with it and laughed most heartily at all the places where I was expected to laugh. That I think it is a very bad sign of the fair Rutledges character for her name to be spelled Sallie. Tell him that I shall be delighted to receive the whole of Bingen, "dear Bingen on the Rhine." By the bye then is not Bingen one of the most darling little Poems in the world.[132] How did W. S. enjoy his visit to George (I beg his pardon) Wimberly Jones?

Today (Thursday) I paid a visit at Stateburg to the Andersons where I got a wheelbarrow full of flowers.[133] They have a beautiful Garden and Greenhouse and I had "great pickings." Miss Anderson is going on to the North in June to be at her brothers wedding. He is to marry a daughter of Judge Gibson and if she stays any time in Philadelphia I want Mary to pay her a visit. There ends the journal of my week and with it must end my letter, which by the bye has grown much larger than I imagined it would from the scanty materials out of which it was composed.

The general neighborhood talk is Mr. Calhoun's death![134] How rapidly news flies in these days! He died at ¼ past 7 in Washington and at ½ past 7 it was known all over Charleston! I have written a letter to Kate[135] which she requested I would direct to Papa's care. I have done so and so has Mrs. Frierson. Will some one see that she gets these letters? I am almost ashamed dear Hen to send you such a grand chain as the one I enclose. The silk was sent to me from Charleston and is of an entirely different color from what I intended. Don't feel bound to wear it. Yours Ever, E.S.

The exchanges between Upper St. John's Parish and Philadelphia included everything from gardening seeds, grits, and fat lighter wood to boxes of newspapers and books. Philadelphia with its Library Company, Philosophical Society, Wistar Parties and Athenaeums was a center of intellectual activity. Emily was envious, even jealous, of her family's access to current literature and societal events. She longed to hear each item of gossip, from weddings to deaths. Every member of her family had a regular letter-writing day and obliged her with accounts of their comings and goings. She in the meantime followed the usual rhythm of her life, with trips to Eutaw, long visits with friends in the Stateburg area, and daily routines of supervising the management of the house, mothering, and gardening. Emily also mentions binding a volume of some of Henry's choicest letters. Emily's letter writing in many ways resembles the self-conscious work of a diary. She hoped to preserve the finest examples of letter writing, an art in which she excelled.

Woodford, May 9th, 1850

My dear Henry,

I cannot tell you how much entertainment your very clever performance gave us. I could not resist showing it to several persons who were unanimous in pronouncing it much more than your modesty would permit me to tell you. I had no idea you had so much talent for drawing. Really those etchings, especially the giant would do credit to an artist. Punch would give his eyes, nose and chin for such a letter! Notwithstanding all its brilliancy however, I have not forgotten the promise made at the end of the letter of another in a simpler style which was to be forthcoming in a few days. I hope you have not forgotten it either. I write this to you today in the hope of refreshing your memory. I intend some of these days to have a small volume of letters bound. You have contributed two which I am determined shall not be hid under a bushel.

Let me now review the events of the past week and see if I can glean anything worth preserving. I wrote to Mary on Wednesday and sent off the letter on Thursday by the Fort Motte P.O. I suppose it has been duly received. On Thursday morning Anna and I returned visits. We went to one place which was worthy of note. It was a beautifully laid out place, with large green flowers and the rarest flowers of all sorts and after walking about the grounds we were entertained with delightful strawberries and cream, all sorts of cakes, and iced lemonade of peculiar flavour being made of lemons fresh picked. I observed in the green house Pineapples, Bananas, Lemons, and Oranges all in fruit. We were at a large dinner party on Thursday when Anna and I regaled the company with music. On Friday morning we left these worthy people preserving an exalted opinion of their hospitality and kind heartedness.

We reached Eutaw at dinner-time and I found a *Neal* awaiting me which had come the night before and which was very welcome. The following three days passed very much as all Eutaw days pass; much feasting on strawberry ice cream and green peas. On Tuesday morning very early we left for the Mannings who we found as we left en status quo. The only thing out of the common run there was a Polish Jew who was travelling and stopped to beg a nights lodging. He was in the room during family prayers and I heard him as he knelt down ejaculate something very earnestly. I suppose it was a prayer for forgiveness for joining in Christian worship. Yesterday (Wednesday) we arrived here after an absence (on my part) of a month and a day. I was amused to see how Bull had employed himself during my absence. I gave him no fixed work but told him to try and make the place look decent. So he had done a little of everything including painting, white washing, gardening and carpentering. I found my garden in a most flourishing condition.

Frank's seeds being well up and quantities of pinks, Heart's Ease and various other plants in full bloom. I wish I could transport to you all some
of our super abundant strawberries. This morning I sent for my green
house plants which have been boarding all winter in a neighbouring
green house. They have increased wonderfully being somewhat like
Lord Bateman's first bride who came to him on a horse but went home
in a coach and three, for tho' they went over to Mrs. Gaillard's in one
cart they came home in two. Bull who has a very pretty turn for flowers is now hard at work putting my geraniums of which I have 40 into
fresh boxes of earth. We are here quite busy now with taking up carpets, putting down mats and stowing away woolens, something similar
to a Philadelphia house cleaning which pleasant time is I suppose still
in prospectus for you.

As you may suppose amid my late journeyings I have not had
much regular reading. In fact not having been in a very reading community I have seen very few books at all deserving to be called new
publications and the most I have done is rereading Irving and Burns
works, two very favourite authors of mine which I borrowed from Eliza
Manning as I went down. I am looking forward to the arrival of the box
by the *Osprey* with the greatest impatience. Think what a treat it will
be. I hope every book and pamphlet has been stuffed in. They will be
well cared for and religiously returned. After all Hen I have a pleasure
which you poor blasé denizens of Atheneums and Librarys have not, the
opening of a box such as I expect. Tell Papa I enclose the Colton note
which he desired me to send him. Tell Frank I will write to him next
week and will then give him a message from Anna about the gloves. Tell
Mary her faithful and in a humble and grateful spirit received letter
arrived on Monday evening. I expect from both Mary and yourself full
accounts of the wedding. I wish the invitation thereto sent to me. I wish
an account of the bridesmaids and groomsmen, of the bride's dress and
of the supper, of the presents she received and of her house. Don't omit
a single item. Mary has not given me a full account of Emily Wiggin
marrying Mr. Balch and I demand to know how long it is since his
wife's death and also what he could possibly find congenial in her. I was
stupefied with astonishment on hearing if it. I cannot let Henry Deas
nuptials pass without a note of exclamation!!

Tempora mutantur et nos mutamur in illis! [The times change, and
we change with them.] This Latin quotation is meant to express my surprise at youths who we have danced on our knee yesterday as it seemed
entering into matrimony today. I was very sorry to hear of poor Julia

Lewis' melancholy death. When you see W. Sargent tell him that we received his last letter and Charles intends answering it very soon. He would have done so before had he not been prevented by the continual succession of company at Eutaw and travelling to and fro. I have got a beautiful air to go with to Bingen with which I know you will be delighted. It was one of Russels but tho' I always admired it the words were so trashy I could not sing it. I must now conclude this homely epistle, hoping to hear from you very soon. Give my best love to all and tell the Mother I love her very much. Vine Vale, Your fond and admiring sister. P.S. I believe I have not said a word about the children. They are perfectly well. While Mary is at N.Y. you will of course take her place and write every Monday.

Emily reported accounts of two fires, one at a wharf in Charleston and one that burned down the house of the Gaillards, her neighbors in Stateburg. Fire was a terrifying and frequent event in the nineteenth century. The Philadelphia and Charleston papers gave graphic descriptions of these destructive occurrences.

> *Direct to Vances Ferry Rd.*
> *Mrs. Thomas I. Wharton*
> *150 Walnut Street*
> *Philadelphia*
> *Pennsylvania*
> *Woodford, May 21st 1850*

My dear Mama,

I have begun my letter two or three days before the usual time as I am obliged to take advantage of any spare minutes as they occur, for reasons which will be obvious before I proceed much farther. Nothing occurred of any consequence out of our usual routine on Friday and Saturday excepting that on Saturday I experienced a sharp disappointment on sending to the R. R. Station and finding no boxes had arrived. On Sunday we received a letter from Mr. Simons saying that they had safely arrived in the *Osprey* and he would send them to the R. R. on Saturday to come up in a freight train the next day.[136] With the letter came a Charleston Newspaper dated the day after the letter which stated that there had been a very large fire in Charleston on Adger's Wharf, the wharf of the *Osprey* and Mr. Simons' Counting House.[137] Altho Mr. Simons' name was not mentioned in the list of sufferers, yet it made me very uneasy lest the boxes should have been wet or injured in the confusion which always attends on a large fire. However I was consoled by Mr. Simons not having written and we resolved to send again to the Station on Tuesday (today).

We went to church and saw Mr. Gaillard's family in excellent spirits, little imagining the calamity which a few short hours was to bring upon them. The last thing that evening that Charles and I talked of was this large fire and the damage it had done to several acquaintances in Charleston. In the night I heard Oliver barking very loud for a long while but thought nothing of it until we were awakened by Bulls knocking and telling us that there was a fire at Mr. Gaillards. It was about 4 o'clock then and we went out in the Piazza and tho there was a loud roaring and bright flames through the trees, I thought it was merely an old field on fire or something of the sort, and laughed very much at Charles for racing off on horseback, all the men on the place following with buckets. I went back to bed but in half an hour was awakened by another knocking and one of the men out of breath informing me that Mr. Gaillard's dwelling house was burnt to the ground and that the whole family would be over at Woodford directly. I must confess that the second (yes it was the second) thought I had was Mr. and Mrs. Gaillard, old Mrs. Gaillard, the Tutor, the five children all with Whooping cough, the nurses and our small house with but two spare rooms, Rachel, my main dependence, sick, and the fact of all the little blackeys headed by Roberty, never having had the disease. However there was not time for thought so I jumped out of bed to consult with Bull about what to have for breakfast, leaving Liz to dress herself and Bud when he awoke, and Lavinia to make fires in the rooms. I sent an imploring message to Rachel to beg her to merely come to the Kitchen and direct Lavinia, but she was inexorable, her weak point being to make the most of her indispositions. So Bull announced that he would take breakfast on his shoulders (and a very good breakfast he gave us too).

The family arrived at about 1/2 after 6 and whatever selfish thought I might have had at first was entirely dispelled by their appearance in the greatest distress, of course, and barely escaping with themselves uninjured. It seems they were all asleep at 4 in the morning and were first awakened by the calls of the Negroes, "for God sake get up the house is burning!" The family ran to the Green House for shelter in their night clothes. The tutor, upstairs, was awakened by his shutters burning. The fire originated in a wing which was not in use, so they have no idea how the fire originated but say that it could not possibly be by design.[138] The Negroes exerted themselves beyond description and saved a surprising quantity of furniture. Mr. Gaillard could hardly get them to leave the house. They even tore off the mantel pieces and I never before heard such instances of thought and exertion. Still his loss is very heavy, exclusive of the house which was large and in complete repair, they can count up 2 thousand dollars in furniture, groceries, etc., etc. Charles saved all the farm buildings by having them covered with wet blankets, but when they first awakened the fire was so far advanced that they did not throw one bucket of water on the house. No insurance. It will make me doubly careful about fire, for I have no doubt that the fire was occasioned by a boy who went into that room that night with a light to get "Aunt Rose's bed." They think he could not have dropped a spark, but I think otherwise. The family will probably stay with us two weeks until Mr. Gaillard's father comes up to his summer residence. I am very glad to be able to show them every kindness and attention for Mr. Gaillard has been a valuable neighbor to Charles, and besides we ought to do things for others in this world besides our own family and friends.

Wednesday. Their losses are heavier than they expected but they bear it very well. I never saw a man show so much feeling as Mr. Gaillard did when he first met his family after the fire, particularly one child, who he did not think of at the time. They give me very little trouble and send every day for the produce of their dairy, vegetable garden and meat. I dare say I have been rather prolix about his fire, but I have talked, thought and heard so much about it, that it was impossible not to write about it.

On Tuesday Charles sent his wagon to the Station for the boxes and some Groceries etc. we had ordered to be there at the same time, but to my great disappointment, again no boxes. The agent said that the freight train was very heavily laden and not yet arrived! So as Charles' corn is calling loudly for work he cannot spare the beasts from the ploughs for two or three days and I must bear the disappointment as well as I can and wait with all the patience I can muster until Saturday.

This morning arrived 5 letters. One from Mr. Simons said that the fire was all around him, even next door but he escaped and had my boxes sent to a gentleman's house. He says they had a most miraculous escape. I received Marys most agreeable letter which you read and of course enjoyed. Was not that great about Lilly Montgomery?[139] Indeed the whole letter was capital. I intended writing to her this week but as I had not received my things thought it best to defer it until they arrived when I could give her a full account of them. I feel penetrated and humble to think of her writing so long a letter while in New York, and especially that she should have written on her usual day. Hen's letter arrived also. Tell him it is as usual worthy of being read by more persons than our family. His letter to Lizzie is a regular Gem, and I anticipate seeing it published some of these days. I am surprised he has not received my letter acknowledging the receipt of his Pictorial Letter. I wrote to him about it and in a letter before to Mary. Oh Hen, how I felt when I read that you had heard the Havana Opera troupe in *Lucia*![140] Of all Operas I should prefer hearing that. Do you think you enjoyed the music sufficiently, Sir! There came also a *Neal* from Papa containing a most exquisite story by Dickens, *Lizzie Leigh*. Did any of the family read it? I think I never read such heart breaking pathos and such gentle Humanity in any story of its length.[141]

Before concluding I must give one characteristic anecdote of Lizzie and Wharton. When I first told Liz of the occurrence on Monday morning, her little face assumed the most anxious expression and she enquired with deep interest if all their lives were saved. Next she wanted to know if Rebecca's baby house had been saved. Soon after I left the room she took Bud and communicated the intelligence to him, and I could hear him receive it with shouts of applause. I have not time to read this long letter over so make excuses for faults, etc. I will write by the next mail after the boxes arrive. Yours ever, E. S.

Mr. Thomas I. Wharton, Esq.
150 Walnut Street
Philadelphia
Pennsylvania
Woodford, May 27th, 1850

My dear Papa,

The long looked for anxiously expected boxes arrived safely on Saturday. Lizzie and I had been so much disappointed about them that we had almost given them up in despair. On Saturday morning Bull went off very early to Stateburg for beef and mutton (Saturday being market day) and returned in much triumph bearing before him on horse-back too, a large wooden box. He informed me that having been deeply interested in my boxes and knowing how anxious I was for them to arrive he went on his own responsibility to the Station and had got one of my boxes from the agent. But wow! On opening it turned out to be a box of groceries which we had sent for to come at the same time. So poor Bull had a ride of 11 miles for nothing (except a pair of pantaloons I gave him as a reward).[142] However, Charles had sent his wagon off at an early hour and by 2 it arrived with the things in it. Unfortunately we had company to dinner that day and I was obliged to sit through dinner knowing that the boxes were in the next room and eating with what appetite I could. Lizzie and Bud's feelings can better be imagined than described. Bud refused to leave them at all and as he made no appearance at the dinner table I presume he made his meal on them.

At last the eventful hour came. The boxes were opened. They were both discovered to be in excellent order, not a speck of dust, no damp, no discompose. I pass over the dresses, etc. as I intend writing to Mary an account of her stewardship, and will proceed to your department.

The books are choice. They are all together and I anticipate taking slow satisfaction out of them for a month, at least. As the box was opened late on Saturday, and yesterday being Sunday, I have scarcely had time to look over any but the serious portion. The rest even to the half sheets of newspapers are carefully stored in a snug corner. *Deck & Port,* of course, adorns one of the parlor tables with the object of bewildering some of my native visitors with the dedication. Charles is delighted with his *Man of War,* and on the strength of its having his name on the title page claims it as his own "property" in the Captain Cuttle way.[143] Many thanks for *H. More* which shall be duly returned— also for those dear little books.[144] By the bye, you forgot the 2d part of *Southey,* and as we broke off in the middle of a sentence of a letter to his brother Tom, would like to know how the sentence ends. So pray send Part 2 by mail, if you can find it about the house. The Henriades were exquisite. I had fortitude and magnanimity of soul sufficient to hand the box round to our worthy guests who would have been quite as well satisfied with Olivers or mixed sugar plums.[145] You knew what I would think of the Inscription which was in the regular Tomb Stone Style!! [146] I was also almost killed with the box of Ginger Lozenges from F. Browns. Such a box, too. Are they meant as Stomachicks or preventives of Cholera? In all events they are very nice. Bud is delighted with his knife, a thing he wanted for a long time, and Liz is equally charmed with her crayons, which she only thinks are too nice to use. But now what shall I say of the beautiful Papeterie?[147] It is entirely new to me and I like Liz cannot yet make up my mind to use it. It adorns the Parlor table being quite too pretty to be shut up in my writing desk. The pens and wax are also very acceptable and nice.

Now if I have omitted anything it is not that I have not appreciated them but that I feel confused among so many things to mention. As I have to write to several others of the family I must stop now, hoping you will soon write to me and thanking you again for all the trouble you have taken. Yours ever, E.S.

❧ ❧ ❧

Miss Mary Wharton
150 Walnut Street
Philadelphia
Pennsylvania
Woodford, May 27th, 1850

My dear P̶á̶p̶á̶ Mary,

(What a bad beginning I make to my letter but these young Orsons are enough to make a Statue dizzy.) At last have the boxes arrived safely, every thing in as perfect order as when they left Philadelphia. I must thank you most warmly for all the trouble you have taken for me. The things are beautiful and Charles is delighted. The hat is very pretty and very becoming. Ditto Lizzie's and Wharton's tho theirs are rather small; still not to any uncomfortable degree.

My dresses are all beautiful and show a great deal of taste. The white is, I think, the prettiest dress I ever saw. I only have the chintz yet tried on but as that fits me so perfectly I am sure the others will. Tell Clem how much pleased I am with them. The scarf is so *comme il faut* and so delicate, so different from the Charleston Mantillas. The Parasol is perfectly to my taste. I never saw such a pretty one before. The fact is I perceive I am getting at a loss for expressions of admiration.

The Ribbons are all choice. Please let me know how to make them up, with ends or without, with hanging ends or straight ends. I mean this ⚬ or this ✿ way. Don't forget to tell me how they are worn. If you could send on an old one in a letter as a model I should be very grateful.

Both the collars are beautiful. The one you made particularly so and tell me about the one lined with silk. It looks rather unfinished without any box at the neck and yet I have none which matches. Is your collar just the same? Thanks for the cuffs you made. They are very neatly made as is also the collar, and I was very much touched at your cutting the others off.[148] Is the stick you sent much too small? The gloves and boots are very nice and fit exactly. All the children's things suit very nicely and I am much obliged for them as I know they were not pleasant shopping. [The remainder of this letter has not been preserved.]

❧ ❧ ❧

Number 33
Miss Mary Wharton
150 Walnut Street
Philadelphia
Pennsylvania
Woodford, May 30th, 1850

Most admired and respected of Marys,

True to its day (which since you have been in New York is Wednesday) your letter arrived. No apology for shabbiness was needed for I assure you it was capital. You must be enjoying yourself a great deal and just in the way I would like. I hope by the time we meet that the details of your adventures will not have faded from your mind for you know that I, like poor little Charley, always like to know "what the gentleman said then." I don't understand why you have not received any letters from me since your visit. I have written regularly once a week and this week twice.

We have had quite cool weather in proportion as you have been groaning under. I say in proportion for the weather is quite warm enough to satisfy any reasonable person, planters and farmers not included, of course, for those worthy individuals incorporate themselves so thoroughly in the feelings of their crops that instead of enjoying the cool nights and mornings and a blanket at night, they are thinking of the shivering cotton which tho it warms others unfortunately cannot warm itself. You can imagine that it is not so very cool when I tell you we have had Raspberries several times.

I am very glad you, remembering my weakness for such things, have kept the cards and answers.[149] I was amused with your account of P.V.D. K's amor patriae and Kate Sergeants. A Miss Tams of Philadelphia, who lately married a Dr. Tucker of this state, a highly respectable family, has been making herself insufferable by her abuse of South Carolina. You never heard such terms as she made use of.

The Gaillard family left us yesterday to go to his fathers house. We did our duty by them during the ten days they were here and they went away very grateful. Their visit will be the cause of keeping away all other visitors this summer for we cannot avoid having Whooping cough on the place, and of course, no one with children will bring them here. Robert, of course, will break out in a few days for he had to assist at table while they were here, and the young worthies insisted on coming to meals altho they would be obliged to make several sorties. I am very sorry on account of Anna and Eliza who were both to pay long visits in June.[150]

Two or three days before the fire occurred we had written to Mr. Simons to choose a Piano for me for the three summer months and he wrote up, the day before to ask what makes I preferred, and also to give the particulars of how it was to come up, etc. The day after the fire the Gaillard's said it would confer a great favor on them if we take charge of and use their Piano until they got into their new House, as it would be utterly ruined if it stayed in their Barn all Summer, and they had no other place to put it in. I was unwilling at first to do so as I was afraid of the responsibility of using other peoples things especially a Piano, but they said so much about it and seemed so anxious that we finally consented, and the Piano is now in the Parlor. It is a Chickering and far better than ordinary country Pianos altho not very new.[151] Still it answers my purpose very well. I have begun to teach Lizzie and am sorry you did not send an Instruction book. However, I think I can get one in Charleston. Theutens is, I suppose, the best. I mean to keep on practicing regularly every day and hope you will find an improvement in my accompaniments. Tell Mama that my most admired song now is Auld Robin Gray.[152] Every one says it suits my voice better than any song I ever sang.

We kept Papa's birthday duly and drank his health in the most approved style. I was quite amused lately in paying a visit at a house where the "Gentleman" has a pretty taste for Law to see *Wharton's Digest* among other law Books.[153]

We are enjoying excessively the books etc which came in the box. *H. More* we are reading together and like very much. I feel so intimate with the Johnson set that when we come to any complimentary allusion to him I feel as flattered and gratified as if it were to Frank or Hen. I have read *Sir Edward Graham* but am rather disappointed in it.[154]

Old Mrs. Gaillard is a character! She condescends to be quite friendly with me on the strength of her mother's having been a Philadelphian. Wayman, I think, was her name and she was a first cousin of the Rev. Mr. Milnor of which she is very proud, especially when I showed her his likeness in his life. The old lady relished very much a cheering cup of green tea with which I used to regale her every afternoon.

One of our neighbors sent us a piece of Kid which we had "dressed" for dinner yesterday, and I suppose Charles and the children

felt quite patriarchal while eating. I confess notwithstanding the associ-
ations with Isaac and Jacob that I could not induce myself to eat it.[155]

The children are quite well. Liz is not much fatter tho her com-
plexion shows how healthy she is. Bud is large and stout and his com-
plexion is really brilliant. I hope the summer will not rob him of it for
I should really like you to see him as he looks now. Two persons who
were here lately who saw Frank at that party he was at said immediately
as they saw Bud that they had never seen a stronger resemblance. Liz is
very busy with her little pursuits and is a real comfort to me. Some of
her observations are killing. I suppose you got my last, giving you an
account of my things. I am delighted with them. Write on. Love to all.
Papa's papers came by the last Mail. Yours ever E. S.

As spring turned into summer Emily began her usual routine of preserving
blackberries and strawberries. Her recipe for Blackberry Jam went thus: "Weigh
berries before washing and to every pound of fruit put 3/4 lb. of sugar. Do not put
any water. Boil until of desired consistency." Sweet corn was enjoyed by the
Sinklers both on the cob as well as in pies and as fritters. Emily's recipe for Corn
Pie called for "six ears corn, salt to taste, 3 eggs, 1 tablespoon butter dessert spoon
flour. Grate corn, add eggs which have been well beaten, then butter salt, flour,
and enough milk to make really soft. Bake in a moderate oven."[156]

Number 36
Woodford, June 20, 1850

My dear Papa,

Here is Thursday and here is my letter. I find it might reach
Philadelphia much earlier if I chose a different day for writing as this
letter which I send to Providence tomorrow morning goes to Stateburg
on Saturday and as there is no mail to Charleston on Sunday does not
go out until Monday and you probably will not get it until Thursday.
Whereas if I wrote on Tuesday the letter would go on directly and you
would receive it on Saturday morning. When I have anything of importance to communicate I can send directly to Stateburg but now that one
letter is pretty much a facsimile of its predecessor I believe I may as well
keep my old writing day. I generally receive letters from Philadelphia in
four or five days after they are written. Our Postmaster Mr. Dinkins has
lately been on a tour to Washington and Baltimore which I hope will
not have the effect of expanding his mind too much. Since his return
one of my newspaper wrappers had a very suspicious look. I dare say

Mr. Hood the P.M. at Stateburg looks with an envious eye at my periodicals as they pass through his hands. He being a Philadelphian and as a natural sequence a very respectable man. Friday was a grand reception day for me. The Post Bag quite groaned under the load of contents which were the *Courier, Sumter Banner(!), Episcopal Recorder, Living Age, Neals Gazette, Ladies Newspaper, Southey* and *Copperfield*. Letters Beside. I am indebted to you for the four last and as Prof Webster says to his daughter about the first good breakfast he got in prison, "I assure you they relished." I received by yesterdays mail a Drawing Room Journal which was very amusing. Now I believe you mean these journals to be in lieu of a letter but I wish you to clearly understand that I am not at all satisfied with such an arrangement and wish to have both letters and papers. Mary's never failing letter arrived on its old day, Sunday; while she was at N.Y. her letters arrived on Wednesdays. I hope she has become more reconciled to the goodly village of Penn. I would advise her to wear magnifying glasses when she walks abroad. I am glad to hear that St. Philip's is at last to have a good organist. If I were in Charleston I should go to Oates, Walters brother in law, to talk the matter over with him. All Walter's movements are of deep importance to Oates. The piece of music which I planned sending Mary was by Walber—*La Melancolie*. I dare say she has it. I wish Mary would send me that music by mail. W. Sargent sent me a piece which was not at all crumpled or spoilt by the conveyance.

We are having now regular summer weather. The thermometer 82 and 83 at 2 o'clock. In the house it is not uncomfortable but the sun is scorching. I allow no playing out of doors after 9 nor before 6. The nights are delightful. There can be no complaint about them.

Thee who is probably just beginning with asparagus will be surprised to hear that on 2d day we had green corn for dinner. It was very sweet being of the sort called Sugar Corn. Today I am busy in putting down Blackberry Jelly, which is a useful article. If it were not for a severe drought I would soon have ochra.

The children are quite well. I wish you could see Bud now. He is really a fine looking little fellow, so stout and fresh looking, but I am afraid this intense sun and glare from which it is impossible to escape will tan us all as brown as it did last summer. The winter took it all off but I am afraid it is all to go over again. Bud is a very cleanly child. I hear him now splashing in a bath and you have no idea of his particularity in dress. Yesterday was a warm day and I wanted him not to wear his drawers which are quite thick. He made the attempt but came to me after a little while saying, "I can't do it, it's too indecent." Liz has him completely under her thumb and consequently thinks him better than most boys. Yesterday we went to dine and spend the day at Mr. James Gaillards and he astonished the company very much by singing quite loud to a little girl there. "Once upon a time when Rebecca was swine!" He is very fond of such witticisms which I am obliged to repress as it often degenerates into vulgarity.

Has no 13 of *Copperfield* come out yet? I am quite interested in it and think it fully equal to any of his late works. Ask Mary if she does not think Traddles the exact prototype of Edward Gardner? I am sure Dickens must have met with him somewhere. I never knew such a likeness. I was very much amused with an advertisement on the back of a French book. There was a list of books for sale and among others the Holy Bible. At the end of the list the publisher remarks that all these fine works can be had for a certain price. We are not accustomed to rank the Bible among other works of a secular character.

I hope soon to hear of the fish being sent. I observe the *Osprey* carries out a large number of passengers every week. When will the new steamer be put on the route? Lizzie is very anxious to write an epistle so I will conclude with much love to all. From your loving daughter, ES

❧ ❧ ❧

Number 40
Woodford, July 18th, 1850
Miss Mary Wharton
150 Walnut Street
Philadelphia
Pennsylvania

My dear Mary

There was a failure in the mail on Saturday night, consequently we got no letters and papers on Sunday and I had to wait with all the patience I could muster for your letter until the next mail day which was yesterday (Wednesday) when it arrived. By the time this reaches you, you will I suppose be either at Cape May or preparing for your departure. I hope each and all of you will have a very pleasant summer. I am astonished to hear of your success with the screens and if there is a fair here shall certainly call on you for a contribution of one. Fairs however, do not seem to flourish here. I am much interested in the Organ business at St. Philip's and your practicing. I shall expect to hear some of my favorite pieces. I am shocked to hear that aunt reads aloud my productions. I request her particularly in every letter to destroy them as soon as read. I will certainly give your message to Anna, but know it will be entirely out of her power to come on this year. William talks a little of going on with us merely to stay a few days and return in the return trip of the *Osprey*. He will do so certainly if circumstances will admit. I will keep Baker in my mind if I hear of anyone wanting a Housekeeper. At present I know of no situation. You see how faithfully I have noticed the various points in your letter. I wish you would do the same. I have asked various questions in my letters lately which have met with no response.

Now for my own affairs. We are suffering very much with the drought. Nearly all the vegetables and fruit are burnt up. The weather has not been as warm as the week before. On Friday arrived the box of Herring. It had been awaiting us for some time at Mr. Gaillards. Tell Papa they are remarkably fine and in good order. Did he write on the box, "by the good ship Osprey?" It was very friendly. We heard on this day of the great fire in Philadelphia and many inquiries were made if my family had suffered by it.[157] The *beau-père* expressed much surprise that the Philadelphia Firemen would allow a Fire to get such a headway. Liz, who occasionally reads the newspapers was very much exercised about your Infant Scholars for she said she knew a great many of them live on Vine Street. What is thought of Webster's confessions?[158] I cannot help believing it truthful. On Sunday we went to church at Bradford Springs where was a large congregation. Everybody nearly being up here at their summer places. We met our friend Mr. Wilkinson there who came home to dinner with us and made himself quite agreeable. He sailed with Charles once. I found in the *Recorder* a letter from Mr. Neville which I dare say you have seen.[159] I should judge from the facetious turn of it that he is quite pleased there.

On Monday afternoon I went up to the school to see Mrs. Hummel who was delighted to see me and who regaled me with some delightful Raspberry Syrup just from Germany. She is expecting her sister over in September who will be a great comfort to poor Hummel in that great menagerie of 96 boarding school girls. She showed me some of the most beautiful specimens of crochet work I have seen.

On Tuesday afternoon we went to pay a visit to a Mrs. Covert and on our return found Mr. and Mrs. R. Richardson[160] and children who had arrived at Woodford a short time before us. They stayed with us until the next evening and paid a very pleasant visit. She is an agreeable, well informed person, lady like and quite pretty. We gave them a very nice dinner and I wished Papa could have seen the piece of mutton of our own killing. It was quite as fine as any of his Proteges. Our neighbor P. G. dined with us also. Tell Papa that three Newspapers he sent arrived yesterday for which many thanks, *Bulletin, Neal, Ladies Newspaper.*

The children are quite well and as the time draws near for us to go to Philadelphia are getting almost frantic on the subject and I was quite amused with Bud yesterday morning. As soon as he awoke he called out, "you know I always tell you I am ready at any minute to go to Philadelphia but as Julia is here this morning I'll just wish you to put it off one day till she goes. Julia Richardson is a little girl of whom both Lizzie . . . [the remainder is missing].

I believe I have written all I can think of. Pray write regularly and long. When you see M. J. Cardeza ask her why she does not write to me. Yours Ever, ES P.S. I heard that the dear little baby died about 2 hours after we left.

ᶬ ᶬ ᶬ

Number 43
Mrs. Thomas I. Wharton
Woodford, August 8, 1850

My dear Mama,

I was very grieved to see by Mary's letter that you have not improved as much as I hoped you would at Cape May. I had gathered from previous letters that your health was better than usual and there-fore was very much disappointed to find that you had been confined to your room for several days. Now let me beseech you not to return to Philadelphia by the time we arrive. I can't tell you how unhappy I would be if I should find Papa and yourself there. It would spoil all my pleasure for the whole visit. As it is, the anticipation of the visit is very much marred by the fear that I have fixed upon too early a time. But this has been such a stormy season and we have had two such experi-ences of September voyages, that I should dislike to try another one.[161] Besides it is a great thing to get rid of the 2 weeks of heat here. This has been the hottest summer known here for 30 years, by the Thermometer. The 90's have predominated all July, and August bids fair to be as warm. I see by the papers that the heat has also been very great in Philadelphia. But by the end of August I hope it will be pretty well over. I am beginning to make preparations for the voyage, and the chil-dren are wound up to the most painful pitch of expectation.

We expect to go down tomorrow to the Sand Hills. I cannot resist Anna's appeals but will merely stay with her until her sister arrives which will be positively on Monday or Tuesday, and then there will be little more than a week for my preparations. I have a good deal to see about. Eliza left her seamstress with me and I want her to do as much sewing as possible before we leave. I wish I could bring her with me. She is such a genteel looking and handy girl. I suppose there will be no difficulty about my getting some one to suit me. I don't want a nurse as much as a servant. Bud is now 5 and Liz 7 so they need some one merely to wash and dress them and take them out occasionally. I want some one who can sew nicely and wash their clothes. Don't trouble yourself about this, I beg.

Yesterday was Wharton's Birthday and I of course took advantage of it to point a moral. He is a much improved child but has many failings yet. What almost kills me is when he, who is the Prodigal son of the family assumes the part of the evangelical Peacock, which happens when Lizzie (very rarely) commits some little faux pas. For instance, the other evening they had both gone to bed and as the doors were all open I could hear every thing that passed. Liz was fretting about something and I heard him begin: "Oh Lizzie you had better get down on your knees and pray God to forgive your fretting temper. How many poor children would be glad to have your comforts. Suppose you were to be struck down with lightning in your sins, what would become of you?" Poor Liz, of course, declined and when I went in the room sometime afterwards, she informed me, in a half querulous, half-amused tone that Buddy had been praying over her the whole evening! Bud notices very intently. Yesterday I was reading to him something about what good clergymen used to do, and he told me that he noticed that when Mr. Elliott came to visit us he did not talk about Jesus or religion. Liz will, I know, entertain you excessively with her wonderful remarks.

This last week we have had a great deal of company. Every day we have had company to dinner. Friday the Nelsons and two gentlemen; Saturday Mrs. Hummel; Monday a gentleman; Tuesday Mr. Elliott and Mr. Wilkinson; Wednesday the Converses, Major Porcher and Mr. Manigault, and to day Mr. Adams (the Tutor in Mrs. Darby's family) and Mr. Gaillard.[162] The Converses paid us a most agreeable visit and brought an immense basket with them filled with the finest fruit of various sorts, which is quite a treat to us for the worms have destroyed all ours. Poor Mrs. Hummel enjoys her visits here so much. She can talk over her old haunts which no one else in the neighborhood cares to hear about.

I have had to write this letter in a very detached way for two separate visitors have interrupted and broken the thread so completely that I seem to have forgotten all I had to say. Our friend Mr. Wilkinson is ordered in the *St. Marys* to sea and as he goes to Charleston today has promised me that he will go over the *Osprey* and write word what he thinks of her since her enlargement. Tell Mary that her last most agreeable letter has been safely received as also Papa's journals including the *Bulletin*. Letter writing takes up a great deal of my time. I received 22 letters in July and of course, they had all to be answered.

I am well aware that this is not the letter it ought to be but I really cannot help it. When we meet I must try to make up for such deficiencies. I hope Papa is quite restored. How is Hen? Yours ever, ES

> Number 44
> Miss Mary Wharton
> Care of T. I. Wharton Esq
> 150 Walnut Street
> Philadelphia
> Penn
> Woodford, August 15th, 1850

My dear Mary,

We returned yesterday from an extensive tour to the Sandhills which I mentioned in my last letter. We went down on Friday and stayed until Anna's sister made her appearance. We were quite favored as to weather for we had the first really cool spell of the season while there, and the days we went down and came back were both cloudy. Of course, we passed an uneventful time, it being not a very lively place and I missed the Manning family very much. We left all quite well and Anna sent many messages to each member of the family. William is very anxious to take a run to Philadelphia in September if circumstances will allow. He looks remarkably well.[163]

On our return I found 6 letters which had arrived during our absence. I had been extremely anxious to get news from you all and felt much relieved to hear Papa was so much better. I trust his recovery will be quick and steady now. I have many plans which I hope he will not be too busy to join in when we arrive, of small excursions etc., and the children want to be taken to see all sorts of things from the Ojibway Indians down to a Pin Man factory, not forgetting a trip to Germantown in the cars where Bud hopes to hear his treasured "Fishers

Lane, etc." Tell Papa I am counting upon many refreshing little trips with him.

We received a letter from Mr. Simons saying that he had engaged a state room on board the *Osprey* for the 14th. He represents the vessel as being much improved as to accommodations, etc. I hope she will not be crowded for although it is late in the season for Travelers, yet she is the only Steamer now running from Charleston, the *Southerner* being up for repairs and the *Northerner* gone to Chagres. If we can only have a smooth time. I don't care for any thing else.

We intended going to Charleston on Friday and passing a night with Sister Margaret, but there is so much Scarlet Fever in Charleston among children that we have determined not to run the risk but go directly from the cars to the boat.[164] I am sorry for it is fatiguing after more than 100 miles in the Cars to go to Sea especially after getting up at 3 in the morning but I think you will agree with me that it is safest. We will probably spend a day with William and Anna and leave from their house as we did last year, they being rather nearer the Railroad and over a better road.[165]

We have now but a week to stay here and many are the preparations which are going on for the important departure. Rachel and Maria are busy with sewing and washing. By the bye I wish you could have seen Maria walking to church last Sunday. Pepys could well have exclaimed "Our girl Pole, monstrous fine." She was dressed in a New Book muslin dress, so full and stiff that it appeared to have a Hoop underneath it and a white straw hat trimmed with light green Satin ribbon.[166]

The children are wild with anticipations of seeing you all and can talk and think of nothing else. I know you will be almost convulsed with some of Lizzie's remarks showing such observations and sense tho not quite so easy as some of Wharton's. The other evening I was hearing him his prayers which were rather long and when he had finished he said, "I do not like these seventy syllable prayers." He had an eruption on his face and body, something like Hives tho smaller and you never saw any thing in your life like the resemblance to James Smith. I assure you he was the image of him, and Anna exclaimed the moment she saw him. Charles and I had noticed it before. The likeness is subsiding with the redness.

Tell Mama I received her letter. Poor thing what a time she must have had at Cape May! I never heard such a concatenation of disagreeable events and for her to be alone there too! With her peculiar feelings too about shocks and happenings! Cape May must have been an entire failure this year from all accounts. I saw by the newspapers that there had been a fracas among the coloured waiters and the visitors.[167] What a summer it has been! I trust we will have an early autumn to make up. According to the Thermometrical accounts it has been the warmest summer in this state for 30 years. Of course the old inhabitants say it is the warmest summer they ever knew.

I saw an account kept by the librarian of the Charleston Library (very much such a worthy as Smith) of the Thermometer in the Library and it appears that in July the Thermometer was 18 times at and above 90 at 3 o'clock.

Thank Papa for *Neal.* There is one number missing which if you see about the house pray keep for me. It has the conclusion in it of a story by Lady Emily Ponsonby which I was rather interested in. You must excuse the paucity of this letter for I really have a great deal to do besides letters to answer. I had three invitations from Charleston which I must decline. With best love to all, Yours Ever, ES

XII

From the Music of Jenny Lind to the Pageantry of Chivalry, Spring 1851

AFTER THE HOTTEST SUMMER on record in South Carolina, Emily spent September and October in Philadelphia, returning to the plantations around November for the usual flurry of fall activity. She was booked on the *Osprey*, all newly renovated, for a trip to Philadelphia on September 15. Despite her fear of stormy trips, she persisted in going North for the early fall months of September and October. Emily was an inveterate traveler, reveling in the extended journeys that were essential to reaching her far-flung destinations. Her depiction of the rice plantations along the Cooper River, with the rice steam mills, flags flying, and musicians playing, is especially evocative of the grand life led by these plantation families. At Lewisfield Plantation Emily and her family dined on delicious wild ducks, and she speaks of the abundance of shad in the river.

During the fall of 1851, Emily divided her time between the Santee plantations, including Belvidere and Eutaw, and the Santee High Hills, where she was at Woodford, close to Manning and Richardson cousins at Homesley and the Ruins. Woodford had sufficient land for cotton farming. Emily describes the spring of 1851 as being so damp and cold that Charles feared for his crops.

Emily also spent time in Charleston, especially enjoying the concerts of Jenny Lind. She shopped regularly for new books and new music at Oates Store at 234 King Street. In Charleston she stayed with Charles's grandmother, Mary Deas Broun, who lived with four generations of family in her house at 39 Society Street. Emily stayed either at Stewarts Boardinghouse or with grandmother Broun. In Charleston she enjoyed especially the company of the Henry Deas Lesesnes, the Russell Middletons, and the Henry Middletons.

Jousting and chivalry were much enjoyed by the South Carolina lowcountry elite. The South especially loved the novels of Sir Walter Scott. He encouraged the planter elite to imagine themselves in the world of gallant knights, loyal chieftains, and faithful lovers. Emily gives a wonderful account of a jousting tournament at Pineville. There were thirty-four knights in shining costume. A special ladies pavilion was set for viewing. For the planting class the tournament was the embodiment of the virtues of manhood, loyalty, and bravery, as well as a way of life from the past.

Emily tells of a wonderful visit to Charleston, where she stayed with her cousins the Henry Lesesnes. In Charleston she sees many Charleston friends, as well as several Philadelphia friends in Charleston on business. The return trip was made by steamboat on the Cooper River, and Emily and the children spent the night at Lewisfield, a Cooper River rice plantation that at this time was being run as an inn. Emily is also anticipating a visit from Mr. Bland, an Englishman. Later Mary Wharton was to marry Mr. Bland and live in England.

❧ ❧ ❧

Number 12
Eutaw February 18th, 1851
Mr. Thomas I. Wharton

My dear Papa,

It was quite impossible for me to write on my last usual writing day and therefore I have been obliged to defer doing so until today (on account of the mail). I am afraid you must have been at some loss to imagine why I had not written when the regular day came round, at least so I flatter myself from my usual punctuality in writing.

Now for an account of our voyages and travels. We left Woodford on Saturday and staid Sunday with the Mannings. We found Eliza with a nice little baby which is to be called William Sinkler.[168] We arrived at Eutaw on Monday and set off early the next morning by way of the R. R. for Charleston. We had intended staying at a hotel as Charles' Grandmother's house where we usually stay was full. But we found at the depot on arriving Mr. Henry Lesesne's carriage with the most pressing invitation to stay at his house, so nolens volens we had to go.[169] I never passed so pleasant a time before in Charleston, the only difficulty was that the time was too short. It is by far the best time to see Charleston to advantage as the Races being just over, the gaieties of the worldly people were by no means subsided and the concourse attracted by the convention had just begun. We had in the cars the usual number of white cravats, with whom we always travel at this season. Nothing could exceed the kindness of Mr. and Mrs. Lesesne and I never before saw her in so favorable a light. They talked constantly of the delightful impression you all made on them in Philadelphia during their visit there and as you might suppose Mr. Lesesne is a strong Union Man. They were both delighted with Lizzie, altho' I could see at first she was a painful sight to them, being just of the age of their only daughter who died last fall.

The first evening we got to Charleston we took tea at Mrs. Frost's, a family party to meet us.[170] We were invited also to a ball at Mrs. Charles Alston's, an aunt of Lizzie Middleton's husband, which I heard was the handsomest ever given in Charleston.

The next morning I sallied out accompanied by Edward whom I have no doubt Mary remembers at Eutaw. The *beau-père* kindly left him in town to attend to us while we were there. He used to walk behind in the Footman style, carrying the parcels and ringing the bells, etc. Liz and Bud had been presented by their Grandfather with a gold piece each. Liz 5 and Bud 2 ½ During the whole of the journey down from Eutaw they were in all the agonies of indecision as to whether they should put them in the Savings Fund or spend them in town. I had previously given Liz a half and Bud a quarter of a dollar which I thought quite enough for them to spend. However, the sight of the shops in King Street quite upset their little remains of prudence and they both relieved themselves of their money very quickly. Prudent, sensible little Liz, however, did not spend nearly all hers. She bought the Girls Own Book, and various other useful things, which example inspired the prodigal Bud with such virtue that he determined instead of toys, to buy himself a little chair and he accordingly got a very pretty walnut chair with a cane seat. The only relaxation he allowed himself was a paint box and a game of lotto.[171]

After these purchases I went to see Mrs. Middleton and Lizzie Smith whom I found looking very well. Mrs. Middleton's family is very much dispersed. The rest of the morning Anna Sinkler and I spent in shopping, I having a good many things to get for the house and servants and Anna requiring my taste in the selection of her spring purchases. In the afternoon I took a drive on the Battery and paid several visits I owed from the last time I was in Charleston.

In the evening drank tea at Mrs. Middleton's. I met Dr. McEuen there who is in Charleston on business. Charles saw him in the morning and thought he looked very badly but I must say I was by no means similarly impressed. There was nothing in his moustache or his manner to convey the idea of a disconsolate widower. He talked of his Journey and residence in the West Indies with admirable composure and when

I asked him some question about Philadelphia, said I must remember how much shut up he had been lately and divers similar remarks. I wanted to send a package by him but he said he was going to Havana and did not know when he would be in Philadelphia. So I sent it by Mr. Ammen who is ordered to the North.[172] We expected him to come up with us, but he could not get detached from his vessel just then. He says he will be at Woodford in a week or two.

Mrs. Middleton's two daughters, Annie and Harriet, are really beautiful girls and very stylish. They went to a ball the evening I passed there and I saw them dressed for it. Mary Lowndes has just met with, what would be considered a misfortune by most people. Her house which was large and convenient was burnt to the ground, week before last and they lost nearly everything. Mary takes it with the utmost sang froid, and says it is a most charming thing to live in a cottage of two rooms.

On Thursday morning we shopped and visited. Among other places I went to Oates' Music Store and had a long talk about our friend Jenny.[173] Oates is brother in law to Walter in Philadelphia and a very agreeable person.[174] It seems Jenny would see no one in Charleston, nor would even take the trouble to answer invitations which were addressed to her. However Oates being one of the fraternity saw her and she said some very soft things to him altho' he says her manner was hurried and irritable. He spoke to me of her singing Home Sweet Home and she gave "the upward look" and said "Ah yes! Home Sweet Home! I love my home too but I am forced to wander in this bleak world alone!" There is a difference of opinion as to her being forced to wander. Oates says she is quite as good a business man as Barnum and has the clearest and shrewdest head imaginable.[175] Tell Mary there is a picture of her which I wish her to look at. It is an exact resemblance of her as she appeared the memorable night we saw her. It is before the Bird Song.[176]

We dined at Charles' Grandmothers on Thursday. The old lady is 88 but I see no failing. There are four generations in the house and her two brothers one 81 and the other between 75 and 80. It is quite a curious house to visit at. In the afternoon I paid some goodbye visits and in the evening went to a very nice party made for us at Mrs Wraggs. Anna and I delighted the company with various duets and I sang Auld Robin Gray. Poor Anna had a wretchedly inopportune hoarseness and took Ipecac lozengers all through the evening. Just before we began to sing I made her run out into the entry and swallow a raw egg. Consequently altho' her voice was quite clear the poor thing was deadly sick. However she managed to get through without an expose (I tell this for Mama's amusement). I was invited to several other places but was unable to go as we left on Friday. I was very sorry to stay so short a time but Charles is anxious to get back to Woodford to get the land prepared for planting. Our friends were quite indignant and we had so many pressing invitations for Friday and Saturday that we would have stayed had not the horses been waiting for us. We had an abundance of fresh shad in Charleston and some of the finest West India fruit I ever saw. The convention was very quiet and uneventful.

The morning we left town (Friday) I wanted a basket to carry some oranges, apples, crackers and stopped at a shop to get one. On asking the price the man said 50 cts. "but I can assure you it is good for we keep none but Philadelphia ware here and this was made by Mr. Dunks near Philadelphia." The man appeared to be much impressed when I told him I was acquainted with Mr. Dunks and was inclined to be very discursive on the subject of Philadelphia, but I had to hurry off.

We took a new route this time. We left in the steam boat and I shall never again go by the cars if it can be helped. The distance from Charleston to Lewisfield where we got out is but 30 miles but the various stopping places all along make it much longer. The river is thickly settled with the celebrated Cooper River Rice Plantations and there are some very handsome residences on it. All the oldest families in the state live on the river and from the time you leave Charleston till you get to Lewisfield there are always plantations in sight. Some of them are so large that you would imagine you saw a village before you and the large steam rice mills, chimneys and other large buildings give an appearance of activity and industry which is pleasing. There is much more style in the appearance of the places on the river than in the interior of the state. The owners are richer and there is more travel. One place in particular was very pretty. On the lawn was a gallery for a band of musicians and the flag flying from the house gave the appearance of an English residence. Sometimes the river is salt all the way up and I noticed on Friday porpoises jumping about as high as 10 miles from Charleston. We did not arrive at Lewisfield until nearly 3 and as it had then begun a cold rain and Lizzie did not feel well we determined to stay all night instead of going on.

Lewisfield is a large old country house belonging to one of the oldest families in the state, formerly very productive. But the present owner (an unmarried man) finding himself left with everything but money, determined to the disgust of his relations and the delight of the travelling community to open a public house at the old family place. It is very well kept and being directly on the river and near a swamp the table is well supplied with fish and game. I never ate such wild ducks before. Charles and I have arranged that when you come on you shall certainly stop at Lewisfield. The house has been full all winter, principally with Northerners. While we were there, there was a Canadian family and a New York family and I was amused when we went to dinner table to hear one of the ladies whisper as Bud made his appearance looking particularly well and rosy, "I am sure that child is not a Southerner." Unfortunately for me, when Henry Sinkler made his entrée I heard the same remark. Henry is a remarkably stout red cheeked child. Bud told me the next morning that he thought the sooner we left that house the better for the ladies ran after him and praised him so much that he would soon be spoiled. I saw at Lewisfield the family Bible of the Simons' beginning from the time they first settled at Lewisfield in 1694. I was not at all surprised at the present poverty of the family for they invariably made it a rule to have families of from 16 to 18 children.

On Saturday morning Lizzie being quite well we left. It is 30 miles from Lewisfield to Eutaw but we wanted to pay a visit we had long promised to a branch of the Porcher family which is connected with old Mr. Sinkler by marriage. We have promised the visit faithfully for the last 4 years and as we had to pass directly by the place which rejoices in the scriptural name of Ophir, we determined to stop.[177] It is 18 miles from Eutaw and the family is a plain country family living in great plenty but no style. They are great "church people" and Miss Porcher is about to marry a clergyman from North Carolina who I think will give them enough of it. Among other things he told the young people of the neighbourhood lately when they were about dancing one Friday evening that it was a greater sin to dance on Friday than Sunday. He is tho' an intelligent man, has been twice to England and stayed the last time with Keble, the Bishop of Oxford and Manning about all of whom he gives many interesting anecdotes. We stayed at Ophir until Monday morning and I left much pleased with a large package of books and papers with which I expect to be much refreshed at Woodford. Dr. Porcher (not our little friend Julius) passed 3 years in Paris and as he still keeps up his French he takes the *Courrier des Etats Unis* and the *Semain Literaire* and various other periodicals. I took away a good quantity and he has promised to transmit to me all the new ones as they come out.

We arrived at Eutaw early on Monday and found Mary and

Henry's letters. I will answer them fully in my next. It is now so late that I must stop this long letter. The *beau-père* is to have a dinner party and it is high time I should dress. I hope Mr. Simons will tell Mr. Bland not to come to Eutaw for we are to leave here on Thursday (day after tomorrow). I wish I had told you in my last how short a time we were to stay at Eutaw. Direct to Providence. I forgot to tell Mary to direct but one letter to Eutaw and how her next letter will go to Woodford. With love to all, I am as ever your devoted daughter, ES

Emily and Charles and the children enjoyed the lowcountry custom of staying with friends and relatives for long visits. Having just stayed at the Henry Lesesnes in Charleston and the Porchers at Ophir, they are now visiting for a week with the Converses at their home and end up spending a night at the Ruins with the Richardsons. At each home they are entertained elegantly with the specialty of the house, from wild ducks to French rolls. Emily is also enjoying the company of Mary's beau from England, Mr. Bland.

Woodford, March 7, 1851

My dear Mary,

I am afraid that my last letter (to Hen) must have arrived several days after it was due, for it was neglected to be sent to the P.O. on the regular mail-day and then had to wait for the next. I wrote just before we were going off on our visit to Mrs. Converse and must now give you the results of our visit.[178] We had a pleasant drive down and arrived at 5 o'clock to a really very handsome and creditable dinner for the country—several courses, soup, shad, etc., all served in the best style on one of the most beautiful dinner-sets you ever saw. They were made in France about 100 years ago for some of the ancestors of the family with the initials on each article. In the evening some of the neighbours were invited. Everything passed off very nicely. We had intended leaving immediately after breakfast the next morning but their breakfast hour is 10 and afterwards there were so many plans for various expeditions and they were so exceedingly pressing for us to stay another day that we agreed to do so. I could easily see that Mr. Bland was quite agreeable to the proposition. We set off at 12 and went first to the new church which is now nearly done and which is of course the lion of the neighbourhood. It is exactly like St. James the Less, I think, and is to be fitted up in very nice style. After looking over the church and rambling in the church yard for some time, the party divided, Charles and Mr. Bland on horse-back to Mr. Singletons and Mr. And Mrs. Converse and myself in the carriage to drive abut the neighbourhood. We assembled again at 5 o'clock to dinner and again in the evening had company. Miss McDuffie and Mr. Singleton arrived from Charleston and the next morning before breakfast came up to the Ruins. We had determined solemnly to go home to Woodford after church, but there was no use in thinking of it. Old Mr. Singleton made a great point of it and the whole party agreed to stay at the Ruins if we did. To cut the matter short Mrs. Converse had the trunk taken off the carriage. We went to church and returned again to the Ruins after service and finally got off on Monday morning after breakfast. We were invited to dine at Mr. Singletons that day but declined thinking we had paid quite long enough visits and also expecting to find a letter from Ammen saying he might be up. We had a delightful visit and I shall never forget Mr. and Mrs. Converses' kindness and attention for without it Mr. Bland's visit to the South would have been very dull. He received an invitation from Mr. Mat Singleton (who married Tom Kinloch's sister) to pay him a visit at his plantation in a different direction which he accepted. You would like the Converses and Miss McDuffie very much. They are intelligent, agreeable and traveled people and I thought every time we sat down to breakfast how your stale bread principles would be tempted. To be sure, at breakfast hour ranging between 10 and ½ past one has a right to eat a little more than at 8 o'clock, especially in the country where one takes more exercise. I counted (internally of course) on the table 7 kinds of breads and cakes all as light as possible—French rolls, flannel cakes, buckwheats, loaf bread, etc. etc., then there would be broiled pigeons, broiled shad, etc., etc. During our stay there were six guest rooms occupied. We invited the whole party to dinner on Tuesday by way of a divertissement for Mr. Bland, but they were all engaged, so we invited the Nelsons and Miss Dickinson who accepted and we had a very nice dinner. You being a sort of Grand-mother to the Omelette Soufflés, would have been gratified with the noble one we had. Mr. Bland went off yesterday morning to Mr. Singletons place, having stayed with us a week. We like him better and better every day and felt quite melancholy about parting with him. Charles particularly misses him very much. I hope he enjoyed himself. Bull avers that he told him it was the pleasantest week he had passed since he left England. I never met with anyone more unaffected and natural, more perfectly gentlemanly and domestic. In several things he reminded me of poor Tom Kinloch. I mean of course in poor Tom's best points. Certainly Englishmen are not nearly as "fast" as Americans and I used to be amused with the manner in which Mr. Bland would take jokes and witticisms. He would be a long time in discovering the point of facetious remarks and I never suffered more than in church on Sunday. Before service I told him that the young ladies of the Congregation, in consequence of the building of the church, which obliged them to hold service in a private house, were without an organ and requested him as a distinguished stranger to set the Psalm and Hymn tunes. He said "certainly." All at once, at the beginning of the service, it occurred to me that he might take me au de la lettre and begin au impromptu which would of course be entirely unexpected to the choir! What I suffered! He was too far from me for me to give him hint that I was only joking and I waited in a state of agonized suspense, until I was relieved by his silence at the critical moment. You would have been amused at his opinions on the subject of the taking of the Communion and he had never before heard that in this country it is not customary for every one to partake of it. He did and he did not see why every one else could, as for preparation he did not see why he was not prepared enough and why every one who had been baptized was not fit for it. He told me I must tell you in consequence of that book on idleness which you gave him to read he had become so industrious that he is now afraid of going into the opposite extreme. I wanted to send a package by him to Philadelphia but he told us he would not be there before the end of May at the earliest. I have instead sent it down to Harris Simons with the request to send it on to Philadelphia by the first private opportunity he hears of. I intended sending it by Ammen but that worthy has not made his appearance yet, and as we have heard he had been ordered suddenly away, I am afraid we will not see him.

The package contains merely your two garments and a cap for Mama. Mr. Bland after his visit to Mr. Singleton's goes to Wimberly Jones and then to New Orleans and up the Mississippi. Why will people travel in those wretched western steamboats. Hardly a newspaper arrives that we do not hear of some accident. I don't think I have fully expressed what I felt about the contents of the box. I am learning the song painfully and shall take great care of it and bring it on with me. Bud's workbox is very appropriate to a trip like that to Mrs. Converses. I took it down with me and used it to baste in his collars to his intense gratification. He keeps his microscope in his pocket and constantly with much dignity inspects flowers, etc. through it. I wish you could hear Lizzie's talk about her portfolio, her little plans about it and determinations about keeping it and her remarks about how she never had expected to own such a thing. I sent the little basket to Daisy today. I know Anna will be delighted with the attention. Tell Papa Bud reads Cobwebs with great gravity and solemnity. He and Lizzie enjoy the "Yes sure" and "good boy!" and other quaintisms as much as we did when children. Tell Hen those caricatures are very diverting and acceptable. Your Indian letter we all think beautiful. I have kept it to show to some friends and Charles is full of starting off next summer to see them. The children have been in convulsions of laughter over that letter of yours written at 9 years. The "Fat Pems of Henry Cuckoos" and the anecdote of the funnels were enchanting to them. But what struck me was what an extremely clever letter it is for a child of 9. I should have thought it the production of one of 13 or 14. Tell Frank his letter arrived by mail before last and I will answer it soon. Your letter to Wharton arrived at the same time and is capital. You can easily imagine the intense excitement of the children when it was opened. They wonder and wonder over it every day and I have put it on the parlour table as I have no idea of its light being hid under a bushel. Lizzie has answered her Party's letter which I enclose but she has made a sad affair of it. Your last arrived this morning and I am truly distressed to hear how sick mama continues. It is too bad to think of her getting Rheumatism on top of everything else. What is to be done about her! If I only could get her here, I know I could cure her, for we have had such delicious weather lately. I must bring this long letter to a close with best love to all, write on, thine as ever, ES

P.S. I will try to make something for the Floating Fair and will try to enlist others.

20
Mary Wharton
Woodford, April 11th, 1851

My dear Mary

I was very much afraid that before sending off your letter to me you would have received mine telling you to direct to Eutaw, but you cannot have done so, for by Wednesdays mail, to my great pleasure I received your last. It came however nearly a week after its time. Why was that? Your next will of course go to Eutaw, but don't be uneasy about it. Anna will take good care of it until we arrive. Our friends arrived here on last Saturday (5th) and I hope are enjoying themselves.

Mr. Lesesne had business in town and returned on Tuesday but will be back again on Wednesday and they will all return I suppose from what I hear, on Saturday making a visit of two weeks in all. The only draw-back to their enjoyment has been that Hal, their eldest child has been a martyr to earache ever since Tuesday and seems to feel so badly today that we have sent for the Doctor who I trust will not say that he is likely to have a fit of serious sickness. The poor child is 8 years old, very good and quiet but delicate from his birth and I am afraid will give them great uneasiness. The other child James, is 3 and one of the handsomest, glow-ing, most exuberant looking children I ever saw. They are accompanied by an Irish nurse very much in the style of Catherine O'Rourke.

I think that Henry Lesesne is certainly what Mama would call one of the finest men in the world.[179] He is so noble and right minded, so just, so deeply religious and with all such expanded views on every sub-ject. No one can know him who has not been in the house with him. Mrs. Lesesne you would I am sure like very much. I don't know any one who has improved more on acquaintance. When we saw her in Philadelphia that summer, which was pretty much all I have ever seen of her until this winter, she was in very bad health, dispirited and lan-guid. The Lesesne family all being, the women especially as strong as possible, never sick, could not understand her lying down and bad feel-ings and from that arose the idea that she was very nervous, complain-ing and fussy, that vulgar word, but which at the same time conveys a very good idea of what I mean. Now I know Mama would have great experiencing with her. There is a great deal in her. She has a remark-ably liberal mind, is very religious and during her sickness has read all Mama's favorite books. Besides she is quite clever naturally. If you only could hear her talk of Mama! I never heard such exalted terms of admi-ration expressed before.

I am afraid from what they say that the Russell Middletons are growing very transcendental.[180] They have both got to undervalue reg-ular church and prayer times to a dangerous degree. The idea seems to be with them that there is no occasion for family prayers, going to church, etc. but that one must keep always in a state of prayer. Russell Middleton's great idea now is the love of God and that provided a per-son loves God everything else is unimportant—creed, profession, etc. I was surprised to hear that Mrs. Middleton was a secessionist and strongly pro slavery.

Mr. Bland's box arrived last Friday and instead of being as we heard a box of preserves, it turned out to be a large French box of sugar plums, with a small box inside of Guava Jelly. It is quite a pretty box with a looking glass inside, but owing to his sending it all the way from Havana here with a paper round it, it arrived in rather a dilapidated condition. However I have glued it up and it looks quite restored. I sent down a trashy box to go by the *Osprey* for the fair, which I hope has arrived safely. In case Mr. Simons did not write beforehand to Papa, I will mention it was to leave in the Steamer of the 12th. The children are deeply interested in the fair and I do wish they could be present.[181]

You say Mama wishes to know how my side is and I am happy to be able to say truly that I have hardly since I left Philadelphia had a sensation in it. The name of the lady who spoke so tenderly of James Smith is Mrs. Wood. Her mother is Mrs. Robertson who also says he is a very fine young man. For Jim's edification I must mention one anecdote of the latter. The day that General [John] Quitman arrived in Charleston he was received at Stewarts and came out on the balcony to address the people. Mrs. Robertson who is a Scotch woman was . . .

[The remainder of this letter is lost]

The lancing tournament that Emily describes in the next letter is similar to those still performed in Orvieto, Italy, today. Elizabeth S. Richardson described another lancing event at Mammus Hall, a Sand Hills plantation owned by Col. Richard I. Manning: "Uncle Jim surprised them one night by having eight young men dance the lancers on horse-back . . . The house was in darkness, when suddenly the yard was a blaze of light with torches held by mounted Negroes, all in fancy dress, and into the open came eight young men in beautiful fancy dress on handsome charges; and the band struck up . . . The Lancers, and these well and wonderfully trained horses with their skillful riders began their dance."

23
Mr. Thomas I. Wharton
Eutaw, April 25th, 1851

My dear Papa,

Your Evelynian and Physian epistle reached me on last Saturday after having been exposed to divers perils by the way. Literally, the Post riders had much to do with it, and it went first to Eutaw and not finding us there was sent to the Mannings, and the next day on to us. However, it and the check arrived safely and caused us a great deal of amusement. As you appear to be really in good faith I will take you so and will not expose the check to the risk of a fourth journey. Therefore

I beg you to pay all the bills which Mary and Henry will present to you and deduct the amount which will not be more than 70 dollars from the next allowance. Charles told me to send back the check by Mrs. Converse, but I feel as if you would do as you have promised and therefore have not done so and now I will drop the subject trusting in your honor to stand by your agreement.

On good Friday we went to Church and afterwards went to what I had never seen before, a country funeral. One of the residents near Stateburg, Mr. Rutledge,[182] died and we were invited to the funeral and as Mr. Lesesne was anxious to be present we went. I was never more struck than the whole scene in that quiet churchyard which is in a beautiful situation, overlooking the distant river, the swamp beyond and the High Hills of Santee between.

On Saturday the Lesesnes left us, after having had I hope, a pleasant visit, and that morning a boy arrived express from Eutaw with the most pressing letters for us to come down immediately, the *beau-père* being extremely anxious for us to see the Tournament. I was privately more anxious to remain at Woodford a week longer so as to be at Miss Fanny Mayrants wedding and thereupon arose a magnanimous rivalry between Charles and myself as to whether we should stay for the wedding or go to the Tournament. However, I insisted upon going for I knew that we were obliged to leave Eutaw on a certain day and therefore could not make up for the week taken off.

Easter Sunday was the most splendid day I ever saw. Too cold for farmers with young crops just up, but not at all too much so for disinterested persons. We went to church having first made preparations to spend the night at Mrs. Converses, which is only a mile from the church but eleven miles nearer to Eutaw. I do wish Mama could have seen the dressing of the church. It is a famous neighborhood for fine gardens and every person brought a large bouquet of roses and these were placed in vases, etc., so that the effect was beautiful. Then the Communion table, pulpit, etc. was dressed with a wreath going all round.

We passed the rest of the day at Mrs. Converses, and I gave her a letter of introduction to Mary. She promised to send word with the letter where she would stay and I will be very much obliged if you and Mary can pay them some attention for they have both been extremely kind to me. Mrs. Converse is not at all a good-looking woman being coarse in her appearance and perhaps so in her manners, but she is clever. Mr. Converse has a cork leg so don't insist upon his warming "that leg" at the fire as old Mr. Sinkler did upon one occasion. I dare say, by the bye that you in Philadelphia had a fire for here it has been until today absolutely necessary to comfort. The coldest April, everyone says known here for years, still as at Mrs. Converses, the strawberries and green peas were in the greatest profusion and it is the case here.[183]

We left the Ruins on Monday morning and arrived at Eutaw in very good time the same day.[184] We found the house quite full of company who had come down from Columbia, en route for the Tournament.[185] The next day after dinner, Anna and William, Charles and I with our respective children, set off, as Pineville[186] is 18 miles from Eutaw and the tilt was to begin at 10:30. We determined to go to a place 3 miles from the ground that evening, and take our time the next morning. Accordingly, we went to Bluford,[187] the residence of Mr. William DuBose (whom Hen met). Mr. DuBose has been a widower for 25 years and his large house is taking care of itself without a lady ever since. He expected us and had made ample preparation for the children, had sent to Charleston for a cart load of cakes, etc. You never saw such an antiquated air as everything wore, old servants, old furniture, old everything. Mr. DuBose is but 62, or 3, perfectly awake to the present day and decidedly the most reading man of the neighborhood.

Wednesday was as bright and beautiful a day as could be desired. Anna and I accompanied by Charles and the *beau-père,* Lizzie, Wharton, and Henry repaired to the ground and took our places in the ladies stand. As we arrived early we got excellent places and had time to inspect the premises before the show began. There were about two hundred ladies present. Some [were] in carriages, but mostly in the stand and from various parts of the country from Charleston and Columbia. There were also strangers. The Judges stands were decorated with flags, etc., and directly in front of the ladies stand was the Ring suspended from something looking it must be confessed very much like a Gallows. At last along the winding road "The Knights" were seen at full speed approaching, the trumpets sounding and as they drew near the Band struck up Yankee Doodle of all things for this anti Yankee state. At last they came before the stage, 30 in all, lances glittering and flags flying and after some maneuvering the steeds were drawn up, lances lowered and the ladies saluted. Mr. Mazyck Porcher,[188] who is now quite well, was the King at Arms, very handsomely dressed in the Sir Walter Raleigh style. He directed the whole affair and deserves great credit. He had copies printed from all the old books that could be found, of the passages on Tilts, Tournaments, feats of arms, etc. He was attended by a Moor in full costume whose business it was to pick up the ring when it dropped which he did with great solemnity. He was a highly respectable old Negro belonging to Mr. Porcher and before going off one of the ladies of the family said to him: "Now, if you do your part well, you shall be rewarded." Upon which he replied: "Thank you ma'am all I wish is to have my Moors dress for my burial suit."

William Sinkler was Herald; his dress was very handsome, blue velvet trimmed with silver, hat and plumes, gauntlets, etc, his horse was beautifully caparisoned. After the saluting was over the Tilting began. The object was to carry off the Ring on the lance, a very difficult matter, and each knight came full speed pointing his lance directly at the Ring, many throwing it off on the ground and many failing entirely. At each attempt the trumpet would sound and the Herald and the Master of the Horse would announce the title of the Knight. When each of the 27 had a trial, they defiled past to the place of starting. There were six trials and when it was all concluded the Judges pronounced that the Knight of Carolina, a young man of the name of Morton Waring, had carried off the Ring the greatest number of times. He was therefore directed to choose a Queen which the poor youth did with much trepidation. He chose Miss Elizabeth Porcher. After this the judges selected the Knight whose costume was the handsomest and he who had ridden the most gracefully. Our friend Julius Porcher,[189] "The Knight of Walworth" was selected for the former and Keating Palmer, "Knight of the Grove" for the latter. Julius Porcher's dress was a full suit of armor which was certainly appropriate and looked extremely well on horseback. He was very ceremonious in his conduct and when requested to choose a maid of honor did so with much circumstance pointing his lance and exclaiming in a loud voice, "I select the fair lady Ingoldsby." And then came the ceremony of crowning. The victorious Knight crowned the Queen with a wreath of white roses and she in return crowned him with a wreath of laurel. The other two Knights then kneeling received from the hands of their maids of honor, the one a scarf for the best costume, and the other a pair of spurs for the best riding.

This over the Herald (William) in the name of the King of Arms, the Master of Horse and himself invited the Knights and the company to a collation, to which of course all repaired. It was by this time 3 o'clock and the collation being very much like a supper at a ball was very acceptable. In the evening there was a regular Ball given by the Knights to which Charles, Anna and I did not go. When the collation was over it was too late to go back to Eutaw, so Anna and I paid two visits and then went back to Bluford where we passed the night and the next morning returned to Eutaw. Charles went to an old friends in the neighborhood and joined us the next morning.

The whole affair to sum up matters was very handsome and went off with but one interruption which nearly broke Lizzie's heart. A young man, Rene Ravenel, "The Knight of Berkeley" rode a vicious horse much against his father's will and on the first trial as he approached the Ring, he lost all command of the animal and in a few seconds was thrown. Fortunately he was only jarred, not hurt and in a few moments mounted another horse, came before the Ladies Stand accompanied by the Herald, and Master of Horse, and after lowering his lance said, "The Knight of Berkeley comes before you without plume or spurs and craves the indulgence of the Ladies for his disgrace." He is quite a handsome young man and looked extremely pale and disconcerted and it was too much for poor Lizzie. She burst into tears and thought of no one else the rest of the day. He went immediately to his father's carriage and Lizzie was somewhat relieved by the ladies sending him a bunch of flowers with a very complimentary message requesting him to favor them with his company on the Stand which he accordingly did and was quite as much the Hero as the real Victor. Women, you know, having always a penchant for Knights in misfortune. The rest of the riders acquitted themselves to admiration. In this part of the world they seem to be one with the horse and there were some splendid horses there. I did so much wish Frank and Hen could have seen the Horses. They were, of course, picked animals and I heard of Mr. Breevoort of N.Y. who was present saying that after seeing such splendid riding and horses he could never mount a horse again. Our friend Fitzsimmons came very near getting the greatest number. He was the "Knight of Erin" dressed in green velvet with gold shamrocks on his hat which was a French affair with plumes and on his coat a scarf on which was embroidered the Harp of Ireland. His dress was very expensive and on horseback you cannot perceive his misfortune. There were many other handsome costumes, particularly Saladin, the Knight Templar, the Hungarian Knight and the Knight of Malta. Now I am afraid I have tired you with this long account. I had no idea of going so much into detail when I began but my pen ran along almost without my being aware of it. I have made a list of the Knights and their order of riding thinking you might be amused to look over them.

We expect to be here about 10 days or two weeks longer so you had all best direct to Providence as we may be obliged to go back sooner for Charles is getting uneasy about his crop. The weather is so cold, he may have to plant over. There is now a regular north easterly November Storm. I must bring this long effusion to an end for there is to be a dinner party here today (of Knights) and I have something to do. I hope you will write soon. The children both send love. Thine ever, Emily Sinkler

   Neal hath arrived. Pray read Wharton's note to me which I enclose in this for Mama.

It was a firm rule that everyone left the plantations by May 15. Emily passed the summer at Woodford, as was the Sinkler custom at this time, and then went to Philadelphia for her usual early fall visit. By October an early frost has killed the vegetation and with it the bugs that so plagued the lowcountry. She is delighted to be setting out again for Eutaw Plantation and a visit with the *beau-père*. Emily, Charles, and the children are spending a night along the way at John Manning's place, Milford. Emily discusses her pastimes in this next letter, including reading, crocheting, pickling shrimp, and preserving flowers. Emily and her circle of friends spent many hours doing sewing and needlework such as crocheting and embroidery. Crocheting was a fine art and consisted of looping stitches formed with a single thread and a hooked needle. Emily made crochet lace in this fashion for her shawls, pillowcases, and collars. She also embroidered hand towels, pillowcases, tablecloths, and napkins with decorative designs. Emily also knitted to make throws and shawls. One of her techniques is preserved in *An Antebellum Plantation Household: Including the South Carolina Low Country Receipts and Remedies of Emily Wharton Sinkler:* "Purl 2 clips and bind; nit two plain throw threads forward; Knit 1 throw thread forward and Knit 2 purl 2 together; repeat."

Moorlands, October 30th, 1851

My dearest Mother,

   I don't think I ever experienced a greater pleasure than on seeing your handwriting on your letter on Monday. It seemed such an evident proof that you were better. I was anxiously looking for a letter for I dreamed the night before that I received a letter saying you had a bad attack by the following day's mail. But this dream was easily accounted for, as Anna and I had been sitting up late the night before talking of you and your sufferings. Anna groans now at everything I tell her about you. And such a sweet letter it was too that you wrote and that post-script was so like you! Your book of flowers has been so much admired that I only wish I had one of your last books to exhibit. It is now at the

Mannings and they are enchanted with it. A Miss Anneley from Charleston is paying them a visit now and she is something of a connoisseur in such matters.[190] She has 4,000 specimens of marine shells. I don't know how many hundreds of alpine plants. She talks in a most knowing way of the various plans of pressing and preserving flowers.

I am now again in what appears to be my natural element, preparing for a journey. It is settled that we are to go from here on Saturday—day after tomorrow—. It is considered perfectly safe to go on the Plantations now for the old fashioned essentials to security have been regularly gone through tho' it is an uncommonly early season. We had ice on Friday and Saturday mornings which killed vegetation. A heavy rain on Sunday which washed away the dead leaves, and on Monday and Tuesday mornings ice again. The *beau-père* went down to Eutaw on Monday to get everything to rights, carpets down, etc., before we arrive on Saturday. Charles and I and the children have been invited to spend tomorrow and tomorrow night at Milford, John Manning's place which we will do and then the next day join William and Anna and proceed on together.[191] I shall stay at Eutaw for a few days while Belvidere gets to rights. I have passed a very pleasant time here. The weather has been delightful and we have dined out constantly and driven out every day. We have had also a great deal of new music to try which you know is a very nice thing. Anna received a present of 13 songs and duets a few days ago and I had several given me in Charleston.

I have been very much, what shall I say, interested will not do, occupied rather in Huntington's new book *Alban*. It is the most extraordinary book I ever read. The first part was very good in its way. The description of New England life, Congregationalism and New Haven Theology, very graphic and well painted but as soon as the Hero turns Roman Catholic the story becomes outrageously absurd. I request Mary most particularly to read the book and to give you a full account of the house haunted by demons and the child possessed by an evil spirit. It is the most enchantingly absurd thing you can imagine and all written in good faith too altho' there is nothing immoral in the story. I think the author has the coarsest and most indelicate mind I ever met with. The lady who lent it me advised me not to read it as it was so intolerably stupid. She had not been able to get through the first few pages of it. I found it anything but stupid.

Lizzie and Wharton are very well and look even better than when they left Philadelphia. They often talk of you and form little plans about you. Lizzie is at present writing a letter to Mary and intends it to go in mine but it is a very doubtful matter for every day she writes epistles which are never finished. Tell Mary to be sure to send on the receipt for Emily Morrell's crochet tidy. I am anxious to be in on yours and I always feel happy while working for you and if I had the pattern here could get through a great deal on Saturday in the carriage.

I am glad the shrimps were nice and I hope you eat and enjoyed some of them. I told Papa to expect them the Saturday after we left but see by JN's letter that he must have forgotten about them. We have just had a very nice jar of them here. I was called off just now and have been able to go out with my letter until now and now it is so late that I must close as the mail closes very early in the morning. Don't strain your eyes to write to me. I am grateful for a letter when it comes and satisfied if it does not. Anna sends her love to you. Give my love to every member of the household and believe me ever yours, ES. P.S. I wrote to Papa a few days ago asking him to get 2 1/4 barrels of Buckwheat. Tell him Charles will be much obliged to him if he will get three half barrels.

A calabash full of eggs on the head of an African American servant at Belvidere Plantation, circa 1914. (Author's collection)

The Santee River from Mitchell's Bluff, near Belvidere. (Author's collection)

Eutaw Creek, which ran between Eutaw and Belvidere Plantations. (Author's collection)

Eutaw Springs, at the point where the springs originate under the hill. (Author's collection)

The Wharton family vacationed at Cape May. This lighthouse was built in 1859 at the entrance to Delaware Bay, Cape May, New Jersey. (Courtesy of Ken Frye)

Cape May, New Jersey. The village of Cape May was known for its Victorian architecture. (Courtesy of Ken Frye)

The Old Mill, built in 1830 by Peter A. Summey, in Flat Rock, North Carolina, frequent vacation site of Emily and Charles Sinkler. (Courtesy of Historic Flat Rock)

Woodfield Inn, Flat Rock, North Carolina. Emily and Charles may have stayed in this inn, which was built in Flat Rock in 1852 on the old Saluda Road. In Emily's day it was called the Farmer's Hotel and was operated by Henry Tudor Farmer. (Courtesy of Historic Flat Rock)

A 1950s reenactment of a jousting tournament, Gippy Plantation. Emily and Charles attended a fabulous lancing, or jousting, tournament on 25 April 1851. Emily's granddaughter, Anne Wickham Sinkler Fishburne, recreated a similar event on the lawn at Gippy Plantation two generations later. (Author's collection)

Another scene from the jousting tournament at Gippy Plantation. (Author's collection)

Carriages at the jousting tournament at Gippy Plantation. (Author's collection)

Singer Jenny Lind. The internationally renowned Lind sang in Charleston in February 1851, at a concert sponsored by P. T. Barnum and the Temperance League and attended by Emily Sinkler.

Emily Wharton Sinkler, 8 October 1823–10 February 1875, "the light and joy" of Belvidere Plantation. (Author's collection)

Charles Sinkler, 8 July 1818–28 March 1894, U.S. Navy lieutenant and owner of Belvidere and Woodford Plantations. (Author's collection)

Caroline Sidney Sinkler, 1860–1948, youngest daughter of Emily and Charles Sinkler, who later became a patron of the arts in Philadelphia. (Author's collection)

Charles St. George Sinkler, 1853–1938, youngest son of Emily and Charles Sinkler. (Author's collection)

Anne Wickham Sinkler, daughter of Julius Porcher and Mary Fanning Wickham of St. Julien Plantation. Anne married Charles St. George Sinkler on 5 December 1883, and they continued the Sinkler cotton farming tradition at Belvidere Plantation. (Author's collection)

Wharton Sinkler, 7 August 1845–1917, oldest son of Emily and Charles Sinkler. Wharton Sinkler fought in the Civil War at the age of seventeen and after the war pursued a career as a neurologist in Philadelphia. (Author's collection)

Henry Wharton, 2 June 1827–11 November 1880, younger brother of Emily. Henry Wharton worked as a lawyer with his father, Thomas Isaac Wharton, and was a board member of the Library Company of Philadelphia. (Courtesy of the Library Company of Philadelphia)

Thomas Isaac Wharton, 17 May 1791–7 April 1857, Emily's father. Wharton was a distinguished lawyer, judge, writer, and leader of the Philadelphia bar. (Courtesy of the Historical Society of Pennsylvania)

The Sinkler family on the lawn at Belvidere, circa 1916. From left to right: Charles St. George Sinkler, Caroline Sidney Sinkler, Arthur Brock, Anne Wickham Porcher Sinkler, Ella Sinkler Brock, Edward Coleman, and Wharton Sinkler. The child in front is Caroline Sidney Sinkler. (Author's collection)

Mary Coré Griffith, Emily's grandmother, in a Thomas Sully portrait. Mary Coré Griffith was a feminist, a utopian, and a friend of Maria Edgeworth and Sir Walter Scott; she distinguished herself as an author and scientist. (Courtesy of David Deas Sinkler, Philadelphia, Pa.)

The residence of Thomas Isaac Wharton, 130 South Sixth Street, Philadelphia. Emily was born in this house in 1823; in December 1824 it was the site of the founding of the Historical Society of Pennsylvania by Wharton and his friends. (Courtesy Historical Society of Pennsylvania)

XIII

A Splendid Christmas, Winter 1851, and Spring 1852

IT IS DECEMBER, AND Emily is collecting ice during a hard freeze to make future ice creams. She also notes that the water in the washbowl at Belvidere froze even though there was a fire in the bedroom. Emily states that the thermometer registered twelve on their porch and that this was the coldest weather since 1835. Later in February there is a regular "Northern" snowstorm on the banks of the Santee, and Emily talks of sleighing.

She is also making preparations for the family Christmas at Eutaw, where she will be helping Anna Linton Sinkler, who had become the lady in charge at Eutaw now that Eliza lived at Homesley. Christmas at Eutaw was a time of great festivity. Her description of the holiday customs—the Christmas tree with candlelight, fireworks, dancing, toasting with eggnog—accords with William Gilmore Simms's *The Golden Christmas: A Chronicle of St. John's Berkeley* (Charleston, 1852). Emily also describes the Sinklers' preparations for Christmas presents for the slaves.

Emily is also looking forward again to race week in Charleston, the third week in February.[192] The *beau-père* had decided to take a suite in the Charleston Hotel for the entire Sinkler family. Emily was no doubt pleased that Charles would be in attendance, as the Episcopal Convention, which he usually attended, had been moved to Columbia for the year of 1852. The *beau-père* was running his horse, Jeff Davis, a four-year-old out of Hero and Marigold. The Eutaw colors were red and white satin. Hercules, the *beau-père's* trainer, was known throughout the South as one of the best racehorse trainers in the business. Emily also hoped to hear Catharine Hayes in concert. The *Charleston Courier* for December 1851 had advertisements for theater, including performances of both *Norma* and *The Barber of Seville*.

Emily had become quite a housekeeper by this time. Her receipt and remedy book, reproduced in *An Antebellum Plantation Household* show that she loved to put on dinner parties and especially enjoyed the finale of three desserts. Emily prepared the desserts with the help of her servants. Her description of a dinner party replete with boiled ham, roast ducks, charlotte polonaise, and plum pudding gives some indication of the lavish spread she hosted at Belvidere.

Emily was fashion conscious. Her letters show that she followed Philadelphia fashions and was anxious to know the manner that ladies were wearing cuffs and collars. She read *Godey's Lady's Book,* which always had samples of embroidery and crochet work that Emily might well have used as patterns for her own handwork. *Godey's* also had full engravings and fashion plates of elegant ladies carrying parasols and wearing regal, long lace and satin dresses. Oates Music store at 253 King Street advertised a year's subscription to *Godey's* for $3. Emily also read *Peterson's Magazine,* which, like *Godey's,* was a ladies' magazine replete with pictures of elegant flounced dresses, beautiful shawls, flower-bedecked hats, and lovely scarves. Finally, Emily would have had a copy of *Frank Leslie's Gazette of Fashion,* which had pictures of I. M. Singer's sewing machine, as well as elaborate patterns for making dresses, collars, cuffs, hats, shoes, fans, necklaces, earrings, and much more. Emily's letters indicate that she was anxious to keep up with the styles and cut a "good figure" in her clothes.

It is also apparent in these letters that Emily was becoming a proficient gardener. She planned and implemented lovely gardens on either side of the front steps at Belvidere, which included matching tea olives which grew to a great height. Her friend Mrs. Marion provided her with cuttings and bulbs. She received cuttings of old-fashioned roses from friends she had made at the lancing tournament at Pineville. Emily's garden at Belvidere was to become a family legacy. On a warm, spring day the glorious blooms of the old-fashioned roses were a rainbow of pinks, mauves, crimsons, blood red, and velvety rose. The garden was alive with the songs of birds—wrens, thrushes, redbirds, and mockingbirds. Emily especially loved the lilacs. Her annual beds of mignonette and heart's-ease were bright with the colors of blue and pink, while the aroma of tea olive suffused the air.

❧ ❧ ❧

12

Belvidere, December 16th, 1851

My dear Mary,

How I wish you could all feel what a cold morning is this 16th of December! I assure you it is with difficulty I can hold the pen in my hand. I am however turning the cold to the best account I can and have a man employed in collecting ice for future ice creams. I have already got a couple of barrels full and of quite thick ice too.

You are probably by this time returned from Baltimore, where I am very glad to find you have had such a pleasant visit. Your letters tho not so long as my rapacious views could have desired, were great treats. Did you see anything of Mrs. Ammen who is also to pay us a visit this winter? She lives with the British Counsel Mr. McTavish and is English or Canadian herself. I saw her for a few minutes in Baltimore but did not think her particularly interesting and have heard since that she is one of the most bigoted Roman Catholics imaginable, which will not be very agreeable in this community which is now devoted to Bible Classes, church practisings, etc. etc. Did you see Mrs. Ulrichs whom I spoke about once before? I feel curious to know something about her, having been so often told I was like her. I received by last mail your letter to Mama, enclosed in one from Papa. Give my love to him and tell him I have enjoyed very much the notes he has sent with your letters. Tell him we are delighted with the Buckwheat. It is capital and tho not quite so white as the last years is equally as light and nice. One of our late guests was quite enchanted with it and declared he had never tasted the like before. If you have preserved the letters you received while at Baltimore, I wish you would send them all to me. I will gain thus little pieces of intelligence which might otherwise be lost.

I am now engaged in preparing a small box of trifles for Christmas for you all. They are mere trifles but I cannot resist sending them. Those provoking steamers, the *Osprey* and *Albatross* are neither running at present so I will have to send the box by Adams Express. I have heard of an opportunity to Charleston towards the end of the week by which I will send the box and will tell Mr. Simons to write a line to Papa the day he sends it by the Express. It is very mortifying about these steamers and I am afraid the line will be entirely broken up soon for I see by the Newspapers that the *Albatross* has been sold.[193]

I have very little to record of the past week. Charles was at Woodford and I stayed here in the day and at Eutaw at night, which gave Anna and myself fine chances for practicing. Eliza and her family arrived last week. She looks well and seems more bright and like herself than she has been for a long time. I had heard a great deal about the Mrs. Thomas you mentioned in one of your letters through Mrs. John Manning. Mrs. Thomas' brother Mr. Douglas Gordon married Mrs. Manning's sister.

I received this week some very fine rose trees, the Cloth of Gold,

Souvenir de Malmaison, etc., a present from a gentleman we met at the Tournament last year. I have also a promise of some delightful French books from the same person who lent me *Helene,* etc. These books are described as perfectly "faut" and yet charming. If they turn out as they are described, I will let you know.

When you see M. Cardeza tell her to send on the patterns of silks I wrote to her about as soon as possible. Poor Anna is waiting in all patience for them. I suppose you must have received the letter in which I asked you to get patterns after you left Philadelphia. The children are very well and deeply interested in every particular of your Baltimore visit. I never saw Liz looking so fat before. She is coming on very well with her music and plays quite a pretty little piece. Bud is grown very boyish, has pockets stuffed with twine and stick, and all sorts of boyish things. He is quite useful in his way too for whenever his father is not here he goes into the stable yard and feeds all the creatures morning and evening. We were all weighed a few evenings ago. I weighed 104, an improvement of 6 pounds since last summer at Germantown. Poor Anna to her horror, found that she weighed 165 lbs., more than she has ever weighed before. Give my love to Hen and ask him why he does not write. Tell him when he sees W. Sargent to thank him for his account of Ellen McIlvaine's wedding.[194] He wrote a long letter to Charles about it, saying that as Hen and you were in Baltimore he supposed there would be no one else to give an account.

How pleased and relieved I am to find Mama continues better. Give my best love to her. I suppose she received my letter last week. Goodbye now, Yours ever, E. S.

13

T. I. Wharton Esq.
150 Walnut Street
Philadelphia, Penn
Belvidere, Dec. 22d, 1851

A happy Christmas to you dear Papa, and to all the household and may you have as many happy returns as I hope you will have. I am rather advancing the season tho of course this will reach you after the day. I dispatched this morning to Charleston a small box directed to your care and as neither of the Philadelphia steamers is running now, Charles requested Mr. Simons to forward it by Adams Express which I hope and trust has an office in Charleston. Charles asked Mr. Simons to endeavor to send it off immediately so that it might reach you on Christmas day or the day after. This box does not contain anything of the slightest value. I merely send it as a remembrance. I dare say you will all be very much amused at the contents. Lizzie and Wharton were in despair at not being able to send anything. Poor Liz had something but mislaid it and tho every place we could think of was searched, it could not be found until this morning after the box was sent. And poor Bud had selected something he thought very beautiful to send to his Marty, a vine covered with bunches of brilliant red berries which had twined very prettily on a smooth stick. I advised him not to pick it until the last day, but when he bustled off into the public road to get it he found that the severe weather we have had, had killed it entirely.

And such weather as we have had—The coldest known in this Latitude since 1835. I know you will scarcely believe me when I tell you that the Thermometer in our Piazza pointed to only 12! The change began on Tuesday night. It blew fearfully and on Wednesday morning it began to snow. It snowed heavily all that day and it was not until Sunday night that the weather moderated at all. The snow remained on the ground for four days, an unusual thing here. The ice was so thick in my room that we could not break it and even in Eliza Manning's room, where she kept a fire burning all night, the water froze hard. She was staying here at the time. I assure you it was entirely too cold to be pleasant. You have had it in Philadelphia much colder, I suppose, tho as your houses there are so much tighter than the houses here, I dare say the water did not freeze in the rooms.

I received by Tuesday's mail a great treat in the epistolary way. Namely two letters from Mama and one from Mary. Tell Mama hers were charming and put me in spirits for the rest of the week. I thought of them constantly. Mary's was as usual, most entertaining. I suppose by this time she has returned from her visit, which I am really glad to find has been so pleasant.

You cannot imagine what a busy time this season of Christmas is here. I have my hands full of divers styles of preparations. In the first place, staying at Eutaw for nearly a week with the house there full of company, involves a good deal of brushing up of the children's wardrobes, etc. Then there is to be the grandest Christmas Tree ever known which is to be hung with wax lights and all manners of gilt things, besides presents for the children. William has gone to town for the express purpose of buying presents having had numerous lists and commissions given him. Then I have to help Anna at Eutaw in her preparations to provide for so many as will be in the house.

Then another thing which takes up a great deal of my time is the servants Christmas. Not only do I give them all rice, sugar, and coffee and Charles kills an ox for them but there is no end of the business of exchanging. They come to me with eggs and chickens for which they wish me to give them sugar, coffee, rice, wheat flour, tobacco, etc. Of course, I never refuse and as they have found me good and immediate pay, they come from far and near and the consequence is I am at a loss to know what to do with all I have. I have now upwards of 100 chickens straggling about and an immense box of salt filled with eggs.

We were talking of Christmas presents lately and what the children would like me to send for to Charleston for them and Bud said: "I want but one present and that is from Party and it is that he should bring himself here; that's all I want." Bud has a little sheepskin saddle and is learning to ride on horseback with his father. He reads very well indeed now and is much animated with Parley's account of the Old French War and the Revolutionary War. Both Liz and Buds reverence for Parley is unbounded and they can hardly believe he is still living.[195]

What are you reading now which is interesting? We are reading *Southey* but it is not to be compared in point of interest to Lockhart's *Life*.[196] There is so much sameness and egotism about those letters. Still we are very much in want of No. 4. If it is in the house I wish you would send it for I am afraid it cannot be bought separate. We have all the rest of the numbers.

That conundrum about poor Sir John Franklin is capital tho I never knew before that Tea Chests were lined with block tin.[197] I thought they were lined with lead. The first exclamation of the children when they found ice in their basins, ice on their toothbrushes, ice on their towels on Wednesday morning was "poor John Franklin!" He is an object of the deepest sympathy and interest to them and was particularly so during that cold spell. Liz who reads the Newspapers carefully wants to know if that account of the little balloon descending into the Lady's garden in England could be true. I suppose it must be a hoax. Please send *Neal*. We did not get one last week. And the *Bulletin* occasionally. What is your opinion of Kossuth? Much talk and divided opinions here.[198] Much love to all. I'll write to Marty next week. Why doesn't Hen write. Yours ever, E. S.

16
Belvidere January 12th, 1852
Miss Mary Wharton

My dear Mary,

Your delightful letter was received by last Mail. I don't know any that I have enjoyed so much for a long time. The same mail brought me the *Bulletins* (tell Party) and Hen's very agreeable letter. The letter, I will answer next week. Since I last wrote nothing has occurred of any moment whatever, the weather has been delightful, just cold enough to make exercise out of doors very attractive and to make it necessary to have a fire in doors all day. Faute le mieux I have taken to riding Tackey again! My former friend the Pony is disabled and I must ride Tackey or nothing at all. The "brute" is not so bad on a regular ride as she is on the short transit between here and Eutaw. The other day I was over there and the ground being wet after a rain, I mounted Tackey to return. She was determined to make my trip as disagreeable as possible until I had recourse to a happy plan which was to make Bob drive her along with a stick in the manner of driving a cow. Rather a disgraceful way of procedure however and very different from the way in which riding is described in books. The provoking animal put me in an awkward position a few days ago. She went along the Nelsons Ferry Road pretty well until we got to Richard Porchers Avenue. When up that she would go and in it she would stay for nearly ¼ of an hour. This week all the gentlemen except Charles go to the Pineville Races and Anna is coming over to stay here. We intend delightful long rides every day, I on Tackey, Anna on Camilla. Now if we only had you here to go on Jeanette how pleasant it would be.

I received a letter lately from Mrs. Converse saying she will be at Belvidere in the course of the winter, tho she cannot fix any time at present. She says Annie speaks constantly in the most grateful terms of the kindness she received from all of you. We were very sorry to receive a few days ago a letter of resignation from Mr. Dehon on account of his health. The Vestry do not intend to accept it however, and have passed resolutions to request him to travel and return to them again. We have not received his answer yet. Mr. Gadsden improves greatly in his preaching. I like him as well as any young clergyman I know, indeed better. The Bible Class goes on and is very interesting. I assure you it requires a great deal of study to keep up. You can imagine how indefatigable the Porchers are in studying.

I hope you have received the letter about Anna's things. The reason she did not like the patterns was that she had set her heart upon a silver grey and none of the silks were of that shade. All that she is anxious about now is that the box should be here in time to have the dress made up for the first week in February when she is going to make a visit to Charleston. The Races take place at that time and it is the only time when Charleston is really gay. I am somewhat in a predicament about going to Charleston. The beau-père goes down every year to the Races and one day being in a very pleasant expansive humor he proposed to William and Anna, Charles and myself to spend a week with him at the Charleston Hotel (which is extremely well kept now) and he would pay the expenses of the whole party. Of course we all accepted and were looking forward to having a very pleasant time. Yesterday arrived two letters, one from Mr. James Simons to Charleston and one from Mrs. Simons to me, containing the most pressing invitations you ever read to stay at their house during our visit to Charleston. Now although they are very nice people I would much rather stay at a Hotel where I can stay out all day etc., than at any private house and yet it is very evident to see from the letters that they will be hurt if we don't come. Indeed Mrs. Simons who was to pay us a visit in April, says if we don't go to her in February she will not come here in April, which she says would be depriving her a pleasure she has had in anticipation all winter. What is to be done!

The convention meets this year in Columbia so Charles does not mean to go. His father, however, who just came back from a meeting of the Vestry says that they are very anxious for Charles to go.

Tuesday morning: If you could be transported here how surprised you would be at the appearance of the place. The snow began early this morning and every thing is now completely white. I suppose the snow is an inch thick and as it is still going on fast I dare say we will have sleighing by tomorrow. I never saw such a Northern looking snow storm before here. Bad weather for the Races. We have company in the house arrived last Night en route and Eutaw is full also. I had several things more to say but must close as I see company coming from Eutaw and the Mail goes at 12. With best love to all, Yours ever, E. S.

The Whartons' gifts greatly increased Liz and Bud's intellectual life. They sent microscopes, globes, and a variety of entertaining reading from geography to bird books. The children obviously relished these extra treats and were immersed in their reading and writing. As part of their education Emily had them keep journals as well as write their own thank-you notes to their grandparents. The children received instruction both from their Irish governess as well as from Emily. Charles taught Bud to ride, while Emily taught Lizzie to play the piano. Emily comments on the unusually cold weather during January of 1852, so cold that the ground had become frozen. She also empathizes with the "blackeys," but assuages her guilt with the note that their access to plenty of firewood puts them in a better position than the poor in cities.

Belvidere Jan. 26th, 1852

My dear Papa,

In the first place let me thank you for your letter and the check for $87 which arrived safely by Saturday's mail. Charles and I were very much pleased with the accuracy of the accounts and I duly showed him the Ground Rent affair. Anna was also excruciated at the accuracy of her account and your having done it all yourself. The box arrived on Sunday (yesterday) afternoon in good order and condition. Tho' it had not been without its adventures. It came from Charleston up to the 31 mile station on Saturday and that night the store it was lodged in took fire and was burned to the ground. They saved the box tho' a vehicle of Charles' which was sent for it got injured and they had some difficulty in saving the mule from the stable. However the damage was trifling to us. You can imagine the excitement the opening of the box caused and the screams of delight which hailed the debut of each fresh object. The note-paper is perfect and just the thing I wanted. I know you think I always say so but this time it is a fact too. I used my last sheet but one of the old note paper today. You cannot doubt but that the stamped envelopes were very acceptable. I know no more useful present you could have sent me. These stamps appear to be universally used. In all my numerous correspondence I have received but two letters unstamped since July. An old lady of our acquaintance carries her use of them rather far for she puts them on the letters she sends by private opportunities. What a treat you have sent Charles and myself in the newspapers, London news magazines and Harpers books. We were literally speaking entirely out of light reading and my mind was growing quite heavy under the weight of the old reading I was undergoing. Even the torn pieces of newspaper are put by to be read (something I must say after the manner of the Prodigal son and the husks). When we have done with the magazines they go to Mrs. Manning and thence to Mrs. Pringle Smith. The children are feasting on the beautiful books you have sent them. But they shall speak for themselves in their own notes. Tho' I know they will not be able to tell half their delight. Liz has with difficulty been able to tear herself away from hers to meals. We think the books entirely too pretty to be shut up in a book case, so they adorn my centre table. Bud feels particularly promoted by his book of birds, never having before owned so large a book. He has immediately taken it for his evening reading book. I will write to the rest of the family about their gifts. Don't forget to say something to Anna about the jar of Pickles she sent you. It has not been mentioned yet.

We intended going to Charleston next week but I feel rather doubtful about it just now. We have heard that the Measles are very prevalent there now, and as the children have never had the disease I do not like to take them. I have written to Mrs. Frost to get her to ask the

Dr's opinion about it for in the country people get very exaggerated accounts of diseases, etc. in town. If Dr. Frost says there is no risk we will go for he is a very prudent man. I would be very sorry to give up the trip for the *beau-père* has engaged rooms for us at the Charleston Hotel and we expect a very pleasant trip. I couldn't go at a better time for the *beau-père* will have his carriage and horses and servants there. Besides I have promised two young ladies to take charge of them and it will be a great disappointment to them. But *que voulez vous*? I shan't go if there is any risk.

Never has such cold weather been known here before this not merely a "cold snap" but the cold keeps on, on, on. The ground has been frozen now for more than two weeks. The blackeys suffer as you can imagine a great deal from the cold, tho' they can always get plenty of wood which is an advantage over the poor in cities. I must bring my letter to a conclusion as I want to write to Mama and Mary and Hen tonight. Write soon again to your ever affectionate, ES. P.S. When you see Aunt ask her what is the meaning of her unusually long silence. I wrote to her a month ago.

The excitement of a trip to Charleston was intense. Emily and Anna spent weeks planning their wardrobes, including silk or muslin dresses with appropriate collars, sleeves, and hats. There was a specific look during this period, and women dressed to conform to the dress code of the day. Clothing was designed to help them look narrow at the waist and wide at the face, hips, and shoulders—an hourglass figure. Women during this period wanted their faces to look full and round, so they wore their hair flat on the top, with fullness on the sides and back, and parted in the middle.

Dresses were constructed with dropped shoulder seams to enhance the appearance of wideness in that area. Skirts were pleated so that the fabric hung in somewhat diagonal lines from the waist, five yards of fabric being used for work clothing and six or more yards used for fancy dresses. As fancy dresses were seldom washed, collars, undersleeves, and cuffs were not only decorative but practical, as they could be removed and laundered, protecting the fine fabric from soil and wear.

The ladies were particularly concerned with their hat ribbons. In *An Antebellum Plantation Household,* there is a procedure for keeping ribbons beautiful: "To wash ribbons make a lather of clean white soap, the water as warm as you can bear your hands. Soap may be applied where there are grease spots on the wrong side. As soon as washed have ready a hot iron and press them out. While wet pressing on the wrong side. To stiffen dip in gum Arabic."

Everyone went to town, including children, servants, and adults. Emily was anticipating concerts, visits with friends, shopping, and, of course, the races. She especially wanted to hear the singing of Miss Catharine Hayes but missed her performance at the Hibernian Hall by only a few days.

Emily loved to entertain and did so lavishly. At the end of this next letter she describes a typical lunch party at Belvidere. She used the produce of Belvidere, including wild ducks, haunch of venison, and trout on her menu. She concluded these celebrations with elegant desserts. Two of the receipts for this wonderful country dinner party were included in *An Antebellum Plantation Household*. They are reproduced below.

Boiled Turkey. Take grated bread, butter, sweet herbs, pepper, salt and a little nutmeg, celery or oysters chopped according to taste. Mix up with yolk of egg. Stuff the turkey, flour it, tie in a cloth and boil an hour and 1/4.

Celery Sauce. Wash and pare a large bunch very clean; Cut into little bits and boil swiftly till tender; add 1/2 pt cream, some mace, nutmeg, and small piece of butter rolled in flour, then boil gently and serve.

Two of the receipts were found in May 1999 along with all the other "missing pages" from Emily's original cooking and remedy book. They are reproduced here for the first time. Emily had a sweet tooth and especially loved to create a grand finale with elegant desserts. The two below were some of her favorites.

Omlette Souffle, Mary Bland. 9 eggs, 1 large lemon. Beat the whites till they turn dry out of the dish. Stand them in a cool place while the yolks are beaten in the same way. Grate gradually in the yolks the rind of the lemon and then squeeze and strain the juice and pour it in beating all the time. Then stir in enough fine powdered sugar to make it very sweet. Prepare your baking pan which should be of tin and wider above than below. Grease and warm it and pour in first the yolks and then the whites beat up together for a moment and bake 20 minutes in quick oven.

Plum Pudding, Mary Bland. One fourth lb. flour (well-sifted), 1/4 lb. bread crumbs, 1/4 lb. currants, 1/4 lb. raisins, and 1/4 lb. suet, 1/2 lb. sugar of which half must be browned to caramel. 1 small glass brandy. Boil 3 hours and 1/2 in a mould tied in a cloth. [1 pound equals 3 1/4 cups of flour.]

18
Belvidere, February 2d 1852
Miss Mary Wharton

My dear Mary,

I wrote last week, acknowledging the receipt of the box but I was so hurried that I couldn't do justice to your share in it and therefore deferred it until this week. I must now thank you most heartily in Anna's name and mine for all you have done. Anna and William are delighted with what you have got for her and Anna cannot send enough messages expressive of thanks. She says you must feel fully compensated for your trouble by the satisfaction you have given. The cloak is very handsome and comme il faut. The silk she has not yet seen, it having remained in town for the purpose of being transformed into a dress. The Ribbons she thinks very handsome and is very much pleased with the shawl, collars, etc. Anna has now a very nice outfit for her visit to Charleston. William bought her a very handsome French hat lately and several other things. He is so extravagant as a shopper, however that she does not employ him often. She asked him to get her a twisting comb and he brought up one for which he paid twenty dollars. To be sure it was a very pretty tortoise shell. I am delighted with my collar and sleeves, and they arrived in the most apropos way for I am always in want of those articles. I suppose the open sleeves are for me as they were with the collar. Under the supposition I have worn them. The only difficulty about the box was that so few things were marked, and being put in books, it was a long time before I found some of them. I knew you were going to send me a collar but was rather puzzled which was mine. But the inside handkerchief determined me. I really am very much obliged to you. The sleeves too were an unexpected pleasure. The box has been a great source of happiness all last week and will be for some time yet, for the books are not near read up yet. Hen's bonbons were the most enchanting things I ever ate. Give my love to the dear Marty and tell her our little circle was full of good wishes for her this morning it being her Birthday. We wished her many happy returns and that the next one might not only find her well, but here at Belvidere.

We are anticipating a great deal of pleasure from our trip to Charleston tomorrow.[199] We heard from Dr. Frost that there is no epidemic there. There were some cases of measles of a mild kind. The reports we heard about Typhus Fever were very much exaggerated. A person who we heard died of it, died of an entirely different thing. The bills of mortality show the city to be perfectly healthy, not a single death from any fever or any catching disease.[200]

Anna and her family went down today and the *beau-père* also. They were very anxious for us to go today too but I could not get ready without doing all my packing and making all my arrangements on Sunday (as we only determined positively to go on Saturday evening after the mail came) and I felt too superstitious to begin my trip under such auspices. We set off tomorrow and in addition to several servants who we are going to treat to a trip to town to see relations, I have to take charge of Mrs. James Sinkler's eldest daughter. It will be somewhat of a bore on me while I am in town but "que voulez vous." Her mother asked me to and I could not refuse. We are all to stay at the Charleston Hotel. It will make it very pleasant for Anna to be there too and have her rooms adjoining. The *beau-père* too takes down his carriage which will be very useful. I hope Catharine Hayes will not leave before we get down.[201] She was giving concerts in Charleston last week and staying at the Charleston Hotel too.

The weather is delightful, so mild that for the last two days we have not needed fires. Very different from last week when it was so bitter cold that I could not have enjoyed myself in Charleston which is a very cold bleak place when it is cold. I shall figure extensively in my new things. Mama's head dress too. How had I best wear it, with the ends down or fastened up. I have only worn my new silk three times in the country, so it is quite fresh, as is also my hat in which I mean to put four violets and get strings to match.[202]

I received your very agreeable letter by Saturdays mail for which many thanks. Keep directing of course to Vances Ferry, for we shall only be gone about a week and by the time you get this we will be back again. I received also a letter from Mrs. Rolands saying that Mr. Rolands had been ordered to the Receiving ship and could get no substitute and that she had been suffering from such bad colds all winter that they would not be able to pay us the visit. I shall not break my heart over it.

We have had as usual few incidents this week. On Tuesday we had quite a large dinner party, mostly ladies. A very nice dinner—Vermicelli Soup, Boiled Turkey, Celery sauce, Bouilli Ham, 2d course, Wild Ducks, Dessert, Omelette Souffle, Charlotte Polonaise, Plum Pudding, etc. etc.

On Saturday we went to the Bible Class which was extremely interesting. I heard there that Mr. Converse has resigned his rectorship of the church at Stateburg. It is a pity after being there 26 years. It is owing I believe principally to some difficulty about the new church symbolism. Both Mr. and Mrs. Converse are in Charleston now so I will see them and hear the particulars.[203]

Lizzie and Wharton are quite well and of course full of the approaching trip. Lizzie is attending to her doll's wardrobe and Bud is trying to think of something sensible to buy with his money. Lizzie says tell Party Cousin Alices book is beautiful. Give my best love to all. Yours ever, E. S.

With the advent of spring, Emily is busy foraging through the countryside for roots and cuttings. She was an avid and talented gardener. While her passion was roses, she was equally successful with irises, jonquils, and other spring bulbs. Charles has provided her with a gardener and a carpenter, and she is relishing the restoration of an old garden whose design, or footprint, still existed, even though the plants were overgrown and old.

❧   ❧   ❧

Mr. Henry Wharton
Belvidere, February 23d, 1852

Do you not feel touched dear Hen with the promptitude with which I answer your letter? Do I suffer one mail to elapse before responding? No. Scarcely has the Messenger departed who brought your letter when behold me at my desk pen in hand. It must be conceded however, that tho your letters are tardy in arriving, they are very pleasant when they do arrive. I was much amused at the dessertation on Sugar Plums—by the mail which brought one of your "Angels visits" arrived one from Mary which was very interesting as usual; also to Wistar Party Invitations which the Recipients were duly gratified at receiving and sorry that they could not accept. Wharton was much confused at the Card. He read it out thus: "Mister Party." Oh said he does Party invite his company so! Mister Party! I request that the Answers be preserved and sent to me by the first good opportunity.

It seems strange to hear of snows in the letters I receive. We have had here for more than a fortnight the most delightful spring like weather, weather in which one feels comfortable both out of doors and in. I am taking advantage of it to improve the place. The ground has been so hard frozen all winter that until now any attempts at gardening have been useless but now I am going at it in earnest. I wish I had you here to consult with. Charles has given me a carpenter to work under my direction for a month, and a person to garden so my hands are full. The old garden is to be restored. It is now nearly forty years since it was tended but it contains many shrubs yet. I have arranged a small garden on each side of the front steps which is to be enclosed with an iron fence, and is to contain the choicest specimens. I have already some very fine roses which have taken so well that they will bloom this spring— The Glory of France, Groille, Harrisonian de Brunnius, Cloth of Gold, and Souvenir de Malmaison. This last is the most splendid Rose you ever saw—as large as a coffee cup, and so firm and rich. I am foraging all through the country for roots and cuttings.

The chief amusement of our household at present is a recruit we have. It being quite clear to everybody that Roberty Bobs province is the Stable yard, and he having announced to me that he could not bear waiting in the house, we have decided to let him remain in his element and to make up the *beau-père* has sent us over a boy of about ten years old who is of a very genteel stock being the Grandson of Maid Lucy. His former life has been devoted to the care of a baby of his mother and until last week he never was in a gentleman's house. He was crazy to come to us and the *beau-père* says had been worrying him for a year to let him come and live with Mas' Charles. You never saw anything to equal his confidentialness and intimacy with every member of the household. The mistakes he makes are very amusing. A day or two ago I sent him into the parlour for something and a few minutes afterwards observed him searching about the front Piazza. On enquiring what he was about he answered "I am hunting about for the Parlour." Yesterday he came to me beaming, telling me he had been planting trees in my garden for me! On examination, I found that he had spent the best part of the morning in sticking worthless little branches of trees in the garden beds.

I never heard yet if you or any of the family heard Catharine Hayes sing when she was in Philadelphia. I missed her by only a few days in Charleston which was a great disappointment. She was not much liked here but there are but very few real judges in the place. We were quite pleased with the singing of two Miss Slomans, teachers. They are English with really fine voices, well cultivated, but ugly to a degree of which you can form no possible conception. The word ugly cannot convey a proper idea of their appearance, for they are by nature frightful and assist nature by their efforts to the last point. They act through each opera in such a style! Imagine them personifying Edgar Ravecesind and Lucia with all the starts, jumps, stares, shakes of the head they could assume. But I cannot describe them to you. Suffice it to say that I was the only person in the room who saw them for the first time, suffered the most intense agony in endeavouring to restrain my laughter, seated as I was in full view of them. And yet one of them (whom I called Eve from her apparent great surprise at every thing in life, especially at the sound of the harp and piano and her own voice) was engaged for a short time to a very respectable young man in Charleston. This family found it out in an amusing way. On Christmas day one of the House Servants who had been told to go out and take a Holiday, returned quite early in the day. On one of the family enquiring the cause of his speedy return, he answered: "I come home disgust, fair disgust; I meet Master Robert do drive out; such a low life, dirty gal, that I jest turn short round and come home, done up." They are just the characters for Dickens to get hold of. One of them informed me when I complimented her on her singing that "music was such a sunny thing." Imagine my feelings when Anna and I sang at knowing that "Eve" was behind me starting and shaking her head and exclaiming, as if she heard music for the first time. I really have said a great deal more about the Slomans than I intended.

We have had company between here and Eutaw all the last week. While they were at Eutaw we stayed over there for two or three days. One of the guests, Dr. Porcher (not Julius), the most reading and cultivated man between here and Charleston brought me a treat in the shape of a large pile of French Books.[204] I have not had time to look at them yet but he says they are delightful and perfectly comme il faut. Anna, Ellen DuBose and myself took a ride on horseback yesterday which was charming, owing principally to poor Ellen's being mounted on Tackey who was worse than ever about gates and ditches. We went 8 miles and passed I suppose at least 20 gates and at each there would be a scene.

Give my best love to Mama and tell her I will write to her next week. I don't like her being so much in her room. She can't be as well as she was when we left in October. Tell Papa Charles is anxious to know if he received from Mr. Simons at the beginning of the month some money. Mr. Simons sent it, but not a word have we heard of the receipt of it. It is a long time since Papa has written to me. Tell Mary write on. The children are very well and send a great deal of love. Lizzie has always great intentions about writing but her time is so much taken up with her multitudinous little pursuits that she seems never to accomplish her intentions. Ever dear Hen, yours affly, ES

Discourse, visits, and marriages between North and South were very common. Emily's letters are full of examples of Draytons, Sinklers, Middletons, and Trapiers visiting Philadelphia, and of Sargents and Ammens visiting Charleston. Emily and Charles's political and cultural views were undoubtedly shaped by the fact that they read Philadelphia newspapers and London magazines and papers. They also visited Philadelphia on a yearly basis and there were exposed to the full range of abolitionist views and liberal political sentiment. Both were undoubtedly distraught by the increasing rancor of regional politics and race. Charles, who fought in the Mexican War, served in the U.S. Navy for fourteen years, and had many northern Navy friends, must have felt substantial loyalty to the Union.

Emily mentions in this next letter how she minced words in order not to create an unpleasant scene. In an earlier letter Emily had stated that she had given up politics as they were not conducive to peace of mind or good temper.

ᴥ ᴥ ᴥ

21
Miss Mary Wharton
Belvidere, March, 1852

My dear Mary,

I feel rather discomposed as to my writing arrangements at present as we have had company all day and it is only now, late in the evening that I can "take up my pen." I am afraid I shall have to write rather a hurried letter for the mail instead of going at 3 o'clock on Tuesday, leaves much earlier in the day and one has therefore very little chance to write on Mail day. I always write on Mondays and I am glad to hear the letters arrive punctually. We seem to have hit on good days for writing, for yours comes invariably on Saturday evening, so I can answer any questions on Monday. I was much relieved to find by your last that Mama is rather better. She is on my mind constantly. I am surprised to hear that you have still such cold weather, for here the winter is completely broken up and everything wears a spring like air. We have no fire in the house except early in the morning and late in the evening.

As usual I have very little to chronicle in the way of happenings altho we have had company several times in the course of the past week. On Tuesday we paid a visit to "the Rocks" to some strangers staying there, two Miss Rogers from Rhode Island, very "banal" girls who are paying their first visit to the South (to some relations in Charleston) and think it necessary to be in ecstasy over everything. They admired everything, very much in the way that Coleman in his book on England did, which made me feel rather crooked. One of them said to me "Of course you like the South much better than the North." I was on the point of giving her a very haughty answer, when I saw two or three pairs of eyes fixed upon me, watching what I would say, so I swallowed my feelings and made a decent and pretty answer about "comparisons," etc., etc.

I gained something from my visit however, for I learned a beautiful way of making frames for engravings, pictures, etc. These frames are made of the burrs of which Mama's little basket is made, arranged in such a way as to make the frame look like a beautiful carved Rosewood frame. Your mouth would water over it. The work is not at all troublesome or difficult.

On Wednesday we dined at Pond Bluff to meet Mrs. Lesesne who is on a visit there. Do you remember a very large child of hers when you were here. I well remember your paying a visit there and being struck with it. She has now the very largest baby I ever saw. When it was an hour old it weighed 17 pounds and has been going on ever since growing in proportion, until now at 8 months it is the size of a child of two or three years.

On Saturday we paid a visit to old Mrs. Marions, an old lady who lives at some distance from here and who is celebrated for her Garden. It is worth seeing. She lives alone and devotes nearly all her time to it, and altho it is too early yet for much of a display, yet the thousands of bulbous roots all in full flower made it look very gay. I supplied myself well with roots and cuttings of different plants. One thing I know you would think pretty is the Rose Hedge. It is of the Daily Rose which is green here all through the winter. It is kept cut and trimmed to a certain size and is the most luxuriant thing you can imagine. I am planning one here.

Yesterday to church where Charles officiated. He is quite used to it now and gets through his "duties" as naturally as possible. I hope to be able to attend some of Mr. Gadsden's lectures during Lent, tho they are at Pineville which is 20 miles from here and rather too long a drive to go and return in one day.

We had made all our arrangements to leave here on Friday or Saturday for a visit to Middle St. John's—the neighbourhood about 18 miles from here. A visit we have promised for a long time, but we have given up the plan, now that we hear the Measles have just broken out on all the plantations in that Neighbourhood. The children escaped getting it from their Charleston Trip and I don't want to put them in the way of it again. They are perfectly well now, looking remarkably healthy.

I enclose you the letter of your Indian friend which I had put away carefully. I was very sorry and so were the children to hear of her death and should like very much to see the sketch of her life. I hope they will publish it in the *Recorder*. By the bye what is the meaning of the Reports we have heard lately about Bishop Doane?[205] Pray give me the Rights of the affair in your next. The *Recorder* had a long article on the subject last week, but still, I should like to know the public opinion on the affair. I must hope that he will be able to come out untarnished, and there is a great deal in Bishop Doane you can't help liking! What is he accused of? Anything besides extravagance in money matters? Bishop Gadsden has been ill lately, and many fear he will not last long. He is quite an old man and very worn out.

I must now come to a conclusion. Write on tho' I must say Miss Wharton, your letters have not been as long as usual for the last two or three times. Give my love to the sweetest little mother and tell her "I feel impressed" as Cop used to say that the spring is going to do her a wonderful deal of good. Tell her she must behave herself tho. Tell Party he has not written me for an age, except little lines on business. I demand therefore a long letter. Tell him that in looking over some old letters I came across on from him (written three years ago) of eight pages. I don't get any such now from him. Yours ever, E. S.

Levy's dry goods store was the source of Emily's silks and muslins for dresses for herself, Anna, and the children. Mary Wharton shopped for patterns as well as cloth, sending it south to Emily and Anna. Ladies' dresses were voluminous, consuming up to ten yards of cloth. Emily followed the styles, trying to keep abreast of what was being worn in Philadelphia through her ladies' magazines such as *Godey's, Graham's,* and *Peterson's,* as well as newspaper columns. The Wharton family was very much involved with both the Library Company and the Historical Society of Pennsylvania. Thomas Isaac Wharton and Henry Wharton were both on the board of the Library Company. Thomas Isaac Wharton founded the Historical Society of Pennsylvania in his home at 130 South Sixth Street. So it is very likely that the reference to taking up a subscription for a new reading room in the following letter refers to one of these two distinguished libraries.

❧ ❧ ❧

22
Miss Mary Wharton
Belvidere, March 15th, 1852

My dear Mary,

Many thanks for your letter which arrived safely on Saturday evening. The patterns gave great satisfaction, so much so, that Charles was keen for my getting four dresses of the sort but I thinking that, rather too much of one good thing, am contented with getting one. Will you therefore get me 10 yards of the blue and Anna 10 yards of the brown. I enclose the two patterns. At the same time that you get these dresses, please get me some patterns of whatever they have pretty at Levy's in the way of Spring and Summer best dresses and send them on in your next letter. You know the spring begins here so soon that one wants thin dresses in April and I have actually nothing to begin on. I am really sorry to give you so much trouble about this matter, especially as

I know you don't like the pattern part of it, but que voulez vous! I must throw myself on your good nature. I enclose in this Ten dollars. After paying for my dress and Anna's there will be a remainder of 4.66.

Give my love to Papa and tell him, I wish he would subscribe to the *Bulletin* for me for three months, the country paper, which appears three times a week, as I see by the advertisement. I have received one of his sending, and am scandalized to think that the Newspaper postage should be so high. Of course the *Bulletin* Editors will now send the paper themselves. I intend the 4.66 for payment of the subscription. If we continue to like it I will begin again next fall to subscribe for it.

Apropos to Newspapers, I saw in a Charleston paper the notice of the death of a "S. P. Pleasants, Esq., stockbroker, who died suddenly in Philadelphia on the 8th." I can hardly suppose it could be Caroline's husband as your letter was written (part of it) on the 9th.

I wish you could send me my dress (the blue cambric) by the first available opportunity you may hear of. I should think it might be made into so small a bundle that a very obliging and yielding individual could be induced to take it. Perhaps M. Cardeza may come! She wrote me a few days ago, saying she was very anxious to pay me a visit and that Mr. Trapier was to leave Philadelphia immediately after Lent and had offered to escort her. Of course I wrote to urge her to do so and arranged in my letter the ways and means for her to get here (I know you would be very much amused at my letter by the bye). I should really be delighted if she could come, tho it would be only for a very short time, as Mr. Trapier is to be absent but two Sundays.

While you are enduring snowstorms etc, things are progressing here to a remarkably early spring. Lilacs, Roses, and many other spring things are in full bloom and the only fear now is, that there will come a "cold snap" and kill everything. We have actually not had a fire in the house since I last wrote, and it is so mild that we always keep a window open in the day. The nights however are cool enough for a blanket. Among the spring things, Shad have come. I do wish you could have some of the abundance. The *beau-père* sent out a fisherman on Friday who brought back eight and one on Saturday who brought four. All very fine ones too.

Tell Frank, Charles received his letter by Saturday's mail and means to answer it. We are delighted with the plan of the new Reading Room. It cannot fail to do a great deal of good. Charles read aloud the circular to me, when Wharton who I did not know was standing by, exclaimed in a most earnest tone, "I will give my dollar to it!" However,

I persuaded him out of it, as he has given away a great deal lately. He has improved in every thing, reads extremely well in any book and gets on well in every study.

We would go up to the Mannings in a few days were it not for the long journey and this being a very important time of the year for Charles to be at home. I don't think Eliza will be able to come down this spring for they seem to have one trouble on another. There was an epidemic on their place this winter, a sort of Pneumonia or inflammation of the lungs, hardly one of the servants escaped, several died and the rest had severe illnesses. Lately two of Mrs. Manning sisters died, one that they were all extremely attached to died last week, and now Mrs. Manning herself, who has been delicate all winter, is so seriously sick that they are extremely uneasy about her. Eliza is only thirty miles from Eutaw and yet in a year's time she can only manage to be three weeks at her father's. During the epidemic they had once but one servant (out of 15) in the house. I must stop now as I want to write a few lines to Mama. Ever thine, E. S.

I enclose the Receipts for Mrs. Coleman which I wish you would get to her. I found that the Tidy Receipt took up a sheet of paper, and nearly two hours to copy.[206] P. S. Oh my Henry!

XIV

The Charleston Races, Spring 1853

IT IS ELEVEN MONTHS before we hear from Emily again. During the eleven-month interval Emily would have returned to Philadelphia for her annual late summer/early fall voyage home. She would then have come back to the plantations, to Belvidere and Eutaw, for the Christmas holidays. Christmas would have been lively with the slaves dancing on the front piazza of Eutaw and the *beau-père* passing a dram of good French brandy to the oldest. There would have been a wonderful Christmas tree with candles and many presents around it.

When we pick up the story again it is February, and the races in Pineville and Charleston are in the offing. The *beau-père* is racing the Eutaw star, Jeff Davis, and with great luck. However, his entry Lot was disqualified from the Jockey Club purse because the jockey failed to strap on his weights.

Emily is anticipating a wonderful visit from Henry and Frank. She is disappointed that her father has not come to visit. Emily is also delighted to be in the age of the personal telegraph dispatch. She has had word from Frank that his ship has been delayed. It is apparent that, with the telegraphic dispatch, communication which had been a seven-day affair was now instantaneous.

Religion was a pervasive element in the Sinkler life. Sunday was strictly observed. The Sinklers read religious magazines and attended Bible classes. Emily's letters show that Charles was very involved with the administration of the church. He was a vestryman and also a warden at the Rocks. Emily, herself, and her fellow ladies were also quite involved in decorating and maintaining the Rocks church. Emily notes that the ladies of the church have even purchased a new melodeon. It is apparent that the ladies' altar guild of the Rocks church was active and involved in church affairs. Emily was actively involved in ladies' organizations, including benevolent societies, altar guilds, and sewing and craft circles. This companionship and association with other women was an important element in the lives of rural women.

❧ ❧ ❧

Mr. Thomas I. Wharton
Belvidere February 8th, 1853

My dear Party,

It really does seem strange that it should so happen that you and Mama should actually be the only ones of the family in Philadelphia and that not any of the four absent ones should be together. I hoped to have heard from Henry by Saturday's mail but was disappointed. I have not heard from him since he set off on his travels. Is it not almost time for me to be looking out for him? I wish you would send me all the letters which have been received from him. From Mary I hope I shall hear tonight, as it is now a fortnight since her last letter was received here. As to the other absent member, we have had quite a disappointment to day. According to Frank's account we expected them to arrive in Savannah on Friday evening and be in Charleston on Saturday morning. We therefore wrote them that the carriage would be in readiness at our station on the following Tuesday (today). Yesterday morning there was much excitement sending off the carriage, which we did the day before so that they could have the horses perfectly fresh the next day, also the cart for their baggage. Fisher (the coachman) provided with a basket of nice wafer cakes for them to beguile the long drive with. Fortunately the *beau-père* came up from town yesterday. We went over to Eutaw to meet him and the first thing he did was to hand me a Telegraphic Dispatch, which announced that the party would not arrive in Charleston until 12 o'clock on Tuesday. The dispatch was from Frank, dated Savannah, Feb. 6th 8:45 p.m. and it reached Charleston at 8:46 p.m. only one minute in traveling. I cannot imagine the reason of the delay, except that the *Georgia* was late getting in to Savannah. I see by the paper that she did not leave Philadelphia until Thursday. I wonder they took the Savannah line! The land route is so much improved and is so much better for winter traveling and if they wanted a sea voyage it would have been much better to have taken the N.Y. Line for the Steamer which left N.Y. at midnight on Wednesday arrived in Charleston very early on Saturday morning. The *beau-père* met our carriage and cart and turned them back, which we were very glad of for the railroad station offers too many temptations to servants. I have just sent off the cavalcade again and hope the trip will be a successful one this time and that they will come up tomorrow. The children were very much disappointed but Lizzie is consoled by thinking she has time now to finish her arch, which is to be after a design from the *London News*.

It is a pity they could not have arrived in Charleston during the races. The *beau-père* had his carriage down, but brought it up yesterday, one of the horses quite sick. He was successful at the Races one day. "Jeff Davis" his famous horse with which he had taken great pains and which was "ruled out" is not allowed to run because the rider had forgotten to put on his belt of shot to make him even in weight with the other riders.[207] While the *beau-père* was at the Charleston Hotel, quite a mistake arose about a certain J. Wharton from Philadelphia, who arrived there by the Savannah boat. He was taken for Frank.

We expect a large party in two or three days, not only all the Mannings but some friends of the Governors who are coming with them: Dr. Thomas of Baltimore, Mr. Gordon, and Mr. Turner of Virginia. Dr. Thomas married a sister of Mr. Basil Gordon and Mary when she was in Baltimore mentioned their house as being the handsomest there. Mr. Gordon is a very rich man, cousin of Mr. John M. Gordon and a widower having married a sister of Mrs. John Mannings. He has a very fine name, Douglas Hamilton Gordon, but I believe in appearance does not come up to it. The *beau-père* met them in Charleston last week. He is as busy as we have been in getting Eutaw house ready for so large a company. William and Anna will be up on Thursday too.

Very little has happened since I last wrote. Saturday's mail brought me no letters, but several papers, among others, *Barnum's Illustrated Paper.* Are not some of the likenesses rich![208]

There were actually only 2 persons in church on Sunday besides Charles and myself, owing to its looking like rain and many families either being in town or having sent their horses to the R. R. Mr. Dehon omitted the sermon, but the service, melodeon and all went on as regularly as if the church were filled. He waited until 12 o'clock for more people and Mr. Mazyck Porcher one of the 2 kept up a lively conversation with me from his side of the church, on current affairs, much to the edification of Mr. Dehon in the vestry room. He informed me among other things that as soon as our friends arrived, he intended coming to Belvidere to spend the day and expected us to do the same at his place, Mexico. Being of a soft and susceptible nature, added to mature years, I have no doubt he will make it a point to fall in love with Mary Paul.

We were sorry to hear from Mr. Dehon that Mr. Potter has declined the call of assistant minister for although he is very worthy and rich in some things. It appears he has had a call to a charge near his own plantation. We are now on the look out again for another assistant minister and I am afraid will not find it easy as the principal object is the preaching to the coloured population which all do not feel "called to."

The ladies of the church have certainly done very well in 1852 in the way of church improvement. They have added a large chancel, communion table, chairs, pulpit, and reading desk, chancel carpet and coverings for the pulpit, etc., and a complete set of new pews, (the old ones being very old and out of repair) a Melodeon, a church carpet and the church entirely painted inside. As I was one of the 9 or 10 ladies who did it all it came pretty heavy as you can imagine. However, I feel completely repaid by the improved appearance of everything. We contracted for the wood work with a person in the neighbourhood, one of the gentlemen of the congregation. I really think it a great pity that the same set of ladies cannot act as vestry-men for church matters would certainly prosper more. They have elected Charles warden and delegate. The convention will be in May and I believe Dr. Atkinson of Baltimore is the prominent candidate. I must now come to a conclusion with much love to Mama and the same from Charles and the children to both of you. Your loving daughter, E. S.

The *beau-père* died on June 8, 1853. The Sinkler family would have grieved terribly at his loss. He was the central "glue" for the Eutaw and Belvidere Sinkler family. He organized the wonderful excursions to Charleston. His horses were the focus of much of the excitement and betting for the Jockey Club races. Without him life must have seemed drab. He put on the wonderful Christmas parties at Eutaw. He is buried in the St. Stephen's graveyard. On his gravestone is the following: "The Angel of the Lord encampeth round about them that fear him and delivereth them."

XV

Life on Sullivan's Island, Spring 1854

THE LETTERS GROW FEW and far between. It is twelve months since the last letter, and again Emily is back at Belvidere and looking forward to the races in Charleston. Mary has now married Mr. Bland and is living abroad in France. Emily mentions that she had recently left Philadelphia, so it is possible that the Sinkler family extended their stay in Philadelphia so that Emily could deliver her new baby there.

In October of 1853 Emily had her fourth child, Charles St. George Sinkler. It had been five years since the death of Arabella, and Emily and Charles were obviously thrilled with the new baby. Lizzie and Wharton were busy with a new tutor, Miss Dawes.

The Sinklers had rented a house on Washington Lane in Germantown for their visit in the summer of 1853. Now they are negotiating for the purchase of a small house in Germantown but want it to be big enough to hold the entire Wharton and Sinkler families.

There is some indication that the Sinkler family was now spending substantial amounts of time in Philadelphia. It is not surprising, given the difficulty of finding a suitable home for the long, hot summer months. It also provides an explanation for the fact that among Emily and Charles's five children, three would decide to make their homes in Philadelphia. Lizzie, Wharton, and Caroline Sidney Sinkler (Carrie, born in 1860) would live in Philadelphia, while Mary Wharton (born 1857) and Charlie would live in South Carolina.

Mr. Thomas I. Wharton
Belvidere February 18th, 1854

My dear Papa,

   I am afraid you think that quite a length of time has elapsed since my last letter. And I have to discipline myself and promise not to let it happen again. The fact is that the Hares arrived just after I sent off my last and as I meant my next to be to Mary and intended making it very long. I never until today could find time to finish it for what with Mrs. Hare's sickness and a thousand other things, I have not had a minute to myself.

Pray send this letter to Mary by the very first steamer after you receive it. I am afraid she will think I have been very neglectful of late, but it has been unavoidable. The first two sheets of the letter are merely an account of our journey here. A recapitulation of what you have already heard. The last sheet beginning at page 9 gives an account of our proceedings since we have been at Belvidere and which you may like to read. I hope I shall receive a letter from her tonight. I have only received a short note from you and a letter from Sidney since we left you and have now written 5 letters and a note, so don't complain too much of me. I have however received a *Bulletin,* some Children's papers and 2 Saturday papers from you. The two latter seem much better than I expected and I would like to continue taking them. Pray enquire if we owe them anything. I don't remember when we began to subscribe. As we have subscribed to the *Herald,* I don't care about the *Bulletin* for the Saturday paper will contain enough sectional affairs.

The Hares went this morning after a visit of 10 days. We did our best to make it agreeable to them by dinner parties etc., etc., and I hope Robert's time passed pleasantly, but I am afraid Mrs. Hare cannot look back to her visit with much pleasure for she was suffering with Asthma nearly all the time. Robert was extremely pleasant and agreeable.

Our various chests, boxes, groceries, Piano etc, etc. arrived safely the second day after The Hares got here with strange to say (for I never expect any letters or boxes to reach their journeys end) not an article hurt or missing. I was very glad to get them as you can imagine.

Lizzie and Wharton are busy at school with Miss Dawes, who professes to be delighted with everything about her and who has certainly improved very much in health since she has been here. Lizzie sends you a letter or note and both many messages which I must keep for my next at which time I will send copies of their Diaries. They are both perfectly well and as for Mr. Baby, he is so much grown that you would hardly know him. He has not had a moments indisposition and takes the greatest notice.[209] Tell Mama my cold is now quite well and I am thankful to say I have had no return of chill or fever. The Postboy is just ready to go so I must conclude now, but will write again by next Mail. Ever Thine, ES.

ᴥ   ᴥ   ᴥ

Mr. Thomas I. Wharton
Tradd Street, May 8th 1854

My dear Papa,

Your delightfully long letter to Charles and myself arrived on last Tuesday evening, just 10 days having elapsed since Charles had written to you on the subject of the G town purchase.[210] We are both much gratified to find that Mama and yourself are pleased with this decision and I trust that there will be a revival next summer of the happy days of Washington Lane. If you do succeed in getting a house before we come you must remember that it must be ample enough to accommodate the family of 150 Walnut St. as well as our family. Charles intends writing a note to you himself as a rejoinder to your letter, but I am afraid it will not be done in time for this package for he has gone down to the Island this morning to arrange matters prior to our removal.[211]

Our family circle was thrown into a state of delightful effervescence at the news of Henry's intention to pay us a visit. I mean to write him a special note this morning on the subject and hope you will not dissuade him from it. He must come as soon as possible. Now that you have thrown out the hope of your joining us at Saratoga[212] or some such place, when we make our Trip, we are also perfectly agog about that too and you may be sure we will keep you up to the point about it. It would be too delightful!

As you see by my date, we have arrived safely in Charleston. For the particulars of our journey I refer you to a letter to Mary which I am about to begin. We arrived on Saturday evening, all well, and were greeted by two very agreeable sights, namely the box and a letter in your handwriting, said letter containing one from Mary, and a note from you. (Apropos to Mary's letter, I cut out of this mornings *Courier* a paragraph concerning foreign letters, which may be a hint to you.) I have scarcely looked into the box enough to thank the different donors for their remembrances. However, the Herrings did not, I can assure you, allow themselves to be overlooked. They have arrived in good order and I believe have only damaged Jane's Parasol, and that can I hope be remedied. I am very much obliged to you for them and anticipate great pleasure in breakfasting off of them. I need not say how attractive and acceptable the sugar-plums are for you know of old how fond we are of them. They have been duly handed round but the greater part are reserved for private enjoyment on the Island. Many thanks also for the *London News,* etc. They will be a great treat too.

I am writing with one of the worst pens imaginable, so stiff that it makes my ideas perfectly so. It is well that the sheet is small. I mentioned in my last that Charles had heard of a Legacy left him by Mr. Seaman Deas. We have heard the amount, nothing very great but still something. The Will is as follows: 4/10ths of the whole property to go to the Sinklers, 3/10ths to the Lesesnes and the rest in annuities and small Legacies. Charles' share will be about $5,500, 5 thousand 5 hundred, which he will invest as soon as he receives.[213] I must conclude now having several other notes to write. Ever thine, ES.

P. S. We expect to move down on Wednesday

Sullivan's Island, May 30, 1854

My dear Papa,

Altho' I have nothing very particular to communicate, yet I do not like to let a longer period than a week elapse without giving you tidings of our goings on. During the past week I have to acknowledge the receipt of several missives from you, some newspapers, (one of them the *Bulletin*) and two envelopes, enclosing sundry letters from Mary accompanied by notes from yourself for all of which many thanks. Tell Henry I have also received from him several pamphlet periodicals which were very acceptable and I beg such favours may be kept up, not forgetting the *Brodeuse* from him and *Leslie's Fashion Monthly* from you, when they come. Also by the bye, do send me any *Illustrated News* or any papers you may have containing accounts of the marriage of the Emperor of Austria. I have seen no accounts of it as yet.[214]

I have not yet got through with the books and papers which came in the box, being on Henry's French Romances, which are very attractive and at the same time strictly comme il faut. By the bye, I did not tell you before of the sad fate of the Herring, from which we anticipated so much. They had to be treated alas, in a very ignoble manner, the voyage and close confinement not having at all agreed with them. I hope the hams had not the same fate! As you surmise there is no regular P.O. on the Island. Letters and Papers are brought down by the boat and deposited at a place called the Point-House where one sends for them.

Ours are brought to the house daily, by an Irishman named Scott, who is a factotum for this part of the Island. He is at the boat each time she arrives and brings up marketing or whatever freight his patrons may have to come up. He is quite a character and keeps three carts quite constantly employed. When I am going to have company to dinner, I get my marketing in Charleston, by means of Mrs. James Sinklers old cook. Otherwise tho' the market here is quite good enough, tho' the meat prices are high. Very nice fish can be bought at the Break-water, nearly in front of our house, daily at very moderate prices. A remarkably nice fish called the whiting and Sheeps-Heads are the most caught—crabs and shrimps in any quantity tho' I have refrained from getting any.

You would be perfectly surprised at the fineness and cheapness of the vegetables. I often say that you would not believe your eyes, were you to walk through the Charleston market as I did a few days ago. Every inch of ground near Charleston is now taken up with English and Northern truck farmers and since the last five years, their success has been wonderful. The white potatoes are really splendid and I am too provoked that there is no steamer running to Phil, for I want so much to send you a barrel. For 6 1/4 cents you can buy a vegetable dish full and each potato the size of a small orange. This springs crop of course. We have had very fine figs too.

I had a visit yesterday from Mrs. James Simons, a person who in general is of a very decided turn of mind incited thereunto by Mr. Simons' intended speedy return. It appears that Mr. Simons has gone with a friend, a Mr. Read, who promised faithfully to be absent a certain length of time, which time Mrs. Simons deems necessary for Mr. Simons recovery. On reaching Phila however, Mr. Read was seized with a fit of homesickness and insisted upon curtailing their journey very considerably—the cause I suppose of their hurrying through Phila—so quickly. Mrs. Simons is staying with one of the notabilities of the island, a certain Mr. Bond I'On. He is a very stout and large old gentleman over 70, the son of an English officer who married in Charleston, during the Revolutionary war. I'On is certainly not an English name however. Talking of notabilities, I hope you read an account of the proposed performances to take place at Mrs. Mowatts wedding. I think it exceeds anything I have ever heard. Among other things, the marriage ceremony was to be performed on a stage in the open air, to be erected in her fathers' garden, which was to be brilliantly illuminated—400 persons invited from N.Y. alone.

Mary's last letters have been very amusing. I hope she will go to England for I am sure a little English life would be very refreshing after the intense French scenes she has gone through lately. What troubles she has had with her servants! But it seems to me she turns them away too easily for merely gossiping. What queer people and unfit people to go to Europe, while we nice and fit people stay at home. However I will not be personal about the last departures. I hope Tom Balshs' health is not seriously affected! Poor fellow! It must have been very sad for him to leave his wife and go to Paris!

One anecdote and I must conclude. You have I dare say heard of Isaac in our establishment, a coloured boy of 11, who does all sorts of odd things. On Sunday he showed Lizzie some candy which he had bought, whereupon she informed him that it was not right to buy things on Sunday. "Oh, but Miss Lizzie, said he, you know I have not joined the church yet, so I can buy as much candy as I like on Sunday."

Tell Henry the best way for him to come will be to take the Tennessee from Baltimore, With love to all, Ever your aff, E.S.

XVI
Winter 1855

IT IS EIGHT MONTHS before we hear from Emily again. In the interval she has likely spent the entire summer and early fall in Philadelphia, where she and Charles intended to purchase a house in Germantown. She is again anticipating her return to Philadelphia and is excited about the house in Germantown, but it seems that instead of purchasing, they rented. Germantown was a delightful suburb of Philadelphia, and apparently all enjoyed spending the summer there for the "season." Emily notes the need to be frugal as the Crimean War has played havoc with the price of cotton.

Emily tells of receiving huge bags of mail. None of this correspondence has been saved. Her own letters often numbered over ten pages, giving some idea of the voluminous nature of her correspondence. It is also interesting to note that she continues to purchase her kettles and other necessities of life from Philadelphia and that her father handled the bills and accounts. Likewise she continued to rely on the Whartons for copies of such periodicals as *Household Words* and the *Brodeuse*.

Mr. Thomas I. Wharton
Belvidere Jan 16th 1855

My dear Party,[215]

As you have doubtless heard, the mail difficulties have all been happily adjusted and Charleston has even been a gainer by the storm, for she now has 2 Northern mails a day instead of 1. Saturday evening brought us the good results of the reconciliation in the shape of all the back mails. The Mail Rider arrived at Eutaw nearly weighed down by the weight of the Mailbag and for Belvidere alone there were 18 letters and 24 newspapers. By the way I must correct Frank's idea that the latter do not reach us. They always do, tho generally by the mail after they are due. Many thanks for those you have sent. Willis' writings are always amusing and apropos.

Of all the letters received that evening nothing could come up to that containing the announcement of Mary's visit. I cannot say how perfectly delighted I am! I have just sent her via Charleston a letter of congratulations, etc. If you or any one is writing soon do mention that I have just sent her an overjoyed 10 paged letter. As you cannot accommodate all at 150 Walnut St. it will be better for me and mine to stay at Frank's and I shall write to him to that effect. I hope he will move before May. We are getting very anxious about our Germantown House. What prospect is there for us now? Charles says he hopes you will be able to get one for $400 for the season. This year it is very necessary for us to be prudent for cotton is in a sad way, which is very hard on those who have made 1/2 crops all through this wretched war.

The Maddock Bill is right—Charles thanks you for attending to Miss Scott's affairs. Lizzie and Wharton were delighted with their letters which also were some older people—Charlie is droller than ever and you would be pleased to see how hearty he looks. I am afraid he has a very jovial turn. The first sound of music sets him dancing and curtseying. As to Murphy and Y's bill, of course you will have to pay it as it is, tho' the second kettle referred to by the "Irish Girl" was an Iron one which came. Well, I must conclude now having several other letters to write, Write soon to your loving, E.S.

❧ ❧ ❧

Belvidere, January 29th, 1855

Thank you dear Hen for the last Number of *Household Words*. I don't know what you think of *North & South*,[216] but I like it exceedingly and am very anxious for "man" as the Baby says. I think all the characters are extremely well drawn and hardly know in the last Number which chapter is the most interesting. I found it very hard work to keep from reading it on Sunday (yesterday) having begun it late on Saturday night.

We had one of those country bugbears, a rainy Sunday—Imagine a steady, pouring rain beginning at 9 in the morning and continuing for 24 hours without a seconds intermission—no leaving the house for anyone and only one religious paper! We were singing hymns in the library in the afternoon when a scene occurred which any one would have been amused with. You have heard of the Baby's great turn for dancing—well he entered, during a very solemn tune and at once began to dance, sometimes ducking down very low then turning round and round and all the time keeping time with one foot. I hope he will not outgrow this accomplishment before you see him, for it is perfectly irresistible.

Thank you for your nice letter relating to the Hanson House—the great point appears to me to be, can we do better? There seems to be a great dearth of places; at least of available ones. One more thank and that is for the *Brodeuse* which arrived in good order. By the bye what is the amount of my indebtedness to you for that valuable periodical for the ensuing year?[217]

We are all jogging on here in a worthy un-interesting style—one day being pretty much like its predecessor. The children, I think, improve under Miss Scott, who is a very good conscientious girl. Lizzie makes steady progress with her music, tho' she always shows very poorly when she plays for anyone. You would be surprised to see how composed she is on horseback! After the first day she indignantly repelled the proposal to have a check rein between her horse and her fathers. And I am sorry to say that it requires great art to persuade Charlie off a horse and then he looks down and sullen. I am so different about horses! Wharton cares much less for riding than the other two.

I was surprised to find that you did not notice in your letter the great fact of Mary's proposed coming. I can scarcely trust myself to count too surely upon it. Ask Papa if he has sent me a letter from her lately? It is now nearly 3 weeks since I have had one. Nothing since the note in K Tilghman's letter announcing her coming. I sent a letter for her which please give Papa. Do write soon again dear Hen. You must not judge of the acceptableness of your letters by the sort of answers I send. If I could I would make them more interesting, but the truth is I have not "de quoi." And now with love to Papa and Mama, believe me to be, Ever thine, E.S. P.S. Please tell Frank he will receive something from me by next mail.

Belvidere, April 3rd, 1855

My dear Hen,

I sent you last week a slight acknowledgement of the impression your epistolary favours have made upon me and wish I could today do full justice to them, and thus give you an encouragement to continue. But alas, as the cherubim's said the "de quoi" is wanting. In these parts the weather is pretty much all one has to write about and as I know that is a matter on which you are supremely indifferent, one has not even that resource to fall back upon.

We are all disappointed that the death of the Czar[218] has produced no more peaceful result. I am afraid too that there is trouble brewing between England and France. In fact the plot seems to thicken all round.

From the last accounts there are several more names with whom it will not do for Charlie to twit Godfrey with, for instance Lucan and Forey. It will be very funny to see those little fellows together. I am teaching Charlie to call Godfrey's name but he does not get any farther than "Concon." The fact is it is a name which one cannot abbreviate. Charlie is far behind his transatlantic cousin in the "gift of the gab" and is by no means so fond of books etc.[219] Music and dancing are his specialties and I wish you could have seen a little incident a day or two ago. Charles went through the parlour to the piazza to speak to some one and Charlie paddled after him full speed. Just as he gained the door which was ajar and had grasped it in one hand, Lizzie struck up a polka on the piano. He immediately arrested and began ducking down and dancing with all his body, keeping time with his head and feet and holding onto the door with one hand.

Did I tell you of the engagement of Fitzsimmons? The fiancée is neither pretty nor particularly young, but they say is clever and cultivated. These two last qualifications did not shine forth when I saw her lately, but still it may be so. She appeared to me to be in very bad health. The fact is there are some singular attendant circumstances to the engagement which are too long for a letter. I don't think it was a love match at first with him tho' he is trying very hard to get up to the point and writes very happily on his prospects—both his family and hers are delighted with the match.

Julius Porcher came here a few afternoons ago in his Philadelphia Phaeton which I believe you ordered for him at Watsons. It is really beautiful and very stylish. Julius is in statu quo and will probably remain there the rest of his life. The people in Charleston are still talking of "Mr. Craft's marriage." Mr. Craft was a bachelor of 40 or upwards, rich, pleasant and given to entertaining and withal a sort of "Beau" of Mrs. King—tho' I believe an unwilling one. Well he has married lately a respectable young lady of a suitable age and determined to decline any intimate acquaintance with Mrs. King. He therefore invited her sister but not herself to the wedding whereupon ensued many ridiculous scenes and notes about all of which I will cause you to laugh when I come on.

I enclose you a note from Lizzie and one from me to the Party. Tell the Marty the children were delighted with her notes which arrived by last mail. Don't forget you owe Wharton one. He is improving every day. I wonder whether letters will be dropped in the dead letter office. According to the new regulation [they will be] if they have only one stamp on them and are a little over weight. I think that would be a very hard case. I shall put 2 stamps on this for fear. Do write soon again to your affy, E.S. P.S. Tell Frank he can have this piece for the Recorder as a lesson to teachers.

XVII

The Coming of War, and the Civil War, 1855–1865

UNDOUBTEDLY THERE WERE LETTERS after the last letter of 1855. Emily and Charles continued to live at Belvidere. There were to be two more children, Mary Wharton Sinkler, born April 25, 1857, and Caroline Sidney Sinkler (nicknamed Carrie), born April 23, 1860. The war years were traumatic ones for Emily and her family. There were also deaths that would have been devastating to Emily. On April 17, 1856, William Henry Sinkler, who was only thirty-seven years old and married to Anna, died. He was buried at the Rocks church graveyard. Then on April 7, 1856, Emily's beloved Papa, or Party as she called him, died.

Wharton, who was only seventeen, had enlisted in the Charleston Light Dragoons. He and his cousin Wade Manning were stationed for many months in the lines of defense of Charleston. When the Dragoons were ordered to Virginia, the younger members of the company, including Wharton, were transferred to Company B, Second South Carolina Cavalry. Captain Chestnut commanded this company. The South Carolina Historical Society has ten letters from Wharton Sinkler to Emily. These letters are full of love and appreciation for the boxes of provisions that Emily and Lizzie sent him. Emily and Charles also sent a servant, Mingo Rivers, to care for young Wharton during his various battle encampments, first in Charleston, then in North Carolina, and finally during the last winter of the war in Virginia, where he was captured and paroled.

Charles did not fight in the war. His loyalties were likely divided because of his lengthy years of service in the United States Navy and his war service in the Mexican-American War. Lizzie recounts the following actions which also indicate divided loyalties: "After the fall of Charleston, my father called up the plantation and told them they had been proclaimed free by Lincoln, but they had better stay quietly in their comfortable homes. He also told them he intended to divide among them most of his provisions, which he did. This, of course, was considered quite quixotic by his neighbours."[220]

Charles's feelings of ambiguity were underscored when a delegation of Union troops from Admiral Dahlgren, who commanded the Union Navy in Charleston, paid him a visit. Lizzie described the scene: "It was a beautiful Sunday in March that I walked out onto the piazza to accompany Papa and Mamma to church . . . when I could hardly believe my eyes to see marching rapidly down the avenue a squad of marines in blue: stalwart men, with flat caps, short muskets on their shoulders and dirks in their belts, and in front of them a tall, slim lieutenant . . . The officer stepped forward and saluted Papa, who went down the piazza steps to meet him. He introduced himself as Lieutenant O'Kane, sent up the Santee with a gunboat by Admiral Dahlgren to bring a letter to Papa. Of course, he was invited into the house, and Papa said he was very glad to hear from his old friend and classmate, Dahlgren, but on reading his letter he said very stiffly to O'Kane: 'I am surprised to see that Dahlgren writes he supposes I am loyal to the United States. He knows very well that my loyalty belongs first to my State and only through my State to the Government.'"[221]

We know much of Emily and Charles's life during the difficult war years because of Lizzie's *Memories of a South Carolina Plantation during the War,* which Lizzie wrote from a diary she kept during the war and which was privately published in 1912. Lizzie describes the depravations of the war in graphic detail. She paints a vivid picture of the family's apprehension in 1865 as Sherman's army approached Orangeburg, South Carolina: "One day one of these scouts, a dashing young Texan, rode up very early one morning and said that the advance guards of Sherman's Army were not more than twenty miles off. Soon after, two shabby soldiers in gray uniform rode up to the front steps and said that they had just ridden down from Orangeburg and had heard the distant drums of Sherman's Army. These men asked for a mouthful to eat but did not dismount, saying they could not afford to be taken prisoners. They said, 'We are sorry to leave you ladies; but we haven't heard that the Yankees are pestering the women folks.' They then rode off, and my mother and I sat in the library with every door and window open so as to hear the first sound of the coming troops. It was a lovely sunny spring day and very warm, but each of us had on two entire suits of clothes, fearing that everything else might be taken from us; and tied inside of our hoop skirts were heavy bags containing all our jewelry and valuable papers. As we sat and tried to sew, a couple of hours later, two more cavalrymen, rode in, this time dressed in blue, and their large brass buckles bore the letter U.S. These, of course, we supposed to be forerunners of Sherman's Army, so what was our surprise when they jumped off their horses and said, 'You did not take us for Yanks, did

you?' These were Northern overcoats that were captured on some battlefield."
They then told us that it was pretty certain that Sherman's Army had turned off
and gone up to Columbia . . . It was not many days after this that a curious dull-
red light in the sky one night gave us the first idea that Columbia had been
burned."222

Belvidere and Eutaw remained relatively unscathed, though both plantations
were raided by Union troops under General Hartwell. Lizzie's account of the raid
on Belvidere is chilling: "At last on this lovely spring day, after hours of anxiety,
we looked out from the piazza and saw a number of Negro soldiers running into
the yard. Of course, the sight of Negroes in uniform seemed to us an appalling
thing, for nowadays it is difficult to imagine what a crime and horrible menace
the arming of the Negroes appeared to the South. Our own coloured servants,
particularly Maumer and her husband Bull and several others came to the piazza
and stood by us, showing us every care and attention. The soldiers whooped and
yelled for all the plantation to gather. They broke open the smokehouse, store-
rooms and barns, and threw out to the Negroes all the provisions and things they
could find. At last several of them ran up the back steps and without even looking at us where we stood on the piazza, went into the house and began throwing things about, cursing and swearing, lashing long carriage whips about our
heads and saying "Damned rebels" very often; also kicking open doors, thrusting
their bayonets into closet and wardrobes; tearing off desk-doors and evidently
looking for wine and silver. Maumer went with my mother after them into the
house and tried to stop their injuring things, continually reproaching them for
their misconduct. One of the Negro soldiers snatched at my mother's watch-
chain, and she took it off and put it into his hands. He looked at the locket hanging on the chain and said: 'Do you value the hair in this locket?' 'Yes,' said she. He
took his knife and picked the hair out and gave it to her. His conscience then
seem to stab him and I am sure her beauty and lovely expression moved him, for
he threw the whole thing, watch and chain back into her hands and ran away as
if from temptation."223

Finally the war came to an end. Emily was instrumental in securing the parole
of her cousin Brown Manning. Emily, who so loved to write and receive letters, was
cut off during the later war years as communication became increasingly impossible.

Mr. Henry Wharton
Belvidere, April 4th, 1865

My dearest Henry,

    I have written you several times lately being very anxious to set
your minds at ease about us. But the opportunities were so uncertain

that I will take advantage of a person going to a point near Charleston in an hour to write you a few lines. We are all well now and getting on very comfortably. Things around us have assumed a quiet and different aspect from when we first wrote. So you must not feel any anxiety about us or take any more trouble for us. We have every hope that with God's help we will do very well for the future.

I should love so dearly to hear from you all. It would be a great comfort, but I fear there are inconveniences in the way of getting letters to us from Charleston. Tho I wrote you of a way which I thought might do—vise Capt. Moultrie of the . . . on Cooper River to the Care of Mrs. Catherine G. White. But I am now unwilling to put any one to any risk or unpleasantness. So pray do nothing that might involve that, as communication has now begun again to Manchester, once a week a mail leaving. Suppose you try the old mode of writing by Flag of Truce, Direct Care of Mrs. R. Manning, Manchester, South Carolina. Of course we have no mail here and do not expect to have again during the War. We are in a remote corner and in a sort of nondescript position, but many mercies have attended us, for which I hope we are duly thankful. Charles is still with us and sends you all most kind messages.

We have not heard from our dear boy since that letter of March 3, but a person who said he was a paroled prisoner (a member of his company) told an intelligent servant of ours that he was captured 2 weeks ago at the same time he was, that he was unhurt and in good hands. That he saw him after he was taken. This all seems straight but we do not give it much credit. But oh dear Hen this state of uncertainty we are in about him. The not being able to hear and yet knowing the constant danger he is in is most harrowing to my soul. Pray for him and for me. Ah when will all these sore and dreadful troubles be over? If we are not to see the end we still thank God to have the blessed hope of a renewed Earth, whose only law will be that of Love. May each of us be partakers in its happiness.

Give much love to dear Kate and each of your Darlings. Kate has been so kind and faithful in writing and I know how much she has felt for us in the last two months. May God bless you and her in every way. Tell dear Mama I wrote her a long letter a few days ago which I trust she has received. Tell dear Frank the same. God bless him. I have not received letters from any of you for a long time. The last being one from Kate and a note from Frank both dated November 16th.

And now dear Hen I dislike to give you and Frank any more trouble but am obliged to do so in this instance. I must beg either him or you to make inquiries and try to assist Capt. Brown Manning who was captured by Sherman's Army on the 27th of February in Chesterfield District in this state. His position is Aid to Gen. Cantey, but he was not on duty when captured, and was attending to some private business. His mother who is an old lady is suffering the most cruel anxiety about him. Has heard all sorts of things to make her anxious. She knows he has lost all his money and his trunk. He is Eliza Manning's brother in law, and you know I am under obligations to the Mannings for uniform kindness and consideration. The old lady has always been most kind to me. Pray assist him if possible. At any rate let him know that the whole family is well in every way. That they are safe and undisturbed (he heard before he was captured that his mother's house had been burned which is an entire mistake), his servant Joe has got home safe, also MCain and many others. His brother is also safe at home and all his children are quite well. (He is a widower.) I heard from the family this morning. His mother thinks that if a personal note could be put in one of the Northern papers assuring them of their well being it would be a great comfort to him. You know dear Hen I would not ask you in this way if I could help it. God bless you again. Ever Your devoted Sister, Emily Sinkler

This 1865 letter is the last known letter written by Emily Wharton Sinkler. For a brief while after the war Emily, Charles, and the five children—Lizzie, Wharton, Charlie, Mary, and Carrie—returned and lived with the Whartons in Philadelphia. Charles hired an overseer, Colonel Chadwick, to run Belvidere. However, this arrangement was not satisfactory, and by 1866 the Sinklers returned to Belvidere and resumed life planting, raising crops, and training horses. Lizzie describes the first winter as one of great deprivation: "During the four years of the war there had been no repairs—painting, shingling, etc.—no renewing of house linen or kitchen utensils or furniture or carpets and in addition to that there had been the injury and destruction by the raids, the pillaging and damage afterwards that a deserted place always suffers. The fences had disappeared and most of the cattle and all the chickens gone. All of our neighbours had immediately come down literally to 'hard pan.' . . . It seemed like a frenzy of despair had fallen upon the people. Mamma had too much spirit to give up anything that could be helped and we had the great benefit of some of our good old servants being too glad to come back to us. But otherwise this was the hardest and most comfortless winter I ever spent."[224]

Eventually Emily and Charles restored the old home to its former state. Charles continued to raise cotton, and many of the former slaves returned to

Belvidere and lived on the "street" working for the Sinklers as hired hands. Their five children grew to maturity. The two older children, Lizzie and Wharton, eventually returned to Philadelphia. Lizzie was to marry Charles Brinton Coxe of Philadelphia on June 14, 1870. Her life was to be one of great adventures. She and her son, Eckley Coxe, financed the University of Pennsylvania's excavations in Egypt and upper Nubia from 1905–1911. Wharton studied medicine at the University of Pennsylvania and became a neurologist. He married Ella Brock on February 10, 1872. They had four sons—Charles, Francis, Seaman Deas, and Wharton. Charlie was to marry Anne Wickham Porcher on December 5, 1883. She was the daughter of the Sinklers' close friends and neighbors, Julius and Mary Fanning Wickham Porcher of St. Julien Plantation. Charles and Anne lived at Belvidere and continued the Sinklers' farming, gardening, and racing traditions. Their children, Anne, Emily, and Caroline (Carrie), were born and raised at Belvidere. Anne carried on the cotton farming traditions of her father and grand-father, living at Belvidere until 1941. Mary Wharton Sinkler was to marry Charles Stevens on February 2, 1884. They were to live first at Chachan and then Lewisfield. Their children were Laura, Elizabeth, and Henry Le Nobel Stevens. Finally, Carrie, who remained unmarried, returned to Philadelphia and became the inseparable, lifelong companion of her sister Lizzie. Carrie lived at the Highlands, a beautiful old estate in Ambler, Pennsylvania, and also had a famous home on the Gloucester Shore where she entertained a circle of intellectual friends. She and Lizzie were to purchase adjoining homes in Philadelphia, at 1604 Locust Street, removing the center wall so that they would share a single space.

Epilogue

Emily died tragically on February 10, 1875. She was only fifty-two years old. Charles survived her by nineteen years, dying on March 17, 1894. Both are buried in the Rocks graveyard, which is now isolated on a small island in the middle of Lake Marion.

Kate Wharton, the wife of Emily's brother Henry, was staying at Belvidere at the time of Emily's death. From her journal she provided a description of the events leading to Emily's death:

> A service had been arranged for Ash-Wednesday morning. There seems to have been some doubt as to whether they would go. Charles said to me afterwards, "Emily was disappointed and said, 'it seems a pity for a Christian family not to keep such a day.' I said; 'Not a word more, you shall go.'" Emily came in and told me they were going to Church, and Lizzie would look after us. Mary went with them, all three in the buggy. Lizzie, Charlie and I established ourselves in the library. Polly took her book on the piazza. It was about one when Jeff came in. "Mass Charlie, de horse am coming up de road without de buggy." When we got to the door the horse was standing still and we saw that the harness was broken. Charlie said he would ride back, while Lizzie was getting him some whiskey to take with him. I caught sight of Charles, rushing out of the wood, looking distraught. "Is any one hurt" we called out. He answered, in a tone of anguish I can never forget, "Your Mother" then becoming calmer, "send for both doctors at once, Let Charlie follow with the carriage." With the help of the girls, I got the rooms ready, warmed the beds, heated water. It was not long before someone called "dey are coming." I went down the steps but Charles said, "Kate you must not come you can do nothing. It is too cold for you here," as Emily was carried to her room. "I don't know whether she is living, she has neither moved or breathed." They brought her up on a mattress. I was able to help getting her into bed. Poor Mary had been terribly bruised and battered. When the doctor came he said, "Charles, she is dead." He fell on the floor, Lizzie kneeling beside him. The doctor said death must have been instantaneous. The accident happened on the way home. They had enjoyed the service and sang the hymns "'In Mercy Not in Wrath" and "Jesus Lover of My Soul." They stopped to warm

themselves at Mr. Fullers. Probably the horse got tired of standing, as there was nothing to frighten him. After they turned in, the horse suddenly dashed off furiously. Charles felt Emily grasp his shoulder and heard her say, "Lord have mercy upon us" and almost with the prayer on her lips her soul took flight. As a moment later the crash came. They struck against a tree, tearing out the seat and part of the buggy and they were all thrown out. When Charles struggled to his feet, Emily and Mary were lying on their faces.

Kate told of the funeral three days later: "A lovely day. It had been arranged to have the service at the house. I cut off some of her hair and Lizzie and I arranged a little cap of soft, white, silk handkerchief to hide the bruises. She so full of love, tenderness and sympathy, lay in peaceful rest. The weeping servants stood round her, but no loud lamentations disturbed her quiet slumber. Charles' sister, Eliza Manning was here, the family from Eutaw, and some of the nearest neighbors. The piazza was full of Negroes. So she was taken away from the home of which she had been the light and joy."

Belvidere, the home of the Sinklers since 1800, was destroyed by the impoundment of the Santee River in 1941. South Carolina Sen. Burnet Maybank and Gov. James Byrnes were avid to get their share of National Industrial Recovery Act funds. They pushed for the creation of a South Carolina Public Service Authority in 1933. With that in place they held out through substantial legal, environmental, and corporate opposition to finally succeed in funding and implementing the Santee-Cooper project. Over one thousand families were resettled. Many were the former slaves of the plantations lining the Santee River. Twenty-four magnificent and historic plantations were destroyed, with their owners receiving paltry sums for their lands and houses. The beautiful and environmentally unique Santee Swamp, the home of the ivory-billed woodpecker, was destroyed and with it virgin stands of cypress, oak, and gum. In its place are now two vast, glittering bodies of water, Lake Marion and Lake Moultrie. The remains of another era and another way of life slumber in their depths.[225] The Rocks church and its graveyard sit on a small island in Lake Marion, and there lie the remains of Emily and Charles Sinkler.

Cast of Characters

Broun, Mary Deas (June 18, 1762–March 12, 1857). Mary Deas Broun was known to Emily as "Grandmother" (she was Charles Sinkler's grandmother), and she lived at 11 Society Street in Charleston. Mary Deas was the only daughter of Elizabeth Allen and John Deas, Jr. Elizabeth Allen had inherited Thoroughgood, a plantation in Goose Creek, South Carolina, of over three thousand acres. John and Elizabeth had eleven children, ten boys and one girl, and spent their time between Thoroughgood and Charleston. Mary Deas, on August 17, 1780, at the age of eighteen, married Capt. Archibald Broun, a Revolutionary War hero. Archibald and Mary had seven children. Their oldest daughter, Elizabeth Allen Broun, married William Sinkler of Eutaw Plantation. Archibald died in 1789, leaving Mary Deas a widow who lived to be ninety-five, dying in 1857. Emily and Charles were the welcome visitors of Grandmother, or Greatie, as she was also known, in her Charleston house on Society Street. Mary Deas Broun is buried in St. Philip's churchyard in Charleston.

Coxe, Elizabeth Allen Sinkler (July 7, 1843–October 24, 1919). Known as Lizzie, Elizabeth Allen Sinkler was Emily and Charles Sinkler's oldest child. On June 14, 1870, she married Charles Brinton Coxe of Drifton and Philadelphia, Pennsylvania. He was to die within two years of the marriage, during which time Lizzie had two babies. Only one, Eckley Brinton Coxe, born May 31, 1872, called Eck, grew to adulthood. He was a graduate of the University of Pennsylvania, and together mother and son financed the major excavations of the university in Egypt and upper Nubia from 1905 to 1911. Eckley Coxe left an endowment for the university's museum of over $600,000. Lizzie took care of her brothers and sisters after her mother's untimely death. She and Caroline, nicknamed Carrie, became inseparable friends, living together at a shared house at 1604 Locust Street in Philadelphia. Lizzie and Eck built a forty-eight-room mansion called Windy Hill in Drifton, Pennsylvania. Each year, Lizzie traveled to Europe on the "grand tour" and carried her southern nieces (Charles and Anne Porcher Sinkler's three girls—Emily, Anne, and Caroline—and Mary Wharton Sinkler and Charles Stevens's two girls—

Elizabeth and Laura) with her to Rome, Genoa, Naples, Cairo, Luxor, and other great cities. Lizzie chronicled her adventures in several short essays about her digs in Egypt as well as her travels across Europe.

Griffith, Mary Coré (d. 1877). Mary Coré married John Griffith, a merchant of Philadelphia, whose father was Dr. John Griffith, born in 1736. The Corés were a French refugee family. Her father was a French immigrant, Joseph Corré, who came to the United States in 1776 as a cook of Major Crew of the Light Dragoons. Joseph ran an ice cream shop in New York. Mrs. Griffith, whose expressive and beautiful portrait by Sully is now owned by David Deas Sinkler of Philadelphia, was the mother of Arabella (1800–February 27, 1866), who married Thomas Isaac Wharton. John Griffith and his wife lived in a large house on the banks of the Delaware River. They occupied, at St. Mary's Burlington Church (in New Jersey, about ten miles from Philadelphia), the pew of the former governor of the province. It was large, square, and high, with a canopy. Mrs. Griffith was early left a widow with large means and bought land on the Delaware River near Bordentown. She called it "Charlie's Hope," named after Charles Edward Stuart, the British prince who was nicknamed Bonnie Prince Charlie, since Mrs. Griffith was a passionate admirer of the Stuarts. Joseph Bonaparte, Napoleon's brother, afterwards bought the adjoining estate. All of her money was spent on Charlie's Hope, where she planted acres of roses in rows, like corn, for her bees. It is said she spent twenty-five thousand dollars on her apiary alone. All of her grandchildren, including Emily and Mary, spent every summer at Charlie's Hope. She was mentioned by Sir Walter Scott in the preface of *The Heart of Midlothian* and by Maria Edgeworth in her *Letters*. Mary Griffith was an author in her own right. Her works included *Our Neighborhood, or, Letters on Horticulture and Natural Phenomena, Interspersed with Opinions on Domestic and Moral Economy; Camperdown, or, News from Our Neighborhood: Being Sketches;* and *The Two Defaulters, or, A Picture of the Times*. Her *Three Hundred Years Hence,* a utopian vision of the world where women made the important decisions, is considered at some length in Vernon Louis Parrington's 1947 study *American Dreams: A Study of American Utopias*. Her grandson Dr. Francis Wharton (Emily's brother) spoke of her as eccentric, French in character, and extravagant.

Manning, Elizabeth Allen Sinkler (September 16, 1821–April 2, 1908). Eliza, as Emily called her, was Emily's best friend and also her sister-in-law. She taught Emily much of what she was to learn about supervising a large plantation house. Eliza married Richard Irvine Manning II of Sumter District on March 3, 1845. She was a tiny woman with a three and one-half shoe size. Richard Manning II acquired 4,100 acres near Manchester, Clarendon, Sumter District, and named it "Homesley." Richard and Eliza had a total of seven children, three of whom died as infants. When the Civil War began in 1861, though Richard opposed secession, he raised and equipped an infantry company known as the Manning Guards, at his own expense. His younger brother, Brown, led the Guards as captain. It is this Brown Manning that Emily refers to in her letter of April 4, 1865. Richard died at his home of typhus fever in 1861, leaving Eliza to manage his estate and raise their children. Eliza was a tower of strength to her family during the Civil War, and persevered to preserve and educate her family after the war. She was described by her daughter Elizabeth Allen Sinkler Richardson as "brave and noble." "My Mother's home 'Homesley' was indeed the home for all . . . My mother was a very remarkable woman; for though my two Uncles and their families and my grandmother and aunt all lived with her, there was never any unpleasantness and all went smoothly."[1]

Porcher, Julius Theodore, M.D. (1829–November 25, 1863). Julius Porcher was the son of Thomas W. Porcher of Walworth Plantation near Eutawville. When Julius married Mary Fanning Wickham of Virginia, his wedding present from his father was St. Julien Plantation, just west of Eutawville. The lovely oak-lined entrance comes up from the River Road in the shape of a *J.* The black Italian marble mantels in the living room were brought back from Italy by Julius Porcher, who had studied medicine in Paris. Julius and Mary Wickham's daughter, Anne Wickham Porcher (September 14, 1860–November 16, 1919), was to marry Charles and Emily's youngest son, Charles St. George Sinkler.

Sinkler, Anna Linton Thomson (November 5, 1823–November 9, 1873). Anna was married to Charles's younger brother and her own first cousin, William Henry Sinkler, on March 4, 1847. She had a beautiful voice, and together Emily and Anna put on many performances at Eutaw and Belvidere. Anna Linton Thomson Sinkler wrote in her unpublished history of the Sinkler family that

> after James' death his widow Margaret Cantey built Belvidere and moved up there early in 1800. Her daughter Margaret Anna was married there to John Linton Thomson Dec. 17, 1816, by the Rev. Charles Snowden. John Linton and Margaret Anna Thomson had two daughters, Margaret Cantey and Anna Linton. The parents died when they were very young and their uncle William Sinkler was their guardian. They were sent to Madame Talvande's school when very young and Anna became an accomplished French scholar and had a beautiful voice . . . Anna had a magnificent contralto voice. Emily Wharton also had a beautiful voice and when they were all living at Eutaw, Uncle Mazyck Porcher who lived at Mexico plantation fifteen miles down the River Road often used to drive up and spend the evening just to hear them sing.[2]

Anna was a large woman, weighing over 165 pounds. She and Emily were inseparable friends. She was described by Elizabeth Allen Sinkler Richardson: "Some of the happiest days of my life were spent with my Aunt, Mrs. William Sinkler [Anna Linton]. One of the loveliest women, possessed of a wonderful voice whose rich and mellow notes sank into your heart; and she and my aunt, Mrs. Charles Sinkler [Emily] with whom I also spent many happy days, used to sing many lovely duets. Aunt Anna's house . . . was always open to her friends and she was always in the midst of them, making herself one of them. Many happy days were spent with my Uncle and Aunt Mr. & Mrs. Charles Sinkler, and the intimacy begun in childhood has ripened into lasting friendship."[3]

Sinkler, Charles (January 8, 1818–March 27, 1894). Charles was the son of William Sinkler and Elizabeth Allen Broun, who had built Eutaw Plantation in 1808. Charles grew up at Eutaw and attended the College of Charleston, graduating there in 1835. He delivered a public oration entitled "On Eloquence" at a special exhibition of the college on April 4, 1834. He served in the United States Navy as a midshipman, beginning March 24, 1836. He passed midshipman on July 1, 1842. He served in the Gulf of Mexico during the Mexican War as the acting master aboard the U.S. brig *Perry.* After Vera Cruz, his squadron was on the lookout for privateers between Havana and the Florida Keys. On October 11, 1846, the *Perry* was wrecked on one of the Florida Keys in a hurricane that devastated the Keys. He resigned on February 20, 1847. He returned to South Carolina, and he and Emily, with three children, moved to Belvidere Plantation in 1848, where he commenced cotton farming. Mr. Sinkler did not fight in the Civil War. He was a Unionist, subscribing to such southern Union newspapers as the *Southern Patriot,* published by Benjamin F. Perry of Greenville, South Carolina. In 1863, when President Lincoln issued the Emancipation Proclamation, he called up the plantation slaves and told them they had been proclaimed free by Lincoln but they had better stay quietly in their comfortable homes. He also told them he intended to divide among them most of his provisions, which he did. On April 11, 1887, he applied for a Mexican War pension. He had previously applied for bounty lands in November 1857, pursuant to an Act of Congress of 1855 awarding bounty land for service in the Mexican War. On March 16, 1854, Charles's brother James Sinkler died and left Charles as the ward of his four children.

Sinkler, Charles St. George (October 20, 1853–July 2, 1934). Born at Eutaw Springs in 1853, he was the second son of Charles and Emily Sinkler. He graduated from the College of Charleston in 1874. He was involved in politics as a Democratic county chairman from 1883–84. He married Anne Wickham Porcher of St. Julien Plantation on December 5, 1883. He was the organizer and commander of the

Eutaw Light Dragoons, a cavalry company of the state. He and Anne lived at Belvidere until their deaths.

Sinkler, Elizabeth Allen Broun (March 17, 1785–June 24, 1824). Elizabeth Allen Broun married William Sinkler of Eutaw Plantation on January 16, 1810. The Sinklers had eight children, only five of whom lived to adulthood. Elizabeth herself died in childbirth. Elizabeth Allen Broun Sinkler was the mother-in-law Emily never knew. When Emily came into the Sinkler clan, William Sinkler, or the *beau-père* as Emily called him, had been a widower for eighteen years.

Sinkler, Emily Wharton (October 12, 1823–February 10, 1875). Emily Wharton was the third child of Arabella Griffith and Thomas Isaac Wharton. She was born in Philadelphia and lived her younger years at 150 Walnut Street, directly across from the statehouse and Independence Square. Thomas Isaac Wharton was the center of a literary circle as well as a legal circle of distinguished friends. He was a founder of the Historical Society of Pennsylvania and was a member of the board of the American Philosophical Society. Emily flourished in this intellectually rich environment. She learned French and Italian in school and became an accomplished pianist and vocalist. She spent her summers with her grandmother, Mary Griffith, at Charlie's Hope on the Delaware River. She met and fell in love with Charles Sinkler when he was stationed as a Navy midshipman in Philadelphia. They were married on October 8, 1842, in St. Stephen's Episcopal Church in Philadelphia. By November 1842 they had arrived in Charleston and were staying in Stewarts, a boarding house. That fall Emily and Charles moved to Charles's father's home, Eutaw Plantation. Charles remained in the Navy until 1847. He resigned after the Mexican War, and the couple moved to Belvidere, an old, decayed plantation that had been built around 1785 by Charles's grandmother, Mary Cantey Sinkler. At Belvidere Emily and Charles renovated the many buildings, adding a church for the slaves. Emily's garden was renowned for its beautiful roses and irises. Belvidere bordered the Santee River and Swamp and was consequently unhealthy in the summer months. Emily and Charles built a home and farm in the Sand Hills at Bradford Springs and called it Woodford. Charles raised cotton at both Belvidere and Woodford. During the 1850s Belvidere and Eutaw Plantations became the center of a vigorous intellectual and cultural life for the surrounding French Huguenot community. Emily and Charles had six children: Elizabeth Allen Sinkler (Lizzie), born July 7, 1843; Wharton Sinkler (Bud), born August 7, 1845; Arabella Wharton Sinkler, born November 1847; Charles St. George Sinkler (Charlie), born October 20, 1853; Mary Wharton Sinkler, born April 25, 1857; and Caroline Sidney Sinkler (Carrie), born April 23, 1860. Emily and Charles remained at Belvidere during the

Civil War. They resumed cotton farming in 1866. Emily died tragically on the way home from an Ash Wednesday service on February 10, 1875.

Sinkler, James (December 28, 1810–March 1854). The older brother of Charles Sinkler, James lived in Charleston and was married to Margaret Huger Sinkler. He was a member of the General Assembly.

Sinkler, James, Captain (1740–November 20, 1800). Captain Sinkler was the son of Mrs. Jean Sinclair, widow, who died in 1769 or later, as her will was signed in that year. She had been granted five hundred acres in South Carolina in 1742 by George II. Her husband, James, was descended from the earls of Orkney and Caithness in Scotland whose name was Sinclair. They left three children, James, Peter, and Dorothy. James was married first to Miss Couhasac, leaving no issue. His second marriage was to Sarah Cantey, the daughter of Charles Cantey of Mattassee. They left one child, Anne, who married Gov. J. B. Richardson. Captain Sinkler's third marriage was to Sarah's sister, Margaret Cantey. Margaret and James had three children, William, Charles, and Anna. A miniature of Margaret, painted by Edward Malbone in Charleston in 1802, shows a lovely matron with huge dark eyes and a fringe of black curly hair under a white frilly cap. Peter and James were patriots in the Revolution and loaned the state of South Carolina nearly $100,000 for the war effort. Peter and James were devoted brothers, and, though they lived twelve miles apart, they visited each other every night. Peter was betrayed by his brother-in-law, Boisseau, and taken a prisoner by the British. He was put in the dungeon of the old Exchange Building in Charleston and died there of typhus fever. Family tradition had it that permission was received from the British to take the body for burial at St. Stephen's, and instead the coffin was filled with powder and shot. Both James and Peter were vestrymen of St. Stephen's Church. Peter lived at Lifeland and James at Old Santee.

After James Sinkler's death his widow, Margaret Cantey, built Belvidere and moved there early in 1800. James and Margaret's child Margaret Anna was married at Belvidere on December 17, 1816, to John Linton Thomson. When Margaret Anna and John Linton Thomson died, they left two daughters, Margaret Cantey Thomson and Anna Linton Thomson, who became the wards of James and Margaret Cantey's other son, William Sinkler of Eutaw Plantation. Anna married her first cousin William Henry Sinkler on March 4, 1841, at Eutaw (see William Henry Sinkler).

Sinkler, Seaman Deas (April 14, 1816–January 1847). The second son of William Sinkler and Elizabeth Allen Sinkler, Seaman Deas Sinkler was a medical doctor who had done his schooling in Paris. He never married and was a well-respected Charleston doctor. The Lodge at Eutaw Plantation was built as his medical office.

He is buried in St. Stephen's graveyard, and his epitaph reads, "Under this stone repose the mortal remains of Seaman Deas Sinkler, Doctor of Medicine. Beloved and cherished son of William Sinkler. To a vigorous intellect, diligently cultivated he united high moral characteristics and endearing social qualities. Having mastered the difficulties which beset the threshold of professional life a bright career of distinction and usefulness opened before him. But in the prime of manhood he was suddenly struck down by disease, in the month of November 1846. After great suffering and anguish which were born without murmuring, breathed last on the 19th of January 1847. Aged 30 years."

Sinkler, Wharton (August 7, 1845–1917). Wharton was Emily and Charles's second child and first son. He fought in the Civil War at the age of 17 on the side of the Confederacy and was stationed in North Carolina. His loyal slave, Mingo Rivers, accompanied him to battle and came home periodically to get new provisions for them both. Wharton left the South after the war and studied medicine at the University of Pennsylvania. He was married to Ella Brock on February 10, 1872. He returned South every year for long hunting parties at Belvidere.

Sinkler, William (November 2, 1787–June 8, 1853). William Sinkler (the *beau-père*) was the oldest son of Captain James Sinkler and his third wife, Margaret Cantey Sinkler. He built Eutaw Plantation in 1808 and married Elizabeth Allen Broun on January 16, 1810. Their children were James Sinkler, who married Margaret Huger; Seaman Deas Sinkler; Charles Sinkler, who married Emily Wharton of Philadelphia; Elizabeth Allen Sinkler, who married Col. Richard Irvine Manning; and William Henry Sinkler, who married his first cousin, Anna Linton Thomson. He had immense landholdings in Upper St. John's, much of it prime cotton land and the remainder pinelands. When William Sinkler died in 1853, he left 103 slaves to his three sons. He left James Sinkler two tracts of land, Brackey and Brushpond. To Charles Sinkler he left Belvidere and four hundred acres of adjoining swampland. He left Eutaw to William Henry Sinkler. He left Charles and William Henry the plantation called Dorcher.[4] He is buried in St. Stephen's Episcopal Church in St. Stephen, South Carolina. On his grave is the following: "In memory of William Sinkler, esq. Who was born on the 2nd of Nov. 1787 and died June 1853 aged 65 years. The Angel of the Lord encampeth round about them that fear him and delivereth them."

Sinkler, William Henry (October 30, 1819–April 17, 1856). William Henry was Charles's youngest brother, who died when only 37 years old. He is buried at the Rocks Church. He was married to his first cousin Anna Linton Thomson, who had been the ward of William Sinkler, the *beau-père*. They lived at Eutaw Plantation, which they inherited from William Sinkler.

Wharton, Arabella Griffith (1800–February 27, 1866). Arabella Griffith was Emily's mother. After marrying Thomas Isaac Wharton, she lived her life at 150 Walnut Street in Philadelphia.

Wharton, Francis (March 7, 1820–February 21, 1889). Emily's older brother, known as Frank, was graduated from Yale University in 1839 and went on to become a clergyman, educator, and author. On November 4, 1852, he married Sidney Paul, daughter of Comegys Paul and Sarah Rodman. Sydney Paul died in September 1854, and Frank then married Helen Elizabeth Ashhurst on December 27, 1860. Two children were born from this marriage, Mary Ashhurst Wharton, born November 13, 1861, and Ella Wharton, born May 29, 1863.

Wharton, Henry (June 2, 1827–November 11, 1880). Henry Wharton was Emily's younger brother, who worked as a lawyer with his father and later as a Philadelphia prosecutor. Henry was graduated from the University of Pennsylvania in 1846 with a bachelor of arts degree and in 1849 with a master of arts degree. He married Katharine Johnstone Brinley on October 21, 1858, and they had six children. A portrait of Henry Wharton is located in the Library Company of Philadelphia. Entries in the Library Company minutes indicate that the picture was commissioned and purchased as a memorial to Wharton, who had been a board member of the Library Company for eighteen years.

Wharton, Mary Griffith (August 24, 1818–March 31, 1899). Mary Wharton was Emily's younger sister. On April 12, 1852, she married George Davison-Bland, son of Thomas Davison-Bland and Apollonia Philip, from Kippax Park, Yorkshire, England. Mary and George had four children, two of whom died in infancy; another, Emily Augusta Davison-Bland, lived only a year. Their only child to grow to adulthood was Godfrey Davison-Bland, born July 26, 1853.

Wharton, Thomas Isaac (May 17, 1791–April 7, 1857). Emily's father was a lawyer and a judge. He was the son of Isaac Wharton and Margaret Rawle. Thomas Isaac Wharton was a distinguished jurist with a specialty in property law. After graduating from the University of Pennsylvania in 1807, Thomas Isaac began the study of law in the office of his uncle, William Rawle, a leader of the Philadelphia Bar. Though he was especially learned in real property law, his knowledge in other legal fields was hardly less profound. Among his early labors was that of compiling a *Digest of Cases Adjudged in the Circuit Court of the United States for the Third Circuit, and in the Courts of Pennsylvania* (1822). In 1830 he was appointed with William Rawle and Joel Jones to codify the civil statute law of Pennsylvania, a task that consumed four years.

Notes

1. T. C. Fay, *Charleston Directory and Strangers' Guide for 1840,* vol. 41, s.v. "Simons, Harris."

2. Dumas Malone, ed., *Dictionary of American Biography* (New York: Charles Scribner's Sons, 1936), 20:34.

3. "For Cape May" [advertisement], *Philadelphia Pennsylvanian,* 21 July 1840.

4. Russell F. Weigley, ed., *Philadelphia: A 300-Year History* (New York: W. W. Norton & Company, 1982), 318.

5. Ibid., 299, 318.

6. "Rydal Mount Female Institute" [advertisement], *Germantown (Pa.) Telegraph,* 4 March 1840.

7. "A. Bolmar's Institute for Boys, West Chester" [advertisement], *Germantown (Pa.) Telegraph,* 1 October 1840.

8. Weigley, *Philadelphia,* 323.

9. "The Great Western Omnibus leaves Germantown every morning returning in the afternoon from Philadelphia" [advertisement], *Germantown (Pa.) Telegraph,* 4 March 1840.

10. "For Savannah, Ga., the fine sailing schooner, Emma, Cpt. Sylver is now loading" [advertisement], *Philadelphia Pennsylvanian,* 1 October 1840.

11. Weigley, *Philadelphia,* 309.

12. Bishop Robert Smith (1732–1801) was the first bishop of the Diocese of South Carolina. He was also the first headmaster of the College of Charleston.

13. Mr. Alfred Huger was the postmaster and resided at 92 Broad Street. John H. Honour, ed., *A Directory of City of Charleston and Neck for 1849* (Charleston, 1849).

14. A map in the author's possession bears a note to this effect.

15. Indenture manuscript in possession of Harriet Claire Sinkler Little, Summerville, S.C.

16. Baker would have been one of the Whartons' house servants. The *Emma* was another of the coastal sail ships that traversed the Philadelphia to Charleston route.

17. Aunt Mary could have been Mary Lesesne, the daughter of Thomas Lesesne and Anna Caroline Broun. Anna Caroline Broun was the sister of the *beau-père's* wife, Elizabeth Allen Broun. The Lesesnes and the Sinklers were cousins as well as friends.

18. Emily read many ladies-only publications that specialized in sewing patterns and fashion designs.

19. Thomas Isaac began the study of law in the office of his uncle, William Rawle, a leader of the Philadelphia bar.

20. The Metcalves were undoubtedly Philadelphia friends of the Sinklers.

21. Rev. William Dehon (1817–1862) was the son of Sarah Russell and the Right Reverend

Theodore Dehon, second Episcopal bishop of South Carolina. He was the rector of St. Stephen's Parish, as well as Black Oak, Middle St. John's, and the Rocks in Upper St. John's from 1842 to 1859. He was the rector of St. Philip's, Charleston, from 1859 to 1862. Albert Sidney Thomas, *A Historical Account of the Protestant Episcopal Church in South Carolina, 1820–1957: Being a Continuation of Dalcho's Account, 1670–1820* (Columbia: The R. L. Bryan Company, 1957), 252–55.

22. H. E. Scudder, *Recollections of Samuel Breck, with Passages from His Notebooks (1771–1862)* (Philadelphia: Porter & Coates, 1877), 288.

23 *Charleston Daily Courier,* 2, and 12 February 1853. The Jockey Club hosted an annual dinner for members on Wednesdays at the Saint Andrews Hall. On the last day of the races they put on the Jockey Club Ball: "The chalked floors, the superb dresses of the company, the furbelows, the flounces, the bouquets of fresh rosebuds and camelias, the exhilarating music, the ceaseless whirl of muslin and of broadcloth in the centre of the hall, the handsome mirrors that decorate the walls of the gay saloon, reflecting graceful figures 'on the light fantastic,' as if in some fairy region, lending enchantment to the brilliant scene!" John B. Irving, *The South Carolina Jockey Club* (1857; reprint, Spartanburg, S.C.: Reprint Co., 1975), 154.

24. "Race Week," *Charleston Courier,* 23, 24, 25, and 27 February 1843.

25. This would have been the Pineville Races, which took place on 7 February and in which Mr. Sinkler ran both Hero and Santa Ana. "Result of the Pineville Races," *Charleston Courier,* 21 February 1843.

26. Reverend Neville married Emily and Charles on 8 September 1842 in Philadelphia.

27. Timothy Shay Arthur (1809–1885) was a temperance crusader and novelist. His most famous novel was *Ten Nights in a Bar-Room and What I Saw There* (1854).

28. This has become the elegant Greenbrier at White Sulphur Springs. Its waters are still a source for good health.

29. Hon. Daniel E. Huger lived at 28 Meeting Street. Fay, *Charleston Directory and Strangers Guide,* s.v. "Huger, Daniel E."

30. Emily was friends with the Hamptons. Mary Cantey Hampton (1780–1863), daughter of John Cantey, was married in 1801 to Wade Hampton of Columbia, South Carolina, the father of the Confederate general and post-Reconstruction governor of South Carolina, Gen. Wade Hampton.

31. Weigley, *Philadelphia,* 352–53.

32. The Philadelphia Know-Nothing Riots of May and July 1844 resulted from dissension between Catholic and anti-Catholic factions; Bishop Kenrick had protested the anti-Catholic school atmosphere and textbooks.

33. Weigley, *Philadephia,* 357.

34. Anne Sinkler Whaley LeClercq, *An Antebellum Plantation Household: Including the South Carolina Low Country Receipts and Remedies of Emily Wharton Sinkler* (Columbia: University of South Carolina Press, 1996), 99.

35. The barque *J. Patton* weighed 168 tons and berthed at Magwood's Wharf. It was from Philadelphia.

36. Weigley, *Philadelphia,* 308.

37. Elizabeth Allen Sinkler married Col. Richard Irvine Manning in December 1845. They were then to settle at Homesley Plantation in the Santee Hills near Bradford Springs. Emily often visited them there.

38. Emily is referring to Washington Irving, the famous American author of such works as *Rip Van Winkle, The Life of George Washington,* and *The Alhambra.* Irving wrote during the period 1832 to 1859 and was thus a contemporary of Emily.

39. Lowcountry African Americans spoke a distinctive language called Gullah. The children who were in their constant care picked up many of the phrases.

40. The Cadwaladers were a distinguished Philadelphia family. Judge John Cadwalader, a Democrat, may well have been a friend of Thomas I. Wharton.

41. Eutaw was not unique in fostering musical performances and celebrations among their servants: "At Mammus Hall my Uncle James Richardson built a bark house where his band played every afternoon. This band was most remarkable; it was formed of his own Negroes who were most wonderfully gifted, particularly one Robin, who could transpose the music to suit each piece. He would transpose it on the sand. Prof. Dover from Charleston trained these musical wonders and lived at Uncle Jim's. Long after Uncle Jim had passed away and these Negroes had been made free, those of them who were left would go every summer to the Virginia Springs and play for the merry throngs gathered from all parts of the country." Elizabeth Sinkler Richardson, "Recollections," four-page, typewritten document in the possession of the author, undated.

42. *Philadelphia Gazette and Commercial Intelligencer,* 7 July 1845.

43. *Germantown (Pa.) Telegraph,* 16 November 1846.

44. *Philadelphia Pennsylvanian,* 2 June 1846.

45. Gaetano Donizetti wrote *Anna Bolena Puritani,* first performed in Milan on 26 December 1830. Gioacchino Rossini wrote *Otello,* first performed in Rome on 25 January 1817. Stephen LaRue, *International Dictionary of Opera* (Detroit: St. James Press, 1993).

46. Secretary of the Navy George Bancroft was responsible for Charles Sinkler's orders.

47. The Philadelphia papers of 1846 show that the North did not favor the war. Texas was granted its independence after the war. Texas became a slave state. Presumably, the North would not have wanted another slave state to join the Union. The Compromise of 1850 was supposed to put an end to the question of slave or free. So one wonders whether Emily's sentiments here are an accurate reflection of Southern opinion.

48. A handsome portrait of the postmaster, Alfred Huger, hangs in the Old Exchange Building at the foot of Broad Street in Charleston, South Carolina. It was painted in 1850 by Alexander H. Emmons.

49. The context of this letter indicates that Joshua Molliston would have been the Whartons' white Irish butler.

50. Mr. Beverly was a Navy colleague of Charles Sinkler and is referred to in Emily's letter of 1 September 1844 from Red Sulphur Springs.

51. John Laurence Manning (1816–1889) served in the South Carolina General Assembly for eight terms and was governor of the state from 1852 to 1854. A prosperous planter, he owned some 648 slaves and had land holdings valued at more than $2 million in 1860.

52. Milford, or Manning's Folly, as it was called, was built by Gov. John Laurence Manning. The Sinklers enjoyed many happy house parties there. Milford is one of the finest mansions in the South. Built on a high sand hill, the foundations are said to have required over three hundred thousand bricks and great quantities of granite. Gregorie tells of General Potter's raid through Sumter County in 1865 in which he burned all seven hundred bales of cotton at Homesley, Eliza Sinkler Manning's home. At Milford, the following scene occurred: "Soon a noisy mob of black soldiers surged into the beautiful hall of Milford from the rear, and a sergeant

in the lead shouted, 'Have you any protection for this house?' 'Our only protection,' replied Manning, 'is from the army of the Confederate States.' Raising his gun, the angered Negro aimed at the elderly gentleman and said, 'You are a dead man!' Just then a Negro officer shouted, 'Halt! The General is at the front door.' Turning his back upon the mob in the hall, Manning walked out on the portico to greet his uninvited guests, and saw Potter and his officers on horseback. 'I suppose,' said the governor, 'this is the commander of the United Sates army?' 'Yes sir,' replied the General, 'and I have come to protect your family and house from injury.' Anne King Gregorie, *History of Sumter County* (Sumter, S.C.: Library Board of Sumter County, 1954), 270–71.

53. Seaman Deas Sinkler is buried in the Sinkler grave plot at St. Stephen's Episcopal Church.

54. The annual Episcopal convention was held in Charleston in February. Charles Sinkler was a warden of the church at the Rocks and also in Charleston. He was frequently a delegate to the convention.

55. The Reverend Christopher Edwards Gadsden was bishop of the Diocese of South Carolina from 1840 to 1852. At the convention of 1847 the bishop addressed the subject of "the worshiping together of all Church people whatever be their creed or station or their mutual relations . . . The Bishop doubted the expediency of having a Church for the exclusive use of only one class of persons . . ." The bishop also was intensely concerned with the ". . . evangelization of the vast numbers of the Negroes in the diocese, both slaves and free . . . He had . . . prepared a suitable catechism to be used in baptismal education." Thomas, *A Historical Account of the Protestant Episcopal Church in South Carolina,* 35.

56. The Reverend William W. Spear of Philadelphia, who had been the assistant and then rector of St. Michael's, accepted a call to become the first minister of the new Grace Church. Grace Church, located at the corner of Wentworth and Glebe Streets, was established for ". . . the use of the school at St. Philip's Rectory on Glebe Street, for sojourners in the city, for residents in the western part of the city between St. Paul's and St. Peter's, and for persons of color." Until its construction was completed, Mr. Spear conducted services at the chapel of the Charleston College, beginning in January 1847. Ibid., 206.

57. Emily's references to her literary tastes show that she read a wide variety of light and popular literature, much of it serialized in *Graham's Magazine* and *Godey's Lady's Book.*

58. The Battery is the sea wall that protects Charleston from the ocean. Its surface is of large, flat, granite stones. The wall is about five feet high and has always been a favorite place for afternoon promenades. In the eighteenth century there was no wall, and the Charleston "neck" had many creeks and inlets. The Battery got its name during the War of 1812 with Great Britain: When the British blockaded Charleston, and Fort Moultrie, Fort Johnson, and Castle Pinckney were garrisoned and armed with federal funds, fifteen guns of large caliber were mounted along the sea wall and aimed toward the open harbor, giving the Battery its name. Walter J. Fraser, Jr., *Charleston! Charleston!: The History of a Southern City* (Columbia: The University of South Carolina Press, 1989), 193.

59. Eliza and Richard Manning's second child was Seaman Sinkler Manning (1 March 1847–18 August 1848).

60. Camden, New Jersey, is across the Delaware River from Philadelphia and would have been a nice afternoon outing in the 1840s.

61. Charles Dickens, *Battle of Life: A Love Story* (London, Bradbury & Evans, 1846).

62. The potato famine of 1845–1848 resulted in enormous suffering and death in Ireland and

in huge numbers of immigrants in the United States, particularly in Philadelphia. In the course of four years, more than 750,000 people died of starvation. Between 1846 and 1855 more than a million Irish men and women emigrated, many coming to the U.S.

63. Under Bishop Christopher Edwards Gadsden, the spirit of evangelism and diocesan missions were important. Under his direction, James Warley Miles ". . . advanced . . . a plan for erecting a house of meditation, study, and work in the West. The plan matured in the Nashotah House Seminary in Nashotah, Wisconsin, in 1842. The express purpose was to organize and extend the Church among the Indians." Thomas, *A Historical Account of the Protestant Episcopal Church in South Carolina,* 39.

64. *Philadelphia Gazette and Commercial Intelligencer,* 10 July 1845.

65. "Progress" in Philadelphia in 1847 brought with it factories, city water, and street illumination, as seen in the following: "Factories making all kinds of goods and machines belched forth smoke. Water channeled through sluices turned wheels which powered looms and powdered chemicals. The use of gas made from coal was general for both house and street illumination. The gas works, taken over by the city in 1841, were enlarged until 1854 when a new facility with a mammoth telescopic storage tank was opened at Point Breeze." Edwin Wolf 2d, *Philadelphia: Portrait of an American City: A Bicentennial History,* ed. Walton Rawls (Harrisburg, Pa.: Stackpole Books, 1975). 187.

66. Charles Dickens, *Dombey & Son* (London, Bradbury & Evans, 1848).

67. Sarah Russell Dehon, daughter of Nathaniel Russell, was married to the Right Reverend Theodore Dehon. Theodore Dehon came to South Carolina from Newport, Rhode Island, in 1810 to be rector of St. Michael's Church and then to be bishop of South Carolina beginning in 1812. Their son, the Reverend William Dehon, ministered to three churches—St. Stephen's Parish, Black Oak Church (Middle St. John's) and the Rocks Church (Upper St. John's). "William Dehon, son of the second Bishop of the diocese, began a notable ministry in this field, serving all three churches, besides five or six chapels erected by planters on their plantations for 1,800 Negroes to whom Mr. Dehon ministered; 300 of these were communicants. The religious tone of the parish rose at this time." The Reverend Dehon served these three parishes from 1842 to 1859, when he became the minister of St. Philip's in Charleston. Thomas, *A Historical Account of the Protestant Episcopal Church in South Carolina,* 404–5.

68. The Charleston Library Society was established in 1748, and from 1835 it occupied the old Bank of South Carolina building at the northwest corner of Broad and Church. Its collections and comfortable reading room are still enjoyed today on a subscription basis. It was "more a gentlemen's preserve than a bibliophiles' retreat . . . Their library grew from about 5,000 volumes in 1830 to 25,000 in 1848, strong in collections of literary and historical works and well stocked with volumes on political theory, philosophy and natural science." Jane H. Pease and William H. Pease, "Intellectual Life in the 1830's: The Institutional Framework and the Charleston Style," in *Intellectual Life in Antebellum Charleston,* ed. Michael O'Brien and David Moltke-Hansen (Knoxville: University of Tennessee Press, 1986), 149.

69. Madame de Sevigne was Marie de Rabutin-Chantal, who lived in Paris from 1626 to 1696. *The Letters of Madame de Sevigne to Her Daughters and Her Friends* is full of anecdotes of seventeenth-century Paris. Robert D. Young, ed., *The Best in World Literature,* vol. 2 of *The Reader's Adviser* (New Providence, N.J.: R. R. Bowker, 1994).

70. Betsey was undoubtedly a seamstress in the employ of the Whartons.

71. The Right Reverend Alonzo Potter was bishop of New York. Bishop Ives was bishop of

North Carolina and later caused controversy by defecting to the Roman Catholic Church. The Right Reverend Christopher Edwards Gadsden was bishop of the Diocese of South Carolina.

72. The sweet olive, or tea olive, blooms in winter and early spring in the lowcountry, perfuming the air.

73. Arabella Wharton Sinkler was born in December 1847 and was christened on 22 December. She died six months later in Philadelphia and was buried on 23 June 1848 in the churchyard of St. Stephen's Episcopal Church, with the Reverend Henry W. Ducachet officiating.

74. "Daguerreotype Portraits—Portraits are taken in every size and style" [advertisement], *Germantown (Pa.) Telegraph,* 27 April 1847. "The first American daguerreotype, a view of Central High School, had been taken in 1839 by the ingenious mechanic Joseph Saxton from the United States Mint where he worked. It did not take long for the art to develop. William G. Mason, an engraver, who made a daguerreotype of a Chestnut Street scene in 1843, is credited with taking the first perfect picture by artificial light. Even better was another photograph of the same shops taken thirteen years later by one of the Langenheim brothers who were then using glass plates. By 1860 there were eighty-four Philadelphia firms engaged in photographic work, most of them supplying carte-de-viste portraits." Edwin Wolf and Walter Rawls, *Philadelphia: Portrait of An American City,* 187.

75. "Herring, 400 boxes, new Digby Herring, 200 boxes Eastport scaled by Nath'l Waldron, 6 South Wharf" [advertisement], *Cummings' Evening Telegraphic Bulletin,* 1 January 1851.

76. Philadelphia was a center of fine cabinetmaking in the mid-nineteenth century, and much of the furniture at Belvidere came from there. A sale close-out advertised in the *Gazette* gives some idea of the range of furniture manufactured in the city: "Large and extensive sale of superior and well made cabinet furniture of the latest patterns and designs . . . in the ware rooms of M. Bouvier & Co, 93 South Second Street above Walnut. Comprising in part, superior wardrobes; spring seat sofas, sofa tables made of rosewood and mahogany; dressing bureaus with oval and square glasses of the most modern styles . . . The principal part of the above furniture has been taken in exchange from most of the best manufacturers in the city." *United States Gazette for the Country,* 9 March 1846.

77. Begun in 1793 and opened in 1801, the Santee Canal was designed by Col. Christian Senf, a Swedish engineer. It was a thirty-five-foot-wide, twenty-two-mile-long ditch with twelve locks and eight aqueducts. The canal connected Charleston, via the Cooper River, to the Santee River. Henry Savage, Jr., *River of the Carolinas: The Santee,* in *Rivers of America,* ed. Carl Carmer (New York: Rinehart & Company, Inc.), 240–53. The furniture would have been unloaded at Nelson's Ferry and brought by wagon to Belvidere.

78. The magazine Emily refers to was *Brother Jonathan,* a weekly magazine which began publication on 13 July 1839. The figures of Brother Jonathan and Uncle Sam were used interchangeably to represent the United States by U.S. cartoonists from the early 1830s to 1861.

79. *Philadelphia Register and National Recorder* (1819–). The *Recorder* was Philadelphia's daily newspaper.

80. Emily may be referring to a performance of Fouqué's popular fairy tale, "Undine." Undine is the tale of the doomed love affair of Knight Huldbrand and the water nymph, Undine. Undine was the daughter of the sea: "Everything about her was bright and glancing. Her pale hair danced and floated around her head, sparkling with waterdrops; her eyes were sea green, her skin as pure and luminous as the white crests of waves." "Fouqué, Friedrich Heinrich Karl de La

Motte, Baron," *Encyclopedia Britannica Online*, http://www.eb.com:180/cgi-bin/g?DocF=micro/216/59 [accessed 6 November 1999].

81. In her letters and receipts Emily speaks of having two types of white potatoes. The tuber is native to South America and was transported to Ireland by Sir Walter Raleigh. There are four basic types of potatoes: russet, long white, round white, and round red. The sweet potato, also grown at Belvidere, is of a different origin, the morning-glory family, and is also native to tropical America. Sharon Tyler Herbst, *Food Lover's Companion: Comprehensive Definitions of Over 3000 Food, Wine, and Culinary Terms* (New York: Barron's, 1990), s.v. "potato." Emily used both white potatoes and sweet potatoes in her many potato receipts. For those receipts see LeClercq, *An Antebellum Plantation Household.*

82. Pond Bluff was the home of the Keating Simons family in 1865 and was between River Road and the Santee River. It was about four miles west of Belvidere. In the 1840s Pond Bluff was owned by the Sinklers' cousins, the Lesesnes. Emily speaks of the two Lesesne children, Francis and Marion, as living there. Private map of Santee River plantations, 1865.

83. There were six major railroad projects undertaken in the antebellum years that made Charleston the hub of a network of railroads that fanned out to the hinterlands of the state and beyond. The passenger station in Charleston was at Mary Street, and the depository was at Line Street. Fraser, *Charleston! Charleston!*, 222.

84. William Henry Sinkler, Charles's younger brother.

85. The races began on Wednesday, 22 February, and lasted until Saturday, 26 February. The Jockey Club purse of $1,000 was for four one-mile heats, a grueling race indeed. William Sinkler, *"beau-père"* to Emily, had entered Shark, a four-year-old by Shark out of Atlanta. The betting was intense, and Shark was the favorite. Before an animated crowd and on a blustery, cold day, Shark carried the field against Countess and Bostona. The Jockey Club Ball was held on Friday night, and it was a bright and interesting scene. "The company consisted of much of the beauty and fashion of our city . . . The supper was elegant indeed. The centers of the tables were set off by pyramids of confectionary and classically formed temples, glittering with pendant bon-bons." "Our Race," *Charleston Courier*, 19, 22–24 February 1848. Here is how Henry Wharton described this race in a letter, March 1ˢᵗ, 1848, to his brother Frank Wharton. "Owing to Emily's friends and Mr. Sinkler's standing, I became acquainted with the best people of Charleston. The races occupied nearly the whole of the day time of the week, and they were to me extremely fascinating from, not only the beauty of the sight, but the part which Mr. Sinkler took in them. His horse "Shark" a most magnificent animal won two purses. . . .But my time was occupied still more agreeably in the evenings. Tuesday evening I went to the St. Cecelia Ball. . . .There I was introduced to a number of young ladies. . . .Wednesday was the dinner of the Race Club, a very splendid affair. Real turtle soup, wild turkies, venison, grouse, partridges, pheasants, shad, and all the smaller fry of delicacies, not forgetting pate de foie gras in great abundance, and wines of great value, such as Johannisberg of 1822. . . .That evening I went to a large ball at Mrs. Pringle's (a daugher of Col. Allston), which is considered one of the most handsome of the houses in Charleston. Rooms, plate, supper, dresses, all very splendid, one carpet cost $700. . . .Friday evening I went to the Race Ball, not very large for a public ball but quite of the first people. The dressing at it was very handsome indeed, much more so then at any of ours. The supper cost $1200. Monday, back again at Belvidere.

86. Samuel Warren, *Works of Samuel Warren* (Leipzig, S. Bernhard Tauchnitz, 1844). The work was issued in seven volumes and included *Passages from the Diary of a Late Physician, Ten Thousand*

a Year, Now and Then—Through a Glass Darkly, The Lily and the Bee, and *An Apologue of the Crystal Palace.*

87. "Within the sprawling county railroads linked the center city with the old market and mill town of Germantown and the new factory settlement of Manayunk. Horse-drawn omnibuses made travel over shorter distances cheap and convenient . . . Gaily painted and fancifully named, the omnibuses started from the Merchants' Exchange, where they drew up beside the tracks of the Columbia Railroad. Until horsepower trolleys were introduced two decades later, omnibuses—literally for all—were the only city-wide public transportation." Wolf and Rawls, *Philadelphia: Portrait of an American City* (Harrisburg: Stackpole Books, 1975), 149, 161.

88. M. Cardeza was a female friend of Emily in Philadelphia, one from whom she apparently learned much choice gossip.

89. Clarendon County was located across the Santee River and Santee Swamp, due north of Belvidere, and was originally within the old Sumter District. C.S. is Charles Sinkler.

90. *The John-donkey* (Philadelphia and New York, 1848). This weekly was only published from 1 January 1848 to 21 October 1848.

91. "Mr. Dehon had for his assistant first the Rev C. P. Gadsden (1848–1853), then Rev. R. P. Johnson (1853–1854) . . . Under Rev. Dehon the 'religious tone of the parish rose' and there were 'over six chapels erected by planters on their plantation for 1,800 Negroes to whom Mr. Dehon ministered.'" Thomas, *A Historical Account of the Protestant Episcopal Church in South Carolina,* 404.

92. "1848 deaths, June 23, Arabella Sinkler, aged 6 months (in church yard, Henry W. Ducachet, Rector)." Roll # X, Ch. 749, St. Stephen's Episcopal Church, 19 South Tenth Street, Philadelphia (in the Historical Society of Pennsylvania), microfilm.

93. Philadelphia was a major gardening center. "From the South had come exotic plants and shrubs since the days of the Bartrams. In that tradition John MacAran built a sophisticated conservatory at Seventeenth and Arch streets where evening entertainments were offered in his long and spacious hot-houses. David Landreth on Federal Street near the Arsenal, Robert Buist at 140 South Twelfth Street, and Henry A. Dreer on Market Street maintained thriving nurseries and carried on an extensive trade in seeds." Wolf and Rawls, *Philadelphia: Portrait of An American City,* 193.

94. "Pineville is, and always has been, a very popular meeting. It has many attractive and peculiar features. It is a meeting conducted entirely unlike any other we know of in our country. It is aristocratic in its character—or, we ought rather to say, the company in attendance is always of so select an order, composed of the gentry of the immediate neighborhood, that it resembles a large united family party, rather than the promiscuous throng of all sorts and conditions of people it is usual to find congregated on a race ground in other places . . . Here you see a people— a primitive people standing by themselves—a type of the feudal past—living upon the lands of their fathers, marrying and intermarrying, continuing to practise that hospitality, and those polite attentions to strangers, which their fathers practised 'in the good old times before them' . . . The present Course, near Pineville, was laid out by Col. Maham. The Course was then called 'The St. Stephen's Course,' and a Club was formed, known as 'The Santee Jockey Club.'" Irving, *The South Carolina Jockey Club,* 157, 158, 159.

95. Emily's remedy for seasickness was as follows: "Generally allow the stomach to discharge its contents once or twice and then if there is no organic disease give 5 drops of Chloroform in a little water and if necessary repeat the dose in 4 to 6 hours. Let the patient sleep and he will awake well." LeClercq, *An Antebellum Plantation Household,* 155.

96. Mr. Agassiz was a Philadelphia friend of the Whartons who was visiting Emily in the South.

97. Emily's prescription for fleas and bedbugs required the use of wormwood, an aromatic plant yielding a bitter extract used in making absinthe: "A writer in the Gardener's Chronicle recommends the use of oil of wormwood to keep off fleas and bed bugs. Put a few drops on a handkerchief or piece of folded muslin and put in the bed haunted by the enemy." LeClercq, *An Antebellum Plantation Household,* 130.

98. The Whartons sent the children many of the best-known children's magazines and books of the mid-nineteenth century.

99. "Their plantations along the Santee Swamp being unhealthy during the summer, Santee River planters and their families flocked to the long triangle known as the High Hills of Santee . . . From early morn until quite dark the sandy roads were kept hot by buggy after buggy and carriages filled with young people from different homes . . . Music and dancing would be kept up until the wee hours . . . In front of each house huge bon fires burned, casting a red glow over the yard . . . How happy these evenings were! For not care had come to the young people and life seemed a bright, beautiful dream." Richardson, "Recollections."

100. Lizzie remembered wonderful occasions in the upcountry. "We always enjoyed our visits to the DeVeaux in Stateburg on the High Hills of the Santee . . . Not only the house and garden and grounds were so lovely, but the mode of life was quite like a great French chateau. Trays of coffee and fruit were brought up to the rooms in the morning by deft, well-trained servants and for those who wandered downstairs early there were in the broad overshadowed back piazza large fanners of splendid peaches and beautiful figs." Elizabeth Allen Coxe, *Memories of a South Carolina Plantation During the War* (privately printed, 1912), 77–83.

101. Woodford was the residence of Isaac Wharton from 1793 to 1808, and Emily probably visited this lovely brick house in the Philadelphia environs on many occasions. Perhaps Emily decided to name the Sinkler place in the Santee Hills after this family home. There is a picture of Isaac Wharton's Woodford in the Sinkler Papers in the South Carolina Historical Society in Charleston, South Carolina. Woodford was forty miles by barge and carriage from Belvidere. As Elizabeth Allen Coxe (Lizzie) noted in her *Memories of a South Carolina Plantation During the War,* "we had no base of supplies but Belvidere, forty miles away, whence Duck Peter plodded up once a week across the swamp with a mule and cart full of vegetables, fruit, butter, and if the weather were cool enough, a butchered lamb, besides several coops of skinny and clucking chickens."

102. Mr. Harris Simons was Charles's lawyer as well as his factor. He lived in Charleston.

103. In the 1850s Charleston had a number of fine hotels, of which the Charleston Hotel was the finest, costing $2.50 per day with dinner at $1.00. Other hotels included Planters, American, Victoria, Carolina, Pavilion, Merchants, and Commercial. The rates of those hotels were $2.00, with dinner at seventy-five cents. *Charleston Daily Courier,* 2 February 1850.

104. Coastwise steamship service between the North and the South began in the 1840s and was regularly advertised thereafter. For example, there was regular service between Philadelphia and Savannah by the Steam Navigation Company's line. In 1853 the steamship advertised was the *State of Georgia,* weighing twelve hundred tons. The cost of cabin passage from Savannah or Charleston was $25, while steerage passage cost $9. In 1853 the *Philadelphia* and the *Osprey,* on which Emily preferred to travel, were steamers in the coastwise service from Charleston to Philadelphia. *Charleston Daily Courier,* 3 July 1852.

105. Taking the cure at one of the Virginia hot springs or traveling to the Sand Hills for the "dryness and Pineyness" of the air were a regular part of the health regime of both Northerners and Southerners, all of whom were plagued by respiratory complaints ranging from asthma to whooping cough to consumption.

106. Richard and Elizabeth (Eliza) Manning (see note 32 above).

107. Emily was a superbly trained musician, playing both the piano and the guitar. The musical evenings at Belvidere and Eutaw were renowned. As Anna Linton Sinkler notes in her *A History of the Sinkler Family* (manuscript in possession of the author, n.d.), "my grandmother, Anna Linton Sinkler, had a magnificent contralto voice. Emily Wharton also had a beautiful voice and when they were all living at Eutaw, Uncle Mazyck Porcher who lived at Mexico Plantation, fifteen miles down the River Road, often used to drive up and spend the evening just to hear them sing." Elizabeth Allen Coxe (Lizzie), Emily's oldest daughter, also remembered the beauty of her mother's voice, as she noted in *Memories of a South Carolina Plantation During the War:* "Mamma and Aunt Anna entertained the guests in the drawing-room by singing duets which sounded to me like the songs of angels. Their voices were so lovely and so well trained, one soprano and one contralto, and they were fascinated with Jenny Lind's songs, of which they had a number. They each had a guitar with a blue ribbon, and sang Italian and German songs on Moonlight evenings in the piazza." Jenny Lind was an established opera singer who toured the United States in 1850 and 1851, giving ninety-three concerts, the final one being in Philadelphia. She sang in English, and Emily would have known many of her popular songs such as "Coming Through the Rye," "The Last Rose of Summer," and "John Anderson, My Joe."

108. Charlotte Brontë completed her novel *Shirley: A Tale* in 1849. It was published by Harper in New York in 1850. The novel is set in the West Riding of Yorkshire during the troubled years of 1811–12, when economic hardships which followed from the war with France, complicated by an embargo on trade with America and the introduction of new machinery, led to massive unemployment and widespread rioting in the wool-producing districts. Herbert J. Rosengarten, "Charlotte Brontë," in *Victorian Novelists Before 1885,* vol. 21 of *Dictionary of Literary Biography,* ed. Ira B. Nadel and William E. Fredeman (Detroit: Gale Research Company, 1983), 25–54. When Emily says that Brontë's "radicalism" in *Shirley* is *"trop fort"* (too strong), she is probably referring to the fact that, in this historical novel of the Luddite uprisings and the manufacturer Robert Moore, Brontë treats the plight of the workers sympathetically and is critical of the callousness and narrow self-interest of the manufacturers who exploit the poor. In *Shirley* there is also an undercurrent of feminism as Brontë, through her two female heroines, pointedly supports women's emancipation from domestic slavery. The phrase "mit die Publicationes" (with the publications, or newspapers) obviously refers to the German newspapers her unknown grantor had included in the bundles of packages with the music and Brontë's *Shirley.*

109. John and William Bartram lived in Philadelphia. John Bartram's botanical garden near Philadelphia was a marvel of the time. William Bartram's *Travels through North and South Carolina, Georgia, East and West Florida, the Cherokee Country . . . Together With Observations on the Manners of the Indians* was a result of trips to those regions to collect botanical specimens. It was first published in 1791. Peter Collinson, to whom Emily refers in her letter, was the Bartrams' principal English contact for marketing American plants and seeds in Europe. Most of the extant information concerning the lives of the two Bartrams is in William Darlington's *Memorials of John Bartram and Humphry Marshall with Notices of Their Botanical Contemporaries* (Philadelphia, 1849).

Possibly Emily is referring to this work. There is a letter from Peter Collinson to John Bartram on 20 December 1737 that is remarkably like the section quoted by Emily. Helen Gere Cruickshank, ed., *John and William Bartram's America: Selections from the Writings of the Philadelphia Naturalists* (New York: The Devin-Adair Company, 1957), 7, 71.

110. "The RG's" were Emily's Woodford neighbors, the Gaillards.

111. Bailey's and Levy's were both stores frequented by Emily in Philadelphia. L. J. Levy & Co. was located at 134 Chestnut Street and for a winter sale had reduced prices on their stock of French and Scotch plaid cloaks, printed mousselines de laines and cashmere, rich silks for dresses and coats, and also cashmere shawls. *United States Gazette for the Country,* 7 January 1847.

112. Emily and Charles attended the Church of the Holy Cross in Stateburg.

113. This comment casts some doubt on the assumption that slaves preferred to work in the house. Apparently on the Sinklers' plantations field hands had greater personal freedom and more time off.

114. The oven Emily is referring to in her 1850 letter could have been either wood- or coal-burning. An advertisement for such an oven was printed in the Philadelphia newspaper: "The Premium Cooking Stove—Thatchers Hot Blast. This stove has two large size ovens, one is used expressly for broiling and roasting . . . The only stove that can be used for boiling, baking, broiling and roasting all at the same time . . . The above stove can be used for either coal or wood. No. 322 Market St." *Germantown (Pa.) Telegraph,* 16 January 1850. Emily's receipts for turkey as well as her Omelette Souffle are both reproduced in LeClercq, *An Antebellum Plantation Household.*

115. The Santee Swamp was a huge area of cypress and gum trees that lay north of the Santee River. Today it is covered by Lake Marion. The many cypress knees protruding above the water attest to the density of the swamp Emily had to cross to go from Eutaw and Belvidere to the Sand Hills and Bradford Springs, where Woodford was located.

116. Grandmother was Charles Sinkler's maternal grandmother, Mary Deas Brown.

117. Clem was Emily's dressmaker in Philadelphia.

118. Charleston had many military companies that paraded with great regularity. For example, on 2 February 1853 the 2d Brigade of Cavalry of Charleston were ordered to "parade at the Race Course, near Charleston on Tuesday 22nd, the line to be formed at 10 a.m." *Charleston Daily Courier,* 2 February 1853.

119. Harriet Horry Huger (1822–1857) was one of Emily's warmest Charleston friends. She was the daughter of Emily's doctor, Dr. Francis Kinloch Huger (1773–1855). Emily was also friends with Dr. Huger's other daughter, Elizabeth Pinckney Huger (1804–1882).

120. The Russell Middletons and the Henry Middletons were friends of Emily and Charles.

121. The annual Episcopal convention. (See note 48.)

122. The *Directory of City of Charleston and Neck for 1849,* printed by A. J. Burke, 40 Broad Street, Charleston, South Carolina, lists the passenger depot as being on Mary Street and the depository on Line Street. There was one train daily for Hamburg (on the east side of the Savannah River from Augusta) and Columbia leaving at 10 a.m., and it cost $6.75.

123. The Mannings to whom Emily refers are her sister-in-law, Elizabeth Allen Sinkler Manning (Eliza), and her husband, Richard Irvine Manning.

124. Hannah More, *The Book of Private Devotion: A Series of Prayers and Meditations* (Hartford, Brown & Parsons, 1845).

125. The Southern Convention of 1850 was a meeting of southern delegates in Nashville, Tennessee, to discuss the issues of the day, including fugitive slaves, the inability to make the Fugitive Slave Act work, and finally whether the South should leave the Union. There was no groundswell for leaving the Union. In the halls of Congress, Daniel Webster, the Massachusetts senator, spoke eloquently in favor of the Compromise of 1850, proposed by Webster, Henry Clay, and John C. Calhoun. It strengthened the Fugitive Slave Act and set a geographical line above which there would be elections in the territories as to whether they would be slave or free.

126. According to the *Germantown (Pa.) Telegraph,* 3 April 1850, Dr. John Webster was tried for the murder of Dr. Parkman. Dr. Webster was a chemistry professor at Harvard, and he murdered Dr. Parkman with a stick of wood in a blackmail scheme. He was executed on 5 September 1850.

127. Emily refers to *Neal's Saturday Gazette.*

128. Mrs. Hummel was the German teacher at the girls' boarding school in Stateburg, which had ninety-six young ladies. A school called the Bradford Institute appears on local property maps of the times. Emily apparently enjoyed speaking German with Mrs. Hummel. Gregorie notes that "Bradford Springs because of its reputation as a health resort, became also a center for schools. The springs took their name from Nathaniel Bradford, who in 1785 had a grant there for 600 acres of vacant land." The Bradford Female Institute occupied 1,246 acres on land that had been formerly Orange Grove Plantation. It was first known as the Bradford Springs Female Academy, organized under Rev. Julius J. DuBose. In 1849 the land was purchased by Rev. Edwin Cater, who hired Mrs. Hummel and Miss E. Spain as teachers. By 1850 there were one hundred girls enrolled. "The Institute reached out into the community as a cultural influence, and Mr. Cater frequently advertised invitations to the public to attend his lectures." Gregorie, *History of Sumter County,* 180–83.

129. Robert Southey, *The Poetical Works of Robert Southey* (Paris, A. and W. Galignani, 1829).

130. François René de Chateaubriand, *Itinéraire de Paris à Jérusalem et de Jérusalem à Paris: En Allant par la Grèce, et Revenant par l'Egypte, la Bárbarie* et *L'Espagne,* (Paris: Le Normant, 1812).

131. The *Perry* shipwreck to which Emily referred occurred in 1846. Charles Sinkler had joined the United States Navy in 1836. Shortly thereafter, when stationed in Philadelphia, he met and married Emily Wharton. In October 1846, while Charles was serving as the sailing master of the United States brigantine *Perry,* which had just returned from the siege of Vera Cruz, the *Perry* was wrecked on Sombrero Reef, about thirty miles from Key West, while on a voyage from Havana to Charleston. One of his brother officers of the Navy, Lt. (later Rev.) R. S. Trapier, was a guest on the *Perry* during that eventful trip and later wrote a graphic description of the cyclone through which they barely escaped with their lives.

132. "Bingen on the Rhine" is by Caroline Elizabeth Sarah Norton (1808–1877). Its four verses are highly sentimental, the last giving some feel for the whole: "Tell my sister not to weep for me, and sob with drooping head, / When the troops come marching home again with glad and gallant tread, / But to look upon them proudly with a calm and steadfast eye, / For her brother was a soldier too, and not afraid to die; / And if a comrade seek her love, I ask her in my name / To listen to him kindly, without regret or shame, / And to hang the old sword in its place (my father's sword and mine) / For the honor of old Bingen, —dear Bingen on the Rhine." For the rest see Ralph L. Woods, *A Treasury of the Familiar* (New York: The Macmillan Company, 1959).

133. The Andersons, who lived in Stateburg, were friends of Emily and Charles. Emily's fascination with gardening was based on an extensive knowledge of botany. Her copy of *North American Botany: Comprising the Native and Common Cultivated Plants, North of Mexico,* by Amos

Eaton and John Wright, published in 1840 by Elias Gates in Troy, New York, is underlined and annotated. Dried herbs and flowers which Emily placed between pages are still there. It is owned by this author, Anne Sinkler LeClercq.

134. John C. Calhoun led the South Carolina nullification movement of the 1830s. Pres. Andrew Jackson considered his efforts seditious. He let it be known that he would hang Calhoun "high as Heyman" if he continued in his efforts to have South Carolina nullify a federal statute, known as the Tariff of Abominations. Calhoun and many Southerners were opposed to the tariff enacted by Congress, which imposed higher tariffs on manufactured goods imported from Europe, thus making the South more dependent on the manufactured goods of the North. In October 1832, in special session, the South Carolina legislature adopted an ordinance declaring the tariff null and void.

135. Kate Wharton was Emily's sister-in-law, married to Emily's brother Frank.

136. The *Osprey* was a steamer in the coastwise service between Philadelphia and Charleston. Mr. Simons was Charles's lawyer and factor and lived in Charleston.

137. The fire that occurred on Adger's Wharf is described in the *Charleston Courier,* 17–18 May 1850. "Destructive Fire! Several Thousand Bales of Cotton Burned. About half past 1 o'clock an alarm of fire was sounded which was found to proceed from the cotton shed on Adger's South Wharf in which was stored a large quantity of cotton . . . The counting houses on the North Wharf took fire . . . It is believed some 4,000 bales of cotton burned, and the loss is estimated at \$350,000."

138. Fire was, of course, a terror in the nineteenth century, when there were inadequate means for preventing its spread. As most homes in the Stateburg area were of wood, and heating was by open fires, the threat of fire was acute. Emily notes, interestingly, that the Gaillards did not think this fire was set by design. There was real fear in South Carolina of slave insurrection. Emily's neighbors were the Jno. G. Gaillards who lived at Ash Hill, a plantation in close proximity to Belvidere.

139. Lilly Montgomery was a Philadelphia friend of Emily.

140. Donizetti's *Lucia di Lammermoor.*

141. "Lizzie Leigh" was attributed by many, including Emily, to Charles Dickens. The mistake probably occurred because it was published in Dickens's first edition of *Household Words* in 1850. "Lizzie Leigh" is a tale of "guilt, remorse, and repentance" and is by Elizabeth Cleghorn Gaskell. Edgar Wright, "Elizabeth Cleghorn Gaskell," in *Victorian Novelists Before 1885,* vol. 21 of *Dictionary of Literary Biography,* ed. Ira B. Nadel and William E. Fredeman (Detroit: Gale Research Company, 1983), 174–89.

142. Emily and Charles's Woodford was in Bradford Springs, as she says, eleven miles from Stateburg. We know that her neighbors were the Jno. G. Gaillards. However, the exact location of Woodford has not been determined. Documents from the Sumter County Courthouse show that Charles Sinkler purchased three hundred acres in Sumter County in 1849 that were bounded on the east by land of Samuel Porcher Gaillard. In 1851 he purchased another 491 acres on the main Sumter County Road.

143. Emily is probably referring to William Thompson Townsend's *The Lost Ship; or, The Man of War's Man, and the Privateer,* published first in 1843. Captain Cuttle was a fatherly, kind, old ship's captain who befriended Florence Dombey and her dog, Diogenes, in Charles Dickens's 1846 *Dombey & Son.* (See note 60.)

144. See note 118.

145. Henriades and Olivers were the names of two confectionery stores in Philadelphia.

146. Tombstone inscriptions might carry an air of the otherworldly.

147. Papeterie is a word used for stylish writing paper.

148. In 1850 women's fashions were in the style of the French Empire. Accessories included lace collars, lace cuffs, umbrellas, shawls, and hats. Wonderful examples of these accessories can be seen in *Godey's Lady's Book, Peterson's Magazine, Graham's Magazine,* and *Frank Leslie's Ladies' Gazette of Paris, London, and New-York Fashions.* Emily would have been familiar with all four of the above periodicals.

149. By cards and answers Emily is referring to invitations and responses. She was avid to know about the social comings and goings of her family and friends in Philadelphia.

150. Anna Linton Sinkler was the wife of Charles's younger brother, William Henry Sinkler. Anna and William Henry were first cousins. They had common grandparents, Capt. James Sinkler and Margaret Cantey Sinkler. Anna's parents, John Linton Thomson and Margaret Anna Sinkler Thomson, died when Anna was very young, and she became a ward of William Sinkler, the *beau-père.* Anna was sent to Madame Talvande's school when very young. She was an accomplished French scholar and had a beautiful contralto voice. She married William Henry Sinkler on 4 March 1841, at Eutaw Plantation, just shortly before Emily and Charles were married. Anna and Emily were best friends as well as sisters-in-law. Elizabeth Allen Sinkler was the *beau-père's* only daughter. She married Richard Irvine Manning at Eutaw in 1845, with the Rocks' minister, Reverend Dehon, officiating. Eliza and Emily were inseparable friends as well as sisters-in-law.

151. "Chickering's Piano: Just received per ship Napoleana fine assortment of 6 and 7 octave iron frame Piano Fortes, exclusively from John Siegling" [advertisement], *Charleston Courier,* 29 April 1851.

152. One of the songs made popular by Jenny Lind, "the Swedish Nightingale." See note 167.

153. Written by Thomas Isaac Wharton, Emily's father.

154. Catherine Sinclair, *Sir Edward Graham, or, Railway Speculators* (London: Longman, Brown, Green, and Longmans, 1849).

155. Emily refers to Isaac, the only son of Abraham and Sarah, in the Bible. At a young age he was taken by his father to be sacrificed in order to test Abraham's faithfulness. At the ultimate moment a kid was substituted. Isaac and Rebecca were the parents of Jacob and Esau. Mircea Eliade, ed., *The Encyclopedia of Religion* (New York: Macmillan, 1987), 7:288.

156. LeClercq, *An Antebellum Plantation Household,* 90, 112.

157. The Philadelphia fire of July 1850 started on Vine Street and spread rapidly in that area.

158. See note 120. *Germantown (Pa.) Telegraph,* 3 April 1850, has an account of the "Trial of Dr. Webster." He had murdered Dr. Parkman, a Harvard chemistry professor, with a stick of wood in a blackmail scheme for importuning of a creditor.

159. Mr. Neville had married Charles and Emily in Philadelphia on 8 September 1842.

160. Emily refers here to Dick Richardson. He lived at DeVeaux, his summer place in Stateburg, with his four daughters, including Julia, a friend of Emily's Lizzie. During the winter he lived at his plantation on the Santee, Big Home. Lizzie describes these two places in her *Memories of a South Carolina Plantation During the War:* "We always enjoyed our visits to the DeVeaux in Stateburg on the High Hills of the Santee, as it was picturesquely called. Their place was one of the most beautiful and luxurious that I knew in the South . . . Not only the house and garden and grounds were so lovely, but the mode of life was, it seemed to me, quite like a great French chateau. Trays of coffee and fruit were brought up to the rooms in the morning by

deft, well-trained servants and for those who wandered downstairs early there were in the broad overshadowed back piazza, large fanners of splendid peaches and beautiful figs . . . The large parties at Cousin Dick Richardson's winter place, 'Big Home,' were equally exciting but quite mediaeval in some ways."

161. The hurricane season lasts from June to October. Emily's first voyage to South Carolina in September 1842 was a stormy, perilous coastwise passage.

162. Mrs. Hummel was the schoolmistress at the girls' boarding school in Stateburg, the Bradford Institute. Mr. Elliott was the minister at the Episcopal church in Stateburg, the Church of the Holy Cross. Mr. Porcher and Mr. Manigault were from Charleston. Mr. Gaillard was Emily and Charles's next-door neighbor.

163. William Henry Sinkler, Anna's husband and Charles's younger brother, was to die at the age of thirty-seven on 17 April 1856. He is buried at the Rocks Church. Anna and William Henry had a son, W. Henry Sinkler, who was born on 5 October 1844 at Eutaw. He fought in the Civil War at the age of seventeen, as did Emily and Charles's Wharton. He managed to make a living for his mother and sisters and was married in June 1865 to Cleremonde Gaillard. Sinkler, *A History of the Sinkler Family.*

164. Sister Margaret was Margaret Huger Sinkler, married to Charles's older brother, James Sinkler. They lived in Charleston. Scarlet fever was a childhood disease of the nineteenth century that killed many. Emily has a preventative for it in her *Receipts and Remedies* that calls for mixing crushed garlic with a pint of "good rye whiskey."

165. Emily would have traveled over the River Road and Nelsons Ferry Road by horse-drawn carriage. The railroad station in Branchville was twenty miles from Eutaw and Belvidere Plantations. One can only imagine the fatigue of such travel, as she describes it, over one hundred miles and then to sea in the most precarious season for travel on the Atlantic.

166. Church and party dress for female African Americans at Belvidere has been captured in photographs of Emily's granddaughter Emily Sinkler's marriage on the Belvidere lawn to Nicholas Guy Roosevelt. The pictures show African American women in highly-starched, long, white muslin dresses much like that described in Emily's letter.

167. Cape May was a fashionable Victorian seaside resort located in New Jersey, south of Atlantic City, between the Delaware Bay and the Atlantic Ocean. In Emily's time, as today, it was a fashionable resort and fishing community.

168. William Sinkler Manning was born 30 January 1851.

169. Henry Lesesne and his wife were among Charles and Emily's best Charleston friends. Charles was Henry Lesesne's first cousin. Elizabeth Allen Broun Sinkler's sister was Anna Caroline Broun. She married Thomas Lesesne, and Henry Deas Lesesne was their child.

170. Dr. Henry Rutledge Frost (1795–1866) was Emily's Charleston doctor. Joseph Ioor Waring, *A History of Medicine in South Carolina, 1825–1900* (Charleston: South Carolina Medical Assn., 1967).

171. Lotto, or bingo, was a child's game of chance using cards on which there is a grid of numbers, a row of which constitute a win when they have been chosen at random.

172. Dr. McEuen and Mr. Ammen were both Philadelphia friends and visited Emily on several different occasions.

173. Jenny was Jenny Lind, "the Swedish Nightingale." Emily loved her songs and sang many of them. Lind was on a tour of the United States in 1851 that was arranged by P. T. Barnum. On Monday, 6 January 1851, Jenny Lind was in Charleston. She was described in the *Charleston*

Courier as a "divine creature causing riots wherever she went. Her voice melted their senses and held them spellbound."

174. "Jenny Lind at Oates, 234 and 236 King St., will be found the following new songs by the Swedish Nightingale" [advertisement], *Charleston Courier,* 20 March 1851. Oates is listed in the *Charleston City Directory* for 1849 as George Oates, bookseller, 234 King Street.

175. Phineas Taylor Barnum (1810–1891) had established the American Museum in New York City, where he exhibited a great variety of freaks. "Eager to change his image from promoter of freaks to impresario of artistic attractions, Barnum risked his entire fortune by importing Jenny Lind, a Swedish soprano whom he had never seen or heard and who was almost unknown in the United States. Dubbing Lind the "Swedish Nightingale," Barnum mounted the most massive publicity campaign he had ever attempted for Jenny Lind's opening night in New York (before a capacity audience of 5,000) and her nine months of concerts across the United States." "Barnum, P(hineas) T(aylor)," *Encyclopedia Britannica Online,* http://www.eb.com:180/cgi-bin/g?DocF=micro/52/88 [accessed 6 November 1999].

176. Jenny Lind's "Bird Song:"

> Birding! Why sing in the forest wide!
> Say Why, Say Why
> Call'st Thou the Bridegroom or the Bride?
> And why, And Why?
> I call no Bridegroom—Call no Bride
> Although I sing in the forest wide
> Nor know I why I'm Singing.

177. Thomas Porcher built Ophir in 1810. It was inundated by the impoundment of the Santee River in 1941. It had broad brick central stairs leading up to a front porch. There was an imposing second story and a third floor with dormers. The house had two end chimneys and two front doors, one entering into the living room and the other into the dining room. There was no central hall in this type of construction. It was unpainted and made of cypress. Harold Tatum, "Buildings and Reminders of Early Day South Carolina" (Sponsored by John R. Todd, 1931), manuscript in SCL.

178. The Converses were friends of Emily and Charles. Mr. Converse was the rector at the Church of the Holy Cross in Stateburg, which was also know as Claremont Episcopal Church. As Gregorie notes, "in ante-bellum times, it was customary for slaves to worship in the same church with their masters, the Negroes being seated in the rear or in the gallery. The Rev. A. L. Converse, rector of Claremont Episcopal Church at Stateburg, in 1841 reported 25 white members of the church and 41 Negroes." Gregorie tells the story of "Big Home" and its association with Reverend Converse. "Like so many of the home-loving citizens of Sumter District, Colonel Singleton expressed his love for the place by naming it 'Home.' There his youngest daughter Sarah Angelica was married on November 27, 1838, to Abraham Van Buren, eldest son and private secretary to President Van Buren. The clergyman who officiated at the splendid wedding, the Rev. Augustus L. Converse, eleven years later also became a son-in-law of Colonel Singleton, when he married the wealthy young widow, Marion DeVeaux of the Ruins . . . Mr. Converse, a northern man with a wooden leg, was the rector of the Episcopal Church in Stateburg, and taught at the local school. His wife, Mary Ann Kellog, died in 1848, and the following year he married Marion DeVeaux, she being then thirty-three years old and he, fifty-one." The wife was

immensely wealthy and signed a marriage settlement giving over all her property to Reverend Converse. The marriage did not last. On one rainy night in January 1854, "he abused the poor lady so dreadfully that, bruised and bleeding, she escaped from the house and hid with one of her daughters in the cotton-house . . . When Mr. Converse sent for hammer and nails to nail up the door, they once more fled and hid in a cotton field in the rain when they were rescued by a neighbor and carried to safety across the river." Gregorie, *History of Sumter County,* 135, 416.

179. The *Directory of City of Charleston and Neck for 1849* lists H. D. Lesesne, attorney at law, 8 St. Michael's Alley or 14 Green. This was undoubtedly Henry Deas Lesesne, who was a close cousin of Mary Deas Broun and a warm friend of Emily and Charles.

180. In New England, Emerson and a group of followers began the transcendentalism movement, which rebelled against orthodoxy and dogma. "The group around Emerson, usually called the Transcendentalists, were defined in one way by Emerson's 1838 Divinity School address, which offended orthodox Unitarians by locating religious authority in the religious nature of human beings, rather than in the Bible or the person of Christ." Robert D. Richardson, Jr., "Ralph Waldo Emerson," in *American Literary Critics and Scholars, 1800–1850,* vol. 59 of *Dictionary of Literary Biography,* ed. John W. Rathbun and Monica M. Grecu (Detroit: Gale Research Company, 1987), 108–29.

181. Fairs were a regular occurrence in Philadelphia. It is interesting that Emily was sending produce and handmade goods from South Carolina for the fair.

182. Emily refers here to John Huger Rutledge (1809–1851), son of Ann Smith and Hugh Rutledge, buried in 1851 at Church of the Holy Cross, Stateburg, South Carolina. *South Carolina Genealogies: Articles from the South Carolina Historical (and Genealogical) Magazine,* vol. 2 (Spartanburg, S.C.: Reprint Company, 1983), 63.

183. *Charleston Courier,* 29 April 1851 gives the "Diary of Weather, at Columbia, past week: 14th: 45, 52, 50, wind South East, rain; 15th: 44, 56, 56, wind North West." This is cold for the lowcountry this late in April. Farmers typically did not plant until after the new moon in April.

184. The Ruins was owned by the Converses. See note 178.

185. A lancing tournament, joust, or tilt evoked images of a chivalrous past when knights and ladies partook in this feudalistic custom. This interest in preserving a pageant from medieval times may show an interest in justifying slavery, emphasizing a feudal, even paternalistic society. The joust was a western European mock battle between two horsemen charging each other with leveled lances, each attempting to unhorse the other. Jousting was replaced by tilting, or riding at the rings, so that the horseman rode at full gallop and inserted his lance through small metal rings. Mark Girouard, "Sir Walter Scott," in *The Return to Camelot: Chivalry and the English Gentleman* (New Haven: Yale University Press, 1981), 29–38.

186. Pineville, like Eutawville, was a pineland summer retreat. Very few of the old summer houses remain today. It is reached by going north from Moncks Corner to St. Stephen and then west to Pineville.

187. "It was a typical plantation home of this section, similar to those nearer Eutawville. Bluford, known as Oakland Club, is midway between St. Stephen and Eutawville. It is a two-story house, built up off the ground with a large back wing. The front yard had huge oaks. The building stands today." Tatum, "Buildings and Reminders of Early Day South Carolina," 68, SCL.

188. Mazyck Porcher lived at his plantation, Mexico. Anna Linton Sinkler, in her *History of the Sinkler Family,* tells this story of him: "Uncle Mazyck was quite a character; if he was dining with anyone and they had a dish he liked he would calmly take it all. The Yankees burned Mexico

and made him walk from Mexico to Eutaw and told him they would hang him at daylight. He said, 'You do not dare do it.' Every year for the rest of his life, he came up to Eutaw on the anniversary and asked to be allowed to go in the wing room where he was a prisoner. We children were dying to know what he did in there."

189. Julius Porcher was the son of Thomas W. Porcher of Walworth. When Julius married Mary Fanning Wickham of Virginia, his wedding present from his father was St. Julien Plantation, just west of Eutawville. The lovely, oak-lined entrance comes up from the River Road in the shape of a J. The black Italian marble mantels in the living room were brought back from Italy by Julius Porcher, who had studied medicine in Paris. Julius and Mary Wickham's daughter, Anne Wickham, was to marry Charles and Emily's youngest son, Charlie.

190. "In 1861 the Museum of the College of Charleton received a cabinet of recent shells, including both native and foreign specimens, from a Miss A.M. Annelly of 'this city'" (Lester D. Stephens, *Science, Race and Religion in the American South* [Chapel Hill: University of North Carolina Press, 2000], 219).

191. Gov. John Lawrence Manning built Milford. It was called Manning's Folly because of the fortune he lavished on it.

192. In DuBose Heyward's *Peter Ashley* (New York: Farrar & Rinehart, 1932), the young aristocrat Peter, who has become a reporter for the *Daily Courier,* gives an absolutely wonderful depiction of the annual races. "At the gate of the course the press became terrific. On a vacant lot across the way, a cock-fight was in progress … The lot was black with Negroes in high excitement at the prospect of enjoying their favorite sport. Most of the house servants would be at the races in the capacity of either maid or groom. But there were the others, the laborers, the great substratum of the city life. They swarmed about refreshment booths. Here and there one would pass with a treasured cock held carefully in the curve of his arm. The air was loud with unrestrained African laughter. Colors seethed, shifting from harmony to discord and back to harmony as cobalt, magenta, purple, flamingo, orange touched and parted with the movement of the crowd." Heyward, 132.

193. The coastwise steam service was essential for communication as well as travel between North and South. Emily's yearly trip home to Philadelphia and her visits from family were all made possible by this service.

194. Ellen McIlvaines was a Philadelphia friend of Emily. Winthrop Sargent was likewise a family friend.

195. Parley's account of the Old French War and the Revolutionary War was by Samuel Griswold Goodrich (born 19 August 1793 in Ridgefield, Connecticut; died 9 May 1860 in New York City), "American publisher and author of children's books under the pseudonym of Peter Parley … In 1827 he began, under the name of Peter Parley, his series of books for the young, which embraced geography, biography, history, science. . . ." "Goodrich, Samuel Griswold," *Encyclopedia Britannica Online,* http://www.eb.com:180/bol/topic?eu=38131&sctn=1&pm=1 [accessed 6 November 1999].

196. J. G. Lockhart, *The Life of Sir Walter Scott* (Edinburgh: Cadell, 1848).

197. Sir John Franklin (1786–1847) was a great early explorer of the Antarctic and Arctic regions. He was lost during an Arctic exploration while searching for the Northwest Passage.

198. Lajos Kossuth (born 19 September 1802, Monok, Hungary; died 20 March 1894, Turin, Italy) was a political reformer who inspired and led Hungary's struggle for independence from Austria. His brief period of power in the revolutionary years of 1848 and 1849, however, was

ended by Russian armies. "Reception for Kossuth in New York City," *Germantown (Pa.) Telegraph,* 15 December 1851 describes the wild welcome and parade for the Hungarian and his bravery in championing liberty against Austrian despotism.

199. Race Week began in 1852 on 4 February. W. H. Sinkler had entered Jeff Davis in the first day's race. *Charleston Courier,* 4 February 1852.

200. Dr. Henry Rutledge Frost was Emily's Charleston doctor. The 1849 *Charleston Directory* lists an H. R. Frost, physician, at 68 Broad Street. The diseases Emily mentions—measles, typhus fever, and more—give an idea of her concern for the health of herself and her family. "Office of City Register—Bill of Mortality, Return of Deaths within the City of Charleston from 13 April to 19 April, 1851." Anemia, apoplexy, tubercles of Brain, cholera, consumption, debility, fever/Typhus, Pneumonia, Teething—these are the diseases listed with the number of persons dying next to each. *Charleston Courier,* 26 April 1851.

201. Catharine Hayes was acclaimed in the *Charleston Courier* of 28 January 1852: "We would remind our readers that tonight, the concert of Miss Catharine Hayes will take place at Hibernian Hall. This, we understand, will be the only opportunity that can be afforded our citizens of hearing this celebrated songstress, who has won for herself a world renowned reputation. From the programme in our advertising columns, it will be seen that she has the aid of talented assistants, and we have no doubt that a large audience will welcome the first and only appearance of 'The Swan of Erin' in this city." In the advertising section it is stated that Catharine Hayes will sing, among others, Meyerbeer's "Ah, mon fils," Wallace's "Happy Birdling," "Auld Robin Gray," a Scottish ballad, and "The Last Rose of Summer," an Irish ballad. It was noted that the piano used on the occasion was from the music store of Mr. Oates. It was here that Emily purchased her sheet music. The store was located at 236 King Street. The price of a ticket was $2.

202. "Madame Pelerin From Paris, 294 King St has just received from France a rich collection of Paris Dress Caps, wreaths, flowers and more for Balls and soirees" [advertisement], *Charleston Courier,* 3 February 1852.

203. Mr. and Mrs. Converse were close friends of Charles and Emily. She speaks of them frequently, and they are often included in her circle of guests at Woodford. He was the minister at the Church of the Holy Cross, where the Sinklers attended church. However, the marriage of Reverend and Mrs. Converse ended unhappily. See note 172.

204. This is probably Thomas Porcher of Ophir Plantation. When Emily visited Ophir she spoke of the Porchers as having sent her off with armloads of French books.

205. Bishop George Washington Doane, second Episcopal bishop of New Jersey, was one of the notable bishops of the American Episcopal Church. His want of business acumen brought him to the verge of disaster. In his efforts to support his educational institutions at Burlington he finally was forced into bankruptcy. His own diocesan convention exonerated him of any culpability, but a persistent effort was made to bring him to trial before the House of Bishops. By using his resources he managed to block proceedings for five years, and eventually the case was dismissed. *Dictionary of American Biography* (New York, Charles Scribner's Sons, 1930), s.v. "George Washington Doane."

206. By tidy, Emily meant a crochet tidy, which was a piece of fancywork used to protect the back, arms, or headrest of a chair or sofa from wear or soil.

207. As usual for the *Courier,* the Washington Races were covered in full, with complete reporting of each race and each heat. On the first day, Col. W. H. Sinkler entered his favorite, Jeff

Davis out of Hero. "The day was fair, mild and lovely, seeming one of Autumn's balmiest days intercalated in the midst of winter. The course was thronged by an array of beauty and fashion . . . We observed in the crowd his Excellency Governor Manning and prominent leading citizens of various portions of the State . . . The entries were Isabella entered by Goldsby of Alabama, Jeff Davis entered by Col. W. H. Sinkler, and Lawson by C & N Green of Richmond. Jeff Davis was the pick and his backers were forced to give odds against the field at the rate of three to one . . . The winner, Jeff Davis . . . It is but justice to remark that the victorious Jeff was put through most admirably by his gallant jockey who steered him with courage, readiness and address that deserved success." *Charleston Courier,* 3–5 February 1853. It is interesting to note that Emily had her facts wrong. Jeff Davis did win, and it was Col. W. H. Sinkler's horse Lot who was disqualified from the Jockey Club Purse for coming in under weight by failing to wear his shot belt.

208. P. T. Barnum's *Illustrated News* was one of the newspapers Emily enjoyed. It was published for only a short while in 1853.

209. Charles St. George Sinkler was born 20 October 1853. He would thus be five months old as of this letter.

210. This abbreviation would seem to be for Germantown in Philadelphia.

211. Emily and Charles by 1854 are spending the hot summers on Sullivan's Island rather than in the upcountry in the Sand Hills. Sullivan's Island is the first barrier island north of Charleston. There were battlements there during the Revolutionary War, including Col. William Moultrie's palmetto log fort. Sullivan's Island was a flourishing summer community reached by daily ferries. An article in the *Charleston Courier* for 12 August 1858 describes the settlement on Sullivan's Island called Moultrieville as having a Planter's Hotel, a Grand Palace "with magnificent piazzas looking out over the sea," Mrs. Fitzsimons's boardinghouse, and a fine old Episcopal church. There was round-trip steamer service six times a day.

212. Saratoga was a summer vacation place in upstate New York.

213. Seaman Deas was Charles's great uncle and the brother of Mary Deas, his grandmother. Seaman Deas was born 8 December 1767 the son of Elizabeth Allen and John Deas, Jr.

214. Kaiserin empress and queen, Elizabeth was born in Munich on 24 December 1837. She was the daughter of King Maxmilian Joseph of Bavaria. On 24 April 1854 she married her first cousin, Emperor Franz Joseph I of Austria. She was an extraordinarily beautiful princess, interested in literature and the arts. *Der Grosse Brockhaus,* vol. 5 (Leipzig, 1930), 475.

215. Emily has gone from addressing her father as Papa to calling him Party. The tradition of calling the older members of the family Party and Marty was continued in the next generation as Charles St. George and Anne Wickham Sinkler were called Party and Marty by their grandchildren.

216. Elizabeth Cleghorn Gaskell's *North and South* was serialized in 1855 in Dickens's *Household Words.* It was a problem novel focusing on the industrial revolution in Manchester, England. There is a conscious comparison between the old rural and new industrial societies of England. Emily would have found interesting analogies to the rural South of the United States and the industrial North of Philadelphia. Wright, *Victorian Novelists,* 182.

217. *The Brodeuse* (Paris, 1834–). Emily subscribed to this French periodical, which provided her with embroidery patterns that were fashionable at the time in Paris.

218. Emily refers here to Czar Nicholas I of Russia, who died on 2 March 1855, and was succeeded by Alexander II. Bernard Grun, *The Timetables of History* (New York: Simon & Schuster, 1975).

219. Emily would appear to be referring to Godfrey Bland, who was the son of Mary and her husband, George Davison-Bland. It would seem that Mary is returning from England for a vacation that will coincide with one of Emily's trips home to Philadelphia. Coxe, *Memories of a South Carolina Plantation,* 36.

220. Ibid.

221. Ibid., 39. There were other Unionists like Charles in South Carolina, many of whom ended up fighting for their state. Elizabeth Sinkler Richardson, in her "Recollections," stated: "Both my father [Col. Richard I. Manning of Mammus Hall] and my husband's father [Col. Richard C. Richardson of the Manor] were bitterly opposed to Secession. But my father responded to his Country's call and enlisted. Having formed and uniformed the "Manning Guards" at his own expense, he went with them as their Captain to Columbia, and from there they were sent to Virginia with my Uncle Brown Manning, as their Captain, and became part of the Hampton Legions."

222. Coxe, *Memories of a South Carolina Plantation,* 34.

223. Ibid., 45.

224. Ibid., 73.

225. Sarah Spruill, "Creating the Santee–Cooper Electric Cooperative: 1934–1941," sixty-one-page paper in the possession of the author, undated.

Cast of Characters

1. Elizabeth Sinkler Richardson, "Recollections," four-page, typewritten document in the possession of the author, undated.

2. Anna Linton Sinkler, "A History of the Sinkler Family," manuscript in the possession of the author, undated.

3. Richardson, "Recollections."

4. "Will of William Sinkler," Record of Wills, Charleston County, South Carolina, vol. 46A (1851–1856), 292–96, Charleston County Library.

Index

Entries in italics denote illustrations.